HERACLES' BOW

Heracles' Bow

ESSAYS ON THE RHETORIC AND

POETICS OF THE LAW

BY JAMES BOYD WHITE

THE UNIVERSITY OF WISCONSIN PRESS

Published 1985

The University of Wisconsin Press
114 North Murray Street
Madison, Wisconsin 53715

The University of Wisconsin Press, Ltd.
1 Gower Street
London WC1E 6HA, England

First printing

Printed in the United States of America

For LC CIP information see the colophon

ISBN 0–299–10410–9

To L. H. LaRue

CONTENTS

FOREWORD

This book is a collection of essays on a set of common themes. I have put them together here in the hope that they will have, as a whole, a shape of their own and make a kind of collective sense, establishing as it were by triangulation a position from which they all proceed. This position is in fact the center of this book. It cannot be adequately summarized here in conceptual form for it is not a conceptual position, but what I call a literary one: a set of attitudes and questions, a way of giving attention to experience, a kind of intellectual identity worked out in performance. But I will try to say something useful here by way of introduction to one who is leafing through this book and wondering what it is all about.

1

The reader may at the outset be puzzled by the analogies suggested by the titles to many of the essays. Law is like, they seem to say, a language, but it is also like drama and poetry and rhetoric and narrative. Each of these analogies, even if in some way attractive, seems in its own terms arguable, but taken together how can they possibly be true? Can these analogies be seriously meant?

I do indeed mean each of these analogies, but I also mean each to be qualified by the others, and I also mean to say something about analogic thinking more generally. Part of my object is to establish a way of thinking by drawing analogies, by making metaphors—by talking about one thing in terms of another—and these essays can be taken in that spirit: not as proposing comparisons between law and other things, each of which is presented as uniquely true and better than any other such comparison, but as manifesting a bent of mind, a disposition and a method, that works by looking at law as one cultural and social activity among others. My emphasis is for the most part on the similarities rather than the differences, partly because many of the differences are self-evident, but also, and more centrally, because one of my aims is to get behind these activities to what they can be seen to share. The kind of analogy I draw is thus not a point-by-point comparison of features, but an attempt by looking at two things to make real and vivid the ground that they share, against which each is a somewhat different figure.

I have no certain name for this ground (or activity, or discipline) and my best definition of it naturally enough lies in my performances in these pages. I would like to call it the art of constituting character, community, and culture in language; if I were to give it a name it would be "constitutive rhetoric," as I suggest in "Rhetoric and Law" (Chapter 2), or perhaps "the poetics of community." But these would be only names, and I would not want to be bound by all their implications, nor by what they seem to omit, as a way of defining the arts of communal and cultural life with which I am concerned. In particular, I want to say that in using such terms as "rhetoric" and "poetics" I do not commit myself to the use of the theoretical apparatus that is rapidly developing in academic circles under those headings.[1]

As for "law," I consciously use that word in a somewhat parochial way, at least at the outset, for by it I mean to speak mainly of modern American law. I do hope that much of what I say about the "law" in this sense can also be said of the law of other cultures and other times, but it is not my purpose to claim that this is so.

2

To put another way what I have just suggested, my aim in this book is to set forth as vividly as I can my sense of the law as a social and cultural activity, as something we do with our minds, with language, and with each other. This is a way of looking at the law not as a set of rules or institutions or structures (as it is usually envisaged), nor as a part of our bureaucracy or government (to be thought of in terms of political science or sociology or economics), but as a kind of rhetorical and literary activity. One feature of this kind of activity is that it must act through the materials it is given—

1. In fact, I think that many academics in both law and literature have become rather too preoccupied with questions of "theory," and in doing so have committed themselves to a language and a set of practices, modeled perhaps on certain social sciences or on analytic philosophy, which actually cut them off from their greatest resource, the roots of their disciplines in ordinary language and ordinary life. For lawyers or readers of literature to become "theorists" in the modern mode is to give away their common birthright, their access to a natural language of many voices. In this book I am trying to work out a way of reading that is not reducible to a technique or technology, but is rather a way of talking about text and language that always assumes the presence of an individual reader's mind, different from others, that is responding to the text and trying to make sense of it, and of the rest of life, in compositions of its own.

an inherited language, an established culture, an existing community—which in using it transforms.[2]

On this view law is in the first place a language, a set of terms and texts and understandings that give to certain speakers a range of things to say to each other. Two lawyers on opposite sides of a case, for example, look at the same statutes, the same judicial opinions, the same general conventions of discourse in the law, and this set of common terms—this common language—is what enables them to articulate to themselves and to each other (or to a third party, such as a judge) what it is they agree and disagree about. And the very fact that the lawyer speaks a legal language means that he or she inhabits a legal culture and is a member of a legal community, made up of people who speak the same way. For this "language" is not just a set of special-sounding words, but a set of intellectual and social activities, and these constitute both a culture—a set of resources for future speech and action, a set of ways of claiming meaning for experience—and a community, a set of relations among actual human beings. The law can thus be seen at once as a language, as a culture, and as a community. What does it mean—what can it mean—to speak this language, to become a member of this culture and this community? These are central questions for any lawyer, and part of my object here is to work out a way of elaborating and addressing them.

To characterize this activity as "rhetorical," as I do, is to claim a somewhat richer meaning for that term than is common. By it I mean not merely the art of persuasion—of making the weaker case the stronger, as the Sophists were said to do—but that art by which culture and community and character are constituted and transformed. It is to be understood in connection with the other key term of my title—"poetics"—by which I mean to suggest that for me the activity of law is at heart a literary one. The law can best be understood and practiced when one comes to see that its language is not conceptual

---

2. I do not mean to suggest that the law is not a set of rules and institutions or that it cannot sensibly be talked about as an instrument of policy. But to talk in those ways is to leave out a lot that is also true about law, and those vocabularies have their own force that can capture the minds that use them and carry them into thinking that they are complete and adequate accounts of what they describe. Talk about law as "rhetoric" has similar dangers, of course, but also certain advantages: its open texture leaves room for uncertainty and variation; and it is naturally concerned with the resources and limits of different modes of speech—with contrast and comparison—and hence with what it itself leaves out. Perhaps rhetorical analysis can even see itself, as it sees other modes of thought, as a discourse that is to some degree artificial, chosen or made, and hence in need of perpetual justification.

or theoretical—not reducible to a string of definitions—but what I call literary or poetic, by which I mean, as I will say more fully below, that it is complex, many-voiced, associative, and deeply metaphorical in nature.

For me it follows that the law is best regarded not as a kind of social science but as one of the humanities. Its practice requires a constant sense of the resources and limits of one's language and culture; a conscious attention to the silence against which all language action takes place, to what *cannot* be said; an awareness of one's own need for an education, particularly for an education from the past that has created our linguistic and intellectual inheritance; a recognition that it is our responsibility to preserve and to improve this inheritance, leaving it fit for use by others; an acknowledgment that the authority of this inheritance is at once real and tentative; and an awareness that others, who are all also users of language, composers of texts, and members of communities, are entitled to basic respect as autonomous and equal persons. All these things mark it as an essentially practical and literary, rather than scientific or theoretical activity.

As I conceive it, the life of the law is thus a life of art, the art of making meaning in language with others. Its goal, like that of other arts always imperfectly attained, is the integration into meaningful wholes of the largest and most contradictory truths—the incorporation into the case of what can be said on both sides of it, the recognition in our discourse of other ways of talking—all under the ruling requirement that what we say make sense. The lawyer must know what the literary person knows, that he or she is always one person speaking to others in a language that is contingent and imperfect. And the excellence of mind required of the lawyer, like the excellence of the composition the lawyer makes, is integrative: a putting to work in the same text of as many of one's resources and capacities as possible, organized in a meaningful way.

The case or controversy to which the lawyer speaks, on which the judge acts, is always a real disturbance in real lives, and our understanding of it and our response to it must both be incomplete. Yet every time we act as lawyers we create and claim a set of meanings: about the events, about the institutions of which we are part, about the very language in which we speak; and for the meanings that we make we are deeply responsible.

A part of the "rhetoric" of the law is rhetoric in a more standard sense, the art of persuading others. Whatever else he or she may be, the lawyer is of necessity a persuader: one who constantly tries to persuade judges, juries, other lawyers, governmental agencies, and sometimes the public at large to take action, or to adopt views, that will advance a client's interests. What does it mean—what can it mean—to devote so much of one's talent and energy to trying to persuade others? (What does it mean for the lawyer, for his or her client, for the world?) Whenever he (or she) organizes his material into persuasive form and addresses the audience he wishes to move, the lawyer gives himself a character and establishes, for the moment at least, a relation with his audience, as well as with his client. What kind of character, what kind of community, does he—can he—establish in these ways? What sort of truth, or justice, or beauty, can he be said to serve?

These are the central questions of this book. They can be summed up by saying that my attention is focused on the expressive and constitutive life that is the center of law—in this sense on the ethics of rhetoric, examined from the inside.

I begin with a reading of Sophocles' *Philoctetes,* a play that considers these questions not in the context of modern law but more generally, and makes a devastating case against a sort of persuasion that looks rather like what modern lawyers do. I end with an explicit defense of the lawyer as rhetorician, framed as a response to Plato's unremitting attack on rhetoric in the *Gorgias.* (As my title suggests, part of my answer lies in the fact that the lawyer can be seen not only as a "rhetorician" but also as a poet.) I hope the intervening essays will be seen as complicating the reader's initial sense of the questions stated above and setting forth the ground upon which the last essay can be said to rest. Even if my defense of the modern lawyer is ultimately thought inadequate, as it may be, I hope that the larger conception of the law as a literary activity by which meaning and community are established can be seen to have a value of its own, especially as a ground upon which criticism of particular laws, of the legal culture, indeed of this book itself, can rest.

This all has a bearing on legal education, for a conception of the law as an art of language and community may help explain why the object of law school is to teach law students "to think as lawyers" rather than merely to teach them "the rules." In their practical lives after graduation, what they will be asked to do by their clients, what they will be paid to do, is to act in the poetic and rhetorical way I describe: to bring to bear the materials of the past upon a present question, remaking those materials as they do so, with the idea of creating a new set of relations in the present and the future—relations between the lawyers themselves and their clients, relations between the clients, and so on. It is the moment of silence, when the lawyer must speak, and in speaking make something new out of his or her language and the world, to which our deepest attention should be directed, in law school and after. And in giving attention to this side of life, we can hope to acquire knowledge of an important kind: not conceptually restatable information—not in that sense theoretical knowledge—but what Wittgenstein would call learning how to investigate our experience and our world and, on that basis, how to go on.

3

A word may be helpful about the origin of these essays and their relation to my other work. As the notes at the beginning of each essay make plain, they are addressed to a rather wide variety of audiences and themselves take a variety of forms. This is from my point of view all to the good, for it functions as a claim that the questions and attitudes at the heart of this book can carry us into rather widely differing terrains.

Five of the essays—"Persuasion and Community in Sophocles' *Philoctetes*" (Chapter 1), "Rhetoric and Law" (Chapter 2), "The Judicial Opinion and the Poem" (Chapter 6), "Facts, Fictions, and Values in Historical Narrative" (Chapter 7), and "Telling Stories in the Law and in Ordinary Life" (Chapter 8)—were composed with this book in mind, and have been published, if at all, only in connection with its preparation. As for the others, with the exception of "The Criminal Law as a System of Meaning" (Chapter 9), they have not been substantially rewritten but stand, with small revisions, as originally published, except that for the most part I have eliminated footnotes. References are collected, where important, in bibliographic notes at the end of each essay.

In the context of my own work, this book is the third in a series. *The Legal Imagination: Studies in the Nature of Legal Thought and Expression* (Boston: Little, Brown, 1973) is a sustained attempt to define the life of the law as a literary one—a life of speaking and writing— through a set of readings and questions and writing assignments. It works by creating a set of difficulties to which (in my view) the only solution is for the student to make himself at once a writer and a lawyer. *When Words Lose Their Meaning* (Chicago: University of Chicago Press, 1984) is an analysis of a wide range of great texts, drawn from different genres and historical periods, in which I attempt to establish a sense of the more general activity—in my subtitle I call it "the constitution and reconstitution of language, character, and community"—of which law is in my view a species, or what I referred to above as the ground against which different arts are figures. This is an attempt to define the law by defining what it is part of, what it is like. In the present book I continue to explore my interest in this general activity but with the aim of directing the reader's attention more explicitly to the nature of modern American law as a field of practice and of life.

I do not mean to suggest that my account of the law is an exhaustive one. Much can be said, for example, about the differences among the various activities that I am interested in seeing in a deep sense as one: law, poetry, drama, narrative, rhetoric, and so on. Law, for example, is explicitly about the use of official power, and it takes place in its own institutional contexts. Much flows from these facts, not only for the purposes of an outside observer like a sociologist or political scientist, but also for the purposes of the legal actors themselves, who are conscious, or should be, that what they do has consequences of special kinds. But these differences are in gross form obvious enough—everyone sees them—and do not need much remark at the outset. In the Afterword I do say something briefly about them, but for me another step comes first, which it is the object of these essays to take: to establish a position from which we are able to see more fully that there is a fundamental identity among the forms of social and verbal action in which we engage and to begin to reflect on the consequences of that fact.

I should perhaps also make explicit, although it should be obvious enough, that my account of law is not meant to be a description of the way it is actually practiced by most judges and lawyers but a representation of the possibilities I see in this form of life both for its practitioners and for the community at large. My apology for the possibilities of the life of the law should thus not be misread as a defense of existing arrangements; rather, it should be taken as an elaboration of the hopes I think we can and should have for the law and for ourselves as lawyers, which may in fact serve as a ground upon which a criticism of law at once idealistic and realistic can rest.

Finally, a word about pronouns and gender. The reader will see that I repeatedly and all too inelegantly struggle with the fact that traditional English speaks as if the male were the norm, the female the exception. I know of no way to resist this insistence that is not itself awkward, but I hope that the reader's understandable irritation with my attempted resolutions will be seen to reveal not merely my own deficiencies of art but also this fact of our common language and culture.

ACKNOWLEDGMENTS

The work that lies behind this book began a long time ago, and more people have contributed to it than I can mention here or even remember. But it is a great pleasure for me to be able to thank at least the following people for their helpful attention to my drafts of various portions (in some instances my drafts of the whole) of this book, or for intellectual assistance of other kinds: Arthur Adkins, Alex Aleinikoff, Theodore Baird, Alton Becker, Walter Blum, Lee Bollinger, Wayne Booth, Clifford Calhoun, Susan Carlton, David Chambers, Homer Clark, John Comaroff, Thomas Eisele, Joseph Epstein, Dan Fader, Robert Ferguson, Stanley Fish, Thomas Green, Bruce Gronbeck, Robert Kaster, Edmund Kitch, Zdenek Krystufek, Robert Ladenson, Arthur LeFrancois, Richard Lempert, Edward Levi, Alfred McDonnell, Andrew McThenia, Bernard Meltzer, Norval Morris, Frances Olsen, Phil Neal, Richard Posner, James Redfield, Donald Regan, Lisa Ruddick, Terrance Sandalow, Frederick Schauer, Kim Scheppele, Steven Shiffrin, Philip Soper, Geoffrey Stone, Cass Sunstein, Stanley Szuba, Joseph Vining, Mary White, Christina Whitman, Hans Zeisel, Franklin Zimring, and the late Malcolm Strachan. My thanks go also to the members of the Law, Language, and Society Workshop and the Seminar in Social and Political Theory, both at the University of Chicago, and to the members of the English Composition Board Advisory Committee and the Language and Culture Seminar, both at the University of Michigan. James O'Hara gave important assistance with the translation and interpretation of the Greek texts, which I acknowledge with gratitude.

I wish to thank especially L. H. LaRue, who read the entire manuscript with care and whose critical comments were of great value to me. For this and many other similar acts of collegial friendship, this book is dedicated to him. Of course, neither he nor any of the others I name is to be held responsible for what I say.

I am also grateful to Jeri Rouse for research assistance and to Terri Shaffer and to Katherine McCreight for their cheerful and accurate work both as typists and as readers of my illegible scrawls.

The Cook Fund of the University of Michigan Law School supported research time for this book, and I am grateful to its donor and trustees for this assistance.

Acknowledgments

Other versions of some of the ideas at work here, especially in "The Invisible Discourse of the Law" (Chapter 4) and "The Judicial Opinion and the Poem" (Chapter 6), can be found in my book *The Legal Imagination*, particularly in chapters 2 and 6. Similarly, there is some overlap between "Reading Law and Reading Literature" (Chapter 5) and the treatment of similar questions in chapters 1 and 10 of *When Words Lose Their Meaning*.

Finally, I am grateful to the following for permission to reprint essays included here, earlier versions of which appeared in their pages:

To The University of Chicago, for permission to reprint "The Study of Law as an Intellectual Activity," which was originally published as a University of Chicago Law School Occasional Paper.

To the *Michigan Quarterly Review*, for permission to reprint "The Invisible Discourse of the Law: Reflections on Legal Literacy and General Education," which appeared in the summer 1982 of the *Michigan Quarterly Review*.

To the *Michigan Law Review*, for permission to reprint "The Judicial Opinion and the Poem: Ways of Reading, Ways of Life," which appeared in vol. 82, no. 7 (1984) of that journal.

To the *Texas Law Review*, for permission to reprint James Boyd White, "Law as Language: Reading Law and Reading Literature," published originally in 60 *Texas L. Rev.* 415 (1982). Copyright © 1982 by the *Texas Law Review*. Reprinted by permission. To the University of Chicago Press for permission to reprint the portions of this essay that also appeared in *When Words Lose Their Meaning*.

To the *University of Colorado Law Review*, for permission to reprint "Making Sense of the Criminal Law," an earlier version of which appeared in 50 *U. Colo. L. Rev.* 1–27 (1978).

To the *University of Chicago Law Review*, for permission to reprint "The Ethics of Argument: Plato's *Gorgias* and the Modern Lawyer," 50 *University of Chicago Law Review* 849–895 (Spring 1983), and "Law as Rhetoric, Rhetoric as Law: The Arts of Cultural and Communal Life," appearing in the summer 1985 issue of that journal.

HERACLES' BOW

1

HERACLES' BOW

PERSUASION AND COMMUNITY

IN SOPHOCLES' *PHILOCTETES*

This essay is meant to frame the book as a whole by establishing themes and questions that will run through it to the end. In it I analyze some of the ways in which character, community, and language are constituted in the speeches that make up the *Philoctetes*, especially in those conversations in which one speaker seeks to persuade another to a particular position. In this connection the play establishes with great clarity a contrast that has been fundamental in Western ethical thought, between treating another person as an object (or an instrument) of manipulation—as a "means" to an end—and treating him (or her) as one who has claims to autonomy and respect that are equal to one's own: that is, as an "end" in himself. This contrast has a special and disturbing significance for someone who, like the lawyer, makes an art of persuading others.

In the course of life it happens again and again—in the family, the workplace, the street, the international arena—that a crisis arises in which we are faced with the possibility of establishing or losing community. Rhetoric as I use the term in this book—the art of "persuasion" in its broadest sense—is the art by which we address these possibilities. As our desires, our senses of ourselves, are seen to work together, we come together, for the moment or for a longer time, making a common world defined by a common set of mutually intelligible roles and activities; or, as we feel ourselves to be opposed, we divide into separate, perhaps hostile, groups or units. A community may be momentary, based upon a sense of common ground that is quickly lost or disproved (or even upon deception), or it may be stable and enduring. How do we—how can we—address these possibilities? What can we say to one another, or to ourselves, about our own desires and those of others, about who we are and who we want to be, and with what possible meanings, what possible successes? Who do we become, what do we risk becoming, when one tack or another is taken? When, for example, is a persuasive success an ethical failure, or an ethical success a persuasive failure? What is the role of truth and sincerity in what we do?

For the lawyer these are especially critical and inescapable questions. A lawyer's professional day is largely made up of conversations, oral and written, in which the object is to persuade another to a particular view. In this sense he or she is a professional rhetorician, and must be concerned with the possibilities of rhetoric as a way of life. In this essay I want to work out a way of thinking about the ethics of persuasion by looking at Sophocles' *Philoctetes,* a play that has much to teach us about how persuasion works, and can work, and what it means to give yourself to a life of persuasion of one kind or another. The play consists of a series of persuasive communities that it contrasts with one another, inviting the audience to approve some, to condemn others. But it is about another activity as well, which it in fact exemplifies: the activity of drama (or of imaginative literature more generally); and we shall have something to ask about the nature of this activity too—is it also a kind of persuasion? An art of community-making? Do the resources of the theater shed light on what happens, and what can happen, in the law?

In both respects the ultimate concern of the play, like my own, is ethical. The central question it teaches us to ask is who we become, individually and collectively—who we can become—in our conversations with one another. What kind of selves, what kind of communities, do we establish with each other in our speech, especially in our persuasive speech? It addresses these questions in the context of a mythological Greek past recreated on the stage; we must address them in the context of modern American law; but the questions themselves, and many of their ramifications, are the same.

To ask these questions is necessarily to ask another, which will be with us throughout these essays: in what terms ought we to judge the communities we see and those we make? How, that is, should we talk about "success" and "failure" in persuasion and community, about what we admire or despise in ourselves and others? In this play we shall see Odysseus succeed in persuading Neoptolemus by using tactics that we cannot ethically admire: he treats him dishonestly and manipulatively, dealing with him, in our standard categories, not as an "end in himself" but as a "means" to another end. But this end, one could argue, involving as it does the taking of Troy and the fulfillment of fate, is a good one; and does Odysseus' despicable conduct not advance its achievement? By contrast, as we shall see, Neoptolemus tries to persuade Philoctetes at the end by a full and frank statement that recognizes the autonomy, worth, and liberty of the other—a very model of "good" persuasion—but this effort fails, at least in the obvious sense that Philoctetes remains obdurate. How are we to evaluate these two forms of persuasion? In forcing this question on our attention the play raises basic ethical issues concerning the degree to which ends justify means; whether ethical thought properly focuses on the consequences of conduct or upon its quality as honest (or otherwise virtuous); and what methods are best for defining such questions and thinking them through to conclusion.

On the point of method, for example, consider the meaning of the standard ethical position, which I invoked above, that one ought never—or at least not without great justification—treat another person as a "means to an end" rather than as an "end in himself." This formulation derives in modern philosophy from Kant, but from another point of view it is a restatement of the basic Christian ethic, and it also has roots in Aristotle's conception of friendship. One basic question about this formula is what it means, not as a matter of conceptual explication but as a matter of moral experience. What does it actually mean, that is, to treat another person as a "means" to an end, or, by contrast, as an "end in himself"? Only when we are clear about that can we even begin to address the question whether we should regard the imperative as absolute or as subject to qualifications, or to think about the proper qualifications, or even to decide whether this is a significant rule at all. But in what terms, by what process, can we best think about the difference between treating others as "ends" and as "means"? How can we best present these activities, these different ways of treating others, to our consciousness? In what terms, what language, can we describe and analyze and judge them?

The implicit position of Sophocles' play is one that I shall also maintain in different terms throughout these essays: that these questions can best be addressed in a language of art, and that a purely conceptual and logical language, like that of modern analytic philosophy, will always be incomplete or defective. I think, that is, that Sophocles' play teaches us what it means to treat another as a means, or as an end, with a clarity and intelligibility—a lucidity—as well as a force, that logical or abstract argument about such questions will of necessity lack. This point connects with another of my themes, which in turn relates to the ethics of legal persuasion: that law is best regarded as an art too, carried on in a language of art, a fact that is in my view large with consequence.

1

The narrative form in which these questions are presented in the play is this. Philoctetes lives alone on an uninhabited island in the Aegean where, because of a foul-smelling and festering wound on his foot, he was cast out ten years earlier by the Achaeans on their way to Troy. His wound was inflicted by a serpent that bit him when he stepped on sacred ground; his cries of pain, we are told, prevented the others from making proper sacrifices and libations. During his years on the island he has been able to live only because he has with him the wonderful bow and arrows of Heracles, given him for a kindness done—Philoctetes lit his funeral pyre—and these are weapons that never miss. Now the Achaeans have been told by a soothsayer that they cannot capture Troy without that bow, and have sent Odysseus and Neoptolemus, Achilles' son, to bring it back.

These two actors are presented with an archetypal question of what I will call "constitutive rhetoric": how to bring into a community an isolated individual who is now outside it. The first question the play addresses is how they are to proceed, and that question is presented both as a practical one—what will work?—and as an ethical one—what is right for them to do?

The most obvious possibility, though the least talked about in this scene, is honest persuasion. For that to succeed, a speaker would have to find a way of talking about what has happened, and what will happen, that Philoctetes and the Achaeans could both accept, and which could thus serve as the ground of a newly constituted community between them. By "way of talking" I mean a whole language: a shared set of terms for telling the story of what has happened and what will happen, for the expression of motive and value, and for the enactment of those movements of the mind leading to a common end that we call reason. Whoever speaks to Philoctetes in this way must find a way to tell the story—the whole story—that leads naturally to his return. Such a common language, such a common story, is in fact what we mean by a community. The art of sincere statement by which this kind of genuine community is established can for our purposes be called, and in a restriction of the range of meaning of the Greek term is called by Sophocles, "persuasion" (*peithō*).

In the play Odysseus says that this kind of persuasion will simply not work against Philoctetes' intransigence—we can see, indeed, that an attempt might only put him on his guard—and that they must therefore practice persuasion of a different kind, a sort of trick or deceitful stratagem (*dolos*). He tells Neoptolemus to win the confidence of Philoctetes by pretending to be sailing back to Greece after a humiliation at the hands of the Achaeans. (He is to say that they awarded his father's armor to Odysseus.) Neoptolemus should offer Philoctetes passage home, and this will enable them to get close enough to get his bow.

Neoptolemus objects that this kind of trickery is inconsistent with his most fundamental conceptions of honor, and urges the use of force (*bia*) or persuasion (*peithō*). But Odysseus explains that they have no alternative: force can never prevail against the weapons of Heracles, and persuasion too is bound to fail. Philoctetes would kill them if he knew who they were, and he could certainly not be talked into coming with them.

Neoptolemus is himself "persuaded" by Odysseus—in which sense of the word we shall soon discover—and goes along with the plan. The rest of the play is about his (and our) discovery of what that decision really means, both in practical and in ethical terms. As things work out Neoptolemus in fact obtains the bow, but he becomes so disgusted with himself that he returns it (over Odysseus' violent objection) and does what he wished to do in the first place: he seeks to persuade Philoctetes to come with them voluntarily, on the grounds that this will be best for him as well as for them. (His wound will be cured by the sons of Asclepius, and he will fulfill his fate and achieve great renown.) But Philoctetes remains obdurate and insists that Neoptolemus keep his promise to take him home. Neoptolemus is about to comply when Heracles miraculously appears and tells Philoctetes that he should indeed go to Troy, where he will be cured and win great glory. Philoctetes complies, and the play ends with his farewell to his island.

Even from this outline it can be seen that the play presents its audience with a real puzzle. We are led to despise Odysseus and to admire Neoptolemus' change of heart; yet Odysseus' way is shown to have "worked"—it got the bow—and Neoptolemus' way to have failed. The play itself seems to require the intrusion of a *deus ex machina* to save it from a chaotic and impossible ending. All this suggests two sets of questions. First, how are we to make sense of the play itself, as a work of art? What is Sophocles asking us to think and feel about the two modes of persuasion—the two kinds of character and community—opposed here, and how does he seek to evoke this response? (What kind of "persuasion" does the play itself engage in?) Second, what ought we to think about the substance of the questions that this play defines, both in general—as a matter of philosophical ethics—and in the context of modern law? To focus on one example of particular significance to us: what kind of persuasion (*peithō* or *dolos*) does the lawyer practice, and what does it mean—what can the lawyer make it mean—that he or she does so?

2

It is worth examining the initial conversation between Odysseus and Neoptolemus in some detail, for their argument about the proper way to approach Philoctetes is itself a performance of one kind of persuasion, one kind of community, and it sets forth the major polarity from which the play will proceed. This polarity, which is still alive for us both in the law and out of it, opposes two kinds of mind: the kind of mind, on the one hand, that naturally thinks in terms of ends and means (how can I get what I want?) and for which justification, if any, lies in results and probabilities (the greater good, or the right likelihood of it, justifies the lesser evil), and the kind of mind, on the other hand, that thinks of right and wrong in terms of general principles (cheating is wrong) or in terms of appropriateness to character (cheating is beneath me).

The circumstance that brings this opposition between Odysseus and Neoptolemus to the surface is another archetypal occasion for constitutive rhetoric. But instead of asking an outsider to join a community, as in their own approach to Philoctetes, this time two members of a community are faced with the task of establishing the terms upon which their own common activity will proceed. The questions are: what form that activity shall take; how, by what process of persuasion, that form shall be determined; what it—and their community—shall be said to mean; whether the enterprise will hold together to its end; and, what will provide part of the answer to all of the other questions, how its "end" should be imagined and defined.

For Odysseus it is all very simple: they are sent to obtain the bow, and the only issue is how they may most certainly obtain it. His is a classic form of ends-means rationality, which naturally focuses on the possible and the impossible, on the probable and the improbable, and regards everything in the world, including itself, as an instrument to obtain the ends it is given. The only question is success. Odysseus does not in fact even argue that the end justifies the means, for justification is not an issue for him. (In the language of modern sports, winning is not the most important thing, it is the only thing.)[1] This is his view not only of the way they should approach Philoctetes, but, as we shall see, of the way he should treat Neoptolemus as well.

Neoptolemus' position, by contrast, is based upon his sense of his own character or identity. His reason for balking at the use of stratagem is self-centered, almost aesthetic: deceit is beneath his dignity. He rests on his nature and paternity: he *is* a certain kind of person, in part by reason of his birth, and it is his sense of who he is that will be his ethical guide.[2] His initial response to Odysseus' suggestion is a kind of instinctive reaction, learned but not wholly understood: for him force and persuasion are both acceptable, but deceit is not. His objection to deceit has nothing to do with recognizing Philoctetes' autonomy or value as a person (for force is by nature coercive) but rests rather upon his sense of what is appropriate for him, Neoptolemus, to do. His central conception of ethics is, naturally enough, an integrated response to circumstance: "when I am pained by hearing advice I hate to do it," he says (line 86). Later, as he contemplates performing the deceitful plan, he asks Odysseus how he could possibly carry himself—*pōs blepōn* (line 110)—while speaking such words; in this he reveals his sense that, like his conduct, his speech must be authentic to him, as indeed it is in his conversation with Odysseus. In this sense dishonesty is not only wrong but simply impossible for him.

He expresses his substantive position in a language of traditional moralism: he would rather fail (*hamartanō*) in a manner appropriate to his class and ideal (the Greek word is *kalōs*) than prevail in a shabby way (*kakōs*) (lines 94–95). At this point these terms simply express his

1. Odysseus does say that if they obtain the bow there will be a gain (*kerdos*) (line 111), and that the Achaeans will suffer if Neoptolemus refuses (line 67). But for him those are both *appeals*, not justifications. Later the Chorus weakly defends him on the ground that he pursues the collective good (line 1145), but not much is made of it; and in any event this justification would work only if Odysseus' plan in fact advanced the greater good, which, as we shall see below, it does not.

If Odysseus were to justify himself, how would he do it? As a utilitarian, says Martha Nussbaum (in her interesting article, "Consequences and Character in Sophocles' *Philoctetes*," *Philosophy and Literature* [1976]: 25–51), and it is true that utilitarianism entails ends-means rationality of Odysseus' kind. But that mode of thought can serve other ends as well, and there is in Odysseus no commitment to the conception of the greatest happiness or to the importance of others. Rather, the overriding stated value is that of the group enterprise, whatever it may be, and without any judgment as to its value. Odysseus is more fascist than Benthamite.

2. The audience of the play would all know his father's remark to Odysseus in the *Iliad*: "As I hate the gates of Hades I hate that man who hides one thing in his heart and says another" (book 9, lines 312–13).

culturally acquired sense of what is appropriate and do not yet have the kind of moral weight they will come to have at the end of the play. While for Neoptolemus the proper ground of ethical judgment is character rather than ends-means rationality, his conception of character is not yet mature. A very young man indeed, he has been properly raised to a set of ideals but has never been forced to think about them and make them his own. Part of the movement of the play is in fact the process by which his acquired instinctive views become truly his own, in the double sense that he is both able to defend them and willing to pay the price they exact. Naturally enough, in the course of this process both the views themselves, and the man who holds them, are transformed.

The method by which Odysseus persuades Neoptolemus to abandon the sense of character upon which he relies, to "give himself" to Odysseus for "a single day" (lines 83–84), is a performance in practice of the doctrine Odysseus espouses. It is a skillful seduction of a standard kind: not *peithō* but *dolos*. Odysseus waits to present Neoptolemus with the issue until the very moment of action, thus depriving him of the possibility of thought and reflection; and he springs upon him now, for the first time, the news that he will not be able to achieve his own great destiny as the destroyer of Troy unless they obtain the bow. This is an end that Neoptolemus cannot deny, and he acquiesces in the means necessary to attain it, shameful to him though they are. Odysseus thus disintegrates Neoptolemus' sense of self, his only ethical guide, by establishing an unforeseen conflict within it. The way this kind of persuasion works here, as elsewhere in the world, is that the successful persuader gets what he wants now and leaves the other to try to put his life and character together again afterwards on his own. This is one performance of what it may mean to regard another as an instrument.

But why is Neoptolemus led so readily to accept a position inconsistent with his character, or what he calls his "nature"? One might say his ambition or selfishness is appealed to against his virtue, but that is not quite right. Rather, Odysseus appeals to his sense of himself as the "one who will overthrow Troy" to meet the force of a resistance that is itself rooted in another instinctive sense of self. He appeals to him against himself. He thus takes advantage of a difficulty that is built into Neoptolemus' mode of thought, which provides no way in which conflicts in his sense of character can be addressed. For one who thinks as Neoptolemus does this difficulty will arise repeatedly, especially where a part of one's self-conception is as "one who succeeds," because it will always be an issue whether the steps that seem necessary to succeed are consistent with the rest of one's character. To avoid being destabilized over and over again, Neoptolemus must rest on something different from instinct and an acquired sense of rightness. His position must be reflected upon, its limits and costs must be acknowledged and made part of the self, before it can become the ground of life.

Disintegration is also enacted in the language that Odysseus brings Neoptolemus to accept. For example, Odysseus accepts Neoptolemus' claim that what he asks is beneath him, and urges him to do it anyway: "since victory is sweet, do what I ask"; "we shall show that we are just another time"; "for one shameless (*anaides*) part of a day give me yourself, and for the rest of life be called the most righteous of men" (lines 80–85)—as though those terms could co-exist in that way! Odysseus' sense of character is so defective as to allow him to think consistency irrelevant. He restates Neoptolemus' willingness to use force but not deceit as a willingness to use force but not words, saying that he himself has found both to be useful instruments. In this he obliterates Neoptolemus' distinction between them, which is not between words and action, but between shameful and honorable action, and thus obliterates the distinction between shame and honor—the central ethical distinction of this world. Odysseus implicitly expresses contempt for Neoptolemus' concern with virtue: he conjoins the verb for being clever in the way that he recommends (*sophisthēnai*) with a word for thief (*klopeus*) (line 77), with which it is utterly impossible to associate Neoptolemus' central values—*agathos, kalos,* and so on. At the end of the interchange, Odysseus claims that by virtue of his conduct Neoptolemus will earn a reputation as one who is wise (*sophos*) and good (*agathos:* here used in the sense of successful person); and Neoptolemus agrees, saying he will throw off all sense of shame (*aischunē*) (lines 119–20). This combination of terms is simply impossible in the Greek of the day, a paradox like the Socratic paradoxes, but unlike those purely destructive, not constructive. The deliberate effect of Odysseus' persuasion (*dolos*) has been the disintegration both of Neoptolemus' language and of his sense of himself.

3

What will it mean for Neoptolemus to do what he has agreed to do? Odysseus has given a simple version—it will mean "success"—but in terms that are impossible to accept, even for a moment. The play now shows us what this deception will mean in other terms.

Philoctetes' appearance is preceded by a choral ode that tells his story of abandonment and endurance, and as this happens the audience suddenly begins to see things from Philoctetes' point of view, and they look very different indeed. When Philoctetes himself appears on stage, as the soul of frankness, warmth, and generosity, we see before us the person who is to be injured. The man who has been spoken of as an instrument in the language of Odysseus now becomes a person: a center of meaning, experience, and autonomy. Our developing sense of who Philoctetes is makes Neoptolemus' deception of him increasingly terrible.

In the opening scene we witnessed the development of a single relationship, that between Odysseus and Neoptolemus. Now we see the simultaneous growth of two relations, both of them between Neoptolemus and Philoctetes: the relation of generous friendship that Philoctetes offers (and Neoptolemus pretends to accept), and the relation of destruction implicit in Neoptolemus' plan of deceit. Neoptolemus' story of injury at the hands of Odysseus and his offer of passage home, indeed his very standing as a Greek and his heroic connections, stimulate in Philoctetes a capacity for generous friendship and trust. We respond to his expressions with warm admiration of our own, and so does Neoptolemus, who is eventually so overcome by his response that he abandons his original plan. The pretended friendship that Neoptolemus originally creates as a matter of strategem or device becomes in this way real. The intended manipulator is persuaded by an unintended appeal that he cannot deny.

What is the nature of this appeal? Philoctetes greets Neoptolemus as a Greek, with a sense of love for his language and culture; he greets him as the son of Achilles, with admiration for his father; he greets him as a member of the Achaean host, with a sense of shared heroic values; he greets his news of Achilles' death, and that of others of his friends, with an authentic grief that Neoptolemus himself must share. As the two men talk they share their stories, and these seem to have a shared meaning: as Philoctetes has been abandoned by Odysseus and the sons of Atreus, Neoptolemus says that he has been deprived of his arms—his inheritance, his manhood—by the same people. The two men thus create a common space based upon a sense of common injury at the hands of the same actors.

But on one side this is all duplicitous. How can it then have the effect on us, or on Neoptolemus, that it seems to? How indeed can it be that Neoptolemus, the open-hearted, authentic young man, incapable of duplicity, is able to carry out this program of cynical deceit? (Remember his question to Odysseus—"how can I carry myself while speaking such things [*pōs blepōn*]?")

The answer is that, despite his conscious intentions, Neoptolemus is at the most basic level in fact not dishonest: both his own story and his responses to Philoctetes' story are in a deep sense true. The false surface version of his story, that Odysseus has deprived him of the arms of his father, has its deeper true version (to which we have just been witness) in the scene in which Odysseus does deprive Neoptolemus of himself—"give me yourself for just a shameless part of a single day." In thus disintegrating him Odysseus has deprived Neoptolemus of his capacity as a man, of his nature and inheritance as a coherent and virtuous self speaking a coherent language—of his "arms" indeed. What Neoptolemus pretends is in fact true: he and Philoctetes are bound together by similar injuries at the same hands.

As Neoptolemus is not yet a man, Philoctetes has been deprived of his manhood; in this scene, they share that plight, and the rest of the play restores both of them to maturity and autonomy. By the end Neoptolemus has his "arms" back, for he acquires control of his own actions and his own moral life. (He has his arms back in a more literal sense as well, for, as we shall see, at one point he successfully stands up to Odysseus' physical threats.) He has also got his language back: the stratagems he has employed are now seen as shameful. "I have taken this bow dishonorably (*aischrōs*) and against justice" (line 1234). At the end of the play Philoctetes has likewise recovered the proper use of his arms, in heroic action, and has accepted both his cure and his role in the world. All this means that Neoptolemus' false story is in a deep sense true; that his response to Philoctetes is not false but true; that the relation of friendship that he starts out to create deceitfully is in fact sincere; and that this relation becomes the center of the play and of Neoptolemus' future growth and health, his ground of action and life.

This explains the dramatic appropriateness of a feature of this play that some readers have found puzzling, namely the scene in which the false trader—the Emporos—appears to warn Philoctetes and Neoptolemus that Odysseus and the Achaeans are after them. This scene renders explicit and vivid—almost in the manner of Aeschylus—the psychological truth that Odysseus is indeed a common enemy in mortal pursuit of both of them, seeking to reduce them to instruments of his plan.

4

But this is to get ahead of ourselves. The stages by which Neoptolemus and Philoctetes move to their final positions are of considerable importance. In presenting this development Sophocles shows us a different kind of persuasive community from the one we saw Odysseus create, a community in which people treat each other as "ends," not as "means"—a community of friendship. When Neoptolemus agrees to take Philoctetes with him, after the report by the Emporos, and they begin to collect Philoctetes' possessions, he asks whether he will be permitted to touch and handle the bow (line 661). Philoctetes says of course: in return for his extraordinary virtue (*aretē*) this will be granted him alone among men. Neoptolemus marks the moment by saying how glad he is to have formed this friendship with Philoctetes, using terms that define the ideal community as reciprocal: "one who knows how to give and receive benefits is a friend beyond price" (lines 672–73). Philoctetes is suddenly overcome by his disease and, terrified that he will lose control of his bow, he gives it to Neoptolemus, not as a favor this time but as a trust, which Neoptolemus accepts. As Philoctetes falls into a coma, Neoptolemus pledges that he will not forsake him (line 812).

The Chorus urges Neoptolemus to take advantage of the moment and leave with the bow, but Neoptolemus refuses. He has come to see that the bow is worth nothing without the man: "his is the crown, it is he the god told us to bring" (line 841). And when Philoctetes awakes to the light and discovers that he has not been abandoned in his sickness, but watched over, he is full of praise and gratitude.

Neoptolemus is full of disgust at himself but nonetheless tells Philoctetes that he must go to Troy, weakly promising that this will lead to Philoctetes' cure. Philoctetes instantly demands the return of his bow; Neoptolemus refuses, justifying himself by reference to necessity, justice, and self-interest, all of which, he says, require him to "obey those in power" (line 925)—that is, to continue to perform the function that has been assigned him. Philoctetes, discovering that he has been betrayed once more, now expresses with an almost operatic grandeur his pain and rage and anguish. This erodes Neoptolemus' resolve further, but just at the moment when he expresses real indecision—he asks the Chorus, "What shall we do?" (line 974)—Odysseus appears on the scene and takes over. He threatens to force Philoctetes to come. For Philoctetes the thought of this is simply torture; in response Odysseus says, in effect, "Very well, we shall give you what you want: we shall leave you, but without the bow by which alone you can live" (lines 1054–62).

Neoptolemus and Odysseus then depart; the Chorus sanctimoniously tells Philoctetes that this is really all his own fault, that Odysseus is really acting for the greater good, and so on. But from this intolerable degradation Neoptolemus rescues Philoctetes and the audience: he returns to give back the bow. His language is now clear: he will undo his prior wrong (*hamartia*: now defined as a moral "missing of the mark," not, as it was earlier in the play, as a merely material failure) by giving back the bow he dishonorably (*aischrōs*) obtained (lines 1224, 1228, 1234); he sees that what is just (*dikaios*) is superior to the merely clever (*sophos*), which Odysseus has been representing and by which both Neoptolemus and Philoctetes have been deprived of their arms, their manhood, and their standing as persons (line 1246). Equally important, from his new position Neoptolemus can now see and understand with clarity the meaning of the soothsayer's statement, for he now understands the circumstance to which it was addressed. What is actually required is of course not the bow—a mere instrument—but the voluntary return of Philoctetes himself; for only this can heal the moral breach in the Achaean community that was caused by the abandonment of Philoctetes.

When Odysseus now threatens him—"see my hand on my sword?" (line 1254–55)—Neoptolemus faces him down, and before this display of resolve Odysseus simply wilts away. Neoptolemus likewise stands up to Philoctetes when he, with bow restored, suddenly takes aim at the reappeared Odysseus. Neoptolemus grabs his arm and restrains him from shooting, saying, "This is honorable (*kalos*) for neither you nor me" (line 1304).

The community established by Philoctetes and Neoptolemus thus includes a wealth of constitutive social practices: expressions of pleasure at a shared language and culture; affirmation of a shared history; participation in shared grief; supplication; expressions of gratitude; pledges and promises (Neoptolemus promises not to leave without Philoctetes, Philoctetes promises to let Neoptolemus touch the bow); the granting of a favor requested (touching the bow); the offer and acceptance of a trust (when the bow is actually given); the movement into a relation between substitute father and substitute son (Neoptolemus never saw Achilles and until the end of the play is in need of a father; Philoctetes constantly addresses him as "child" or "son"); and—a practice for which we have no name but which is essential to

healthy life—the solicitous attendance at the side of one incapacitated by illness. The protective concern, maternal in character, that
Neoptolemus here grants Philoctetes is just what the Achaeans denied him. And in one wonderful moment Philoctetes shows what it
is to pay attention to another person and his story: when Neoptolemus tells his false tale about being deprived of his father's arms, Philoctetes says, "But how could Ajax have allowed that to happen?"
(line 410–11). For him the story is real, and he responds to it fully; in
so doing he both recognizes the experience of another and, in his
admiration for Ajax, activates his own heroic values (which are now
overridden most of the time by his sense of injury). Contrast with all
this the social practices established in the conversation between
Neoptolemus and Odysseus: a kind of competitive and deceptive argument between them and a shared participation, on unequal terms,
in a manipulative plot (*dolos*). One can easily see how Neoptolemus
was persuaded to abandon his original aim and to commit himself to
a different kind of life.

One consequence of the fullness and beauty of Neoptolemus' developing friendship with Philoctetes is that his abuse of it is a wrong
even worse than Odysseus' abuse of his relation with Neoptolemus.
Odysseus destabilized for a moment the character of one who trusted
him by suddenly activating an unsuspected conflict that the other
could not handle, in this way persuading him to engage in conduct
of which he would later repent. But Neoptolemus' self-disgust, his
ultimate repudiation of his own conduct was almost certain; in some
sense the seduction was thus likely to prove, as it did prove, educational, teaching Neoptolemus his own true values and something of
his own—and others'—susceptibilities to shameful action. But
Neoptolemus' planned deception of Philoctetes works in a different
and far more destructive way. It stimulates trust, hope, and generosity in a damaged man only to trample on them; it calls forth a person's central capacities for social and personal life, and then deliberately injures them. The natural consequence is the destruction of
Philoctetes' capacity for community and all that depends upon community. This deception threatens a real destruction of the self; it is
perhaps a form of what a Christian would call the sin against the
Holy Ghost.

5

When Neoptolemus restores the bow he gives himself the opportunity to do what he thought should have been done in the first place, that is, to achieve his mission of bringing Philoctetes back to the Achaean community not by deceit (*dolos*) nor, as he now sees, by force (*bia*), but by persuasion (*peithō*). And what he means by persuasion is not the art of manipulating others to adopt one's position, but the art of stating fully and sincerely the grounds upon which one thinks common action can and should rest.

I am very pleased to hear you praise my father and me, but now hear what I want from you. It is necessary for men to bear the fortunes that the gods give. But if someone willingly clings to his injuries, as you do, it is not right to have either forgiveness or pity for him. You have become wild, and reject all advice, even from one who counsels you in good will, whom you hate as if he were a hostile enemy.

All the same I will speak, and I call upon Zeus who supports the Oath; you mark what I say and write it in your mind.

You suffer this disease by the fortune of the gods, for you came too near the guardian of Chryse, the snake that secretly protected the roofless sacred ground, watching over it. Now know this: from this terrible disease there shall be no relief, so long as the sun rises in one place and sets in another, until you of your own free will go to the plains of Troy and meet the sons of Asclepius among us. By them you will be calmed from your disease, and you will then emerge, with this bow and with me, as the destroyer of the city.

I shall tell you how I know these things. We captured a Trojan, Helenus their best seer, who said plainly that these things should happen; and he added that Troy must fall this very summer, or he should give himself up to be killed for speaking falsely.

Now that you know these things, yield willingly. Great is the increase of your honor: to be chosen as the best of the Greeks and by taking Troy, the source of sorrow, to win the highest fame. (Lines 1314–46)

What are the characteristics of this speech? Neoptolemus begins by calling upon the kind of willingness to engage in sincere conversation that has been defined by him, by Philoctetes, and by the play itself as a central feature of proper community, proper character, and proper persuasion. He seeks to constitute his audience as one who will attend, and do so in his own interest. He claims that Philoctetes is harboring his sense of injury, and he justifies this view, to Philoctetes and to us, by locating his present request in a transformed narrative of Philoctetes' life. This story defines Philoctetes not as one who simply "suffers terribly" nor as one who "suffers at the hands of the hated Achaeans," as Philoctetes wants to do, but as one who suffers for a reason that can be understood and stated. He suffers because he stepped on the sacred ground. It is not an issue whether he was at fault in doing so, for the point of Neoptolemus' statement is neither to blame nor to excuse Philoctetes for taking that step. Similarly, it is not an issue whether the Achaeans were right or wrong to abandon him: there is no discussion of the necessity of the abandonment—for example, whether their sacrifices really were disturbed, as Odysseus claimed (lines 8–9)—or of available alternatives to it. The question is seen as one of causation, not blame, and this implicitly suggests that cure, rather than revenge, can be the aim. To stop the obsessive (if understandable) process of blaming and excusing frees the mind to think about how the wound can be healed: by the "arts of Asclepius" as Neoptolemus puts it, or, more significantly for us, by Philoctetes' reintegration into the community of which he was once a part. On Philoctetes' side, he must give up his love for his own illness. What is required of him, before he can be cured, is forgiveness—forgiveness of others and forgiveness of himself, for it was his own misstep that brought about the injury and the subsequent abandonment.

Neoptolemus' speech thus operates at once as a recognition of Philoctetes' experience; as a reinterpretation of it in light of what else is known; and as a conversion, by narrative, of the intolerable into the tolerable. It has obvious parallels with psychoanalysis, and in both cases the ruling values are truthfulness, recognition, and integration.

But this persuasive statement in fact fails, and fails for reasons that Neoptolemus should be able to understand. As he asked of Odysseus, "How can I carry myself in making this deception (*pōs blepōn*)," Philoctetes now in essence asks, "How can I come before the others, how can I possibly join with them, after what has happened?" (lines 1352–57). He insists that Neoptolemus keep his promise to take him home. Neoptolemus is about to comply when Heracles appears and restates to Philoctetes the story of his life and the necessity and propriety of his return. This time Philoctetes accepts and is persuaded.

6

How are we to read and understand this sequence of events, especially Neoptolemus' ultimate failure and the need for Heracles' intervention at the end? And what of the fact that Odysseus' method of persuasion succeeded? What do these events mean as part of what Sophocles is saying in the play, and what do we, independently of the play, think of the issues it presents? We can start by returning to the initial polarity between Odysseus and Neoptolemus, out of which the play moves.

In reading the opening scene one quickly sees that Odysseus habitually regards everything and everybody as an instrument, as a means to an end, but the consequences of this habit of thought emerge only gradually in the course of the play. Consider, for example, his mistake as to the meaning of the soothsayer's prophecy, which provides an assumption essential to his argument in the opening scene. Odysseus reads the prophecy as requiring the two men simply to "get the bow" as though the weapon had a kind of magic that would automatically win the war for them. This kind of reading is natural for a mind given to his instrumental way of thinking. But as the play proceeds we learn that the soothsayer's command is to obtain not just the bow but Philoctetes and that Philoctetes' return to the community must be voluntary. And we learn this fact in an interesting way: partly by a kind of accident, as one speaker or another states the authoritative command differently and with varying degrees of reliability—the first time we learn that the Achaeans must persuade Philoctetes himself is from the Emporos, whom we know to be in some respects dishonest—but much more importantly in another way, which has great relevance to the interpretation of all authoritative texts, legal among the rest. For the true meaning of the command is most reliably discovered by Neoptolemus gradually, as he matures, not by learning more about the actual words the soothsayer uttered but by learning more about the situation to which he spoke.

To one who learns to see things and to think about them as Neoptolemus does, and as we do too, it is not only immoral but unrealistic to think that all that is required here is the physical acquisition of an instrument, an inert bow and its arrows. What is required, as anyone with eyes can see—and this is after all what the soothsayer saw—is that the breach in the community created by Philoctetes' abandonment must be healed, and it can only be healed by his free and voluntary return. He must become a member of the community once more. This means that deceit cannot get the Achaeans what they want (nor indeed can Neoptolemus' original alternative, force): only persuasion, and persuasion of the sincere and authentic kind by which community is established (*peithō*), can work.

To conceive of what goes wrong as a matter of reading: Odysseus shows that he is incapable of reading a perfectly sensible directive in an intelligent way.[3] In the law, we call such readers literalists: they are given to reading authoritative texts as "literal" commands without regard to their evident purpose and nature and without regard to the universe of understandings and commitments that render them comprehensible. Such a reader, then as now, is in fact likely to miss not only the true meaning of a text but its very words, as Odysseus does: to fail even at the task of literalism itself. The modern lawyer can perhaps thus take some heart from what Sophocles shows him: Odysseus is not a model of the crafty lawyer after all, unscrupulous but effective, rational but base, but an example of a lawyer who is bad in both senses of the term. At just the level where his claims for himself are most seriously made, that he is a pragmatic success, he is in fact a total failure.

What Odysseus misses is the reality of the social world, and its power. His cast of mind, which itemizes the world into a chain of *desiderata* and mechanisms, is incapable of understanding the reality and force of shared understandings and confidences. This error appears today in the common idea that our "wealth" is material—the bringing of resources under individual control for purposes of exchange or consumption—while in fact our most important wealth is social and cultural: confidence in the reliability and good sense and generosity of our neighbors; trust in the reciprocal practices by which community is established; pleasure in finding, and making, shared meanings, and in elaborating them cooperatively; or, in terms of this play, confidence and pleasure in those activities by which Neoptolemus and Philoctetes create a world of action and significance. Think of our own desire for physical safety: whether one speaks of international relations, city streets, the workplace, or the family, the healthy and just community achieves a kind of security that mere force can never attain.

The ultimate fact about Odysseus is his disappearance into nothingness at the end. Once Neoptolemus faces him down, he evapo-

---

3. This is made especially plain in the Emporos' account, in which Helenus says that Philoctetes must be persuaded to come, whereupon Odysseus instantly undertakes to go get him, by force if necessary (lines 610–18).

rates off the stage, to reappear only as a possible target for Philoctetes. The man whose great claim is to be a source of competent energy ends up literally nothing at all. The power of evil is only apparent, for in the realm of character and community it has no force, no actuality, against an integrated mind.

This beautifully dramatized evaporation is implicit in Odysseus' mode of thinking, for one thing ends-means rationality cannot do is choose its ends. They must be taken as givens. Compare the most systematic modern version of this kind of thought, market economics, in which ends are explicitly taken as external to the system: preferences are whatever any person happens to prefer, and all preferences are equal until given different values through the prices paid or obtained for them. Because Odysseus cannot think about the proper choice of ends, his whole being is spent in the service of ends that he cannot examine. At one point he claims to be one who aims to "conquer always" (line 1052), but this is not inconsistent with what I have said. It is the statement of the purely competitive mind, who has no values except as those are defined by what other people want, like the little boy who wants nothing in the world but what his brother happens to have. As for the choice of means, Odysseus' attention to probability and improbability, cost and benefit, locates the authority for that choice outside the self, in the world, for the only question is what will work best. Such a mind cannot constitute a self.

Odysseus in fact makes this consequence of his thought explicit when he tells Neoptolemus to give himself for just one shameful day, then to be the most honorable of men, and when he says that he himself is capable of virtue when that is the game, but not when it is not: he says that he *is* whatever the situation calls for (line 1049). From one point of view this is familiar cynical advice not to be a goody-goody. From another, however, it is a horrifying statement of a person without a self, without a soul, for Odysseus seems wholly unaware that who he is today has, or can have, any relation to who he will be tomorrow, or was yesterday. For him the self has no continuity but is a series of discrete and unconnected actions and moments of consciousness, a set of fragments. This means that rational thought about, and action in, the social and cultural realm is impossible. Think of the social practices that Neoptolemus and Philoctetes share: could Odysseus pledge, or promise, or give or receive a trust?

The central value of this play is integration: the putting together of parts of the self, parts of experience, parts of language, into meaningful wholes—like Heracles' version of Philoctetes' story and Neoptolemus' final version of his own language of value—and putting together people into communities. But Odysseus stands for disintegration, not only in his methods of persuasion, by which he momentarily disintegrates Neoptolemus for the moment and by which Neoptolemus threatens Philoctetes with disintegration, but in himself: he ends as a disintegrated nonentity.

If Odysseus is the pure "consequentialist" who fails to understand consequences of the most important kind, Neoptolemus is an exemplar of what can be called "character ethics" who at first fails to maintain his character. But as Odysseus becomes an increasingly destructive and empty version of himself, Neoptolemus is shown to develop, largely through the friendship of Philoctetes, into a mature and autonomous person who knows and can defend his own values. When Philoctetes' intractability presents him with a conflict between two different futures for himself, as one who is successful in destroying Troy and as one who is true to his pledge to and friendship with Philoctetes, Neoptolemus knows which to choose. This time he does not disintegrate.

As for Philoctetes, he is carefully placed with respect to each of the others. As Neoptolemus is too readily persuaded, Philoctetes is too intransigent: he should, as Heracles says, be willing to be persuaded in the way Neoptolemus ultimately seeks to do. And as Odysseus too narrowly focuses his attention on "the bow," and in doing so fails to see the reality of social life and of shared meaning, when Philoctetes focuses obsessively on his injury and gives it a priority over all other facts he misses much of the same reality. At the end Neoptolemus acquires some of Philoctetes' resolve, Philoctetes some of his amenability to persuasion: they both achieve maturity and health.

As we saw above, what ultimately persuades Philoctetes is a new narrative, a version of his life that recognizes what is at the moment most real to him about his experience—his injury—but also places it in a context consisting of what else is real to him, and about him: his heroic valor, his love of his comrades, his fated role as the destroyer of Troy. The past, the present, and the future are put together in a new order, the central force and achievement of which is its combination of recognition and integration.

What are we then to make of the fact that Neoptolemus' noble form of persuasion fails and Odysseus' ignoble form succeeds? Does this not upset the whole structure of value I have just outlined and undermine what seems to be the most important meaning of the play?

This is the central difficulty to which the play is written, and understanding it requires two initial clarifications. Despite what I have just suggested, the play makes clear that Neoptolemus' ultimate attempt to persuade Philoctetes in fact fails not because it is weaker than some alternative, but either because nothing would ever have succeeded against such intransigence or because the prior deception has alienated Philoctetes irreparably. We simply do not know what the result would have been had Neoptolemus come to Philoctetes at the beginning, explaining that Helenus had prophesied his cure, and so forth, and urging his return. As it is, Philoctetes has just suffered a terrible abuse of trust at the hands of Odysseus and Neoptolemus, and it may be this that makes him so intractable. The proper kind of persuasion might have led to successful reconciliation and a proper reading of the play will keep that possibility in mind, at least as part of the background. (The failure may be the consequence, that is, not of the use of Neoptolemus' methods but those of Odysseus.) And in any event, as I suggested above, Odysseus' methods proved not to be successful. The play in fact shows that they will fail every time that true cooperation is required, for all that can possibly be obtained this way is an instrument or object, a "bow," and not the creation of a functioning community. The failure of Neoptolemus' persuasion, if failure there be, is thus not to be taken as argument for the methods of Odysseus, which will fail even more certainly, at least on occasions like this one.

Where this leaves us is with the enforced recognition of certain central ethical and practical truths: that there is no sure-fire method of attaining your ends when those ends require the cooperation of others and that to recognize the freedom and autonomy of another, which is the only real possibility if one is to succeed at all, is necessarily to leave room for the exercise of that freedom and autonomy in ways you do not wish.

But there is more to it than that, for the play is at its heart about the conditions under which ethical and practical thought take place, about their ontology and epistemology if you will. Here its major point is that the only circumstances under which ends-means rationality might be rational never exist, for our thought must always take place on conditions of uncertainty that render that kind of "rationality" worse than useless. These conditions require us to think in other, more difficult, ways and to attend first and last to questions of character and community. The only rational "ends"—the only ends we can confidently use as guides to conduct—are conceptions of ourselves and of our relations with others, not materially describable states of affairs.

How does Sophocles establish these conditions of uncertainty and make them vivid? In this connection consider our initial mistake about the meaning of the prophecy, and the dominance of Odysseus' interpretation of it over us and Neoptolemus alike in the opening scene. As readers (or as an audience), we at first share Odysseus' mistake, for how could we do otherwise? We accept his statement of the premises of the expedition and only gradually come to perceive the conditions of life that render those premises impossible. We are led to misread so that our reading can be corrected.

When we learn that the meaning of the prophecy is uncertain, we at first want to know "what it says," that is, what its words are. This, we think, will enable us to judge what the characters should do. But in the real world we live always in uncertainty, without such clear prophecies or other directives; our hunger for clarity will not be sat-isfied; and we must accept the fact that our ethical and moral imper-atives must in part be constructed by us—as the meaning of the prophecy in this play ultimately is—out of the materials of the world with which we are presented, out of the evident meanings and de-mands of the situation. In not giving us a reliable version of the prophecy until the very end—and even then giving it to us in a dif-ferent form—and in showing us that we can nonetheless judge what is right, the play teaches us to accept the responsibilities of maturity and the conditions of uncertainty on which human life is led.

This suggests an answer to one who responds to the play by say-ing: "But don't we sometimes need only the bow and not the man? And *then* what Odysseus does would be justified, wouldn't it?" The answer is this: we do not know—we can never know—that we need the bow and not the man. To think that we do, or might, need only the bow, and to contrive on that basis is to commit ourselves to a course that is irrational as well as unethical.

Our thought about ethics and justice, about our practical social and political lives, must acknowledge that the facts, the imperatives, and the motives of ourselves and others are not fixed but uncertain, in a sense always made by us in conversation with each other. The con-ditions for pure ends-means rationality never exist. The habit of mind that yearns for these methods and their certainties is bound to be delusive, and ultimately—despite its claims to superior rationality—to be irrational, because it will not be in accordance with the nature of our world and our experience. The only way to function rationally in these domains is to recognize the radical uncertainty in which we live; to proceed by trial and error; to operate with a constant pressure towards openness; to acknowledge the necessity of community and cooperation both to the definition and to the attainment of any of our "ends"; to realize that one aim of life is the transformation of our own perceptions, wishes, and selves; and to regard the central intellectual imperative as the integration of all we can perceive, of all that we are, into meaningful wholes.

A second reality made vivid by the play is its insistence that all social action requires community and that community can never be compelled. Slaves will revolt, spouses will divorce, workmen will unite, partners will resign, allies will default, and often they will do so in the face of death itself. Our practical and moral lives are radically communal—unless perhaps we live alone on an island—and this means that our thought about what we want and who we are must reflect the freedom and power of others, without whose free cooperation we can have nothing of value, be nothing of value. This in turn means that hardheaded practical thought and sound ethical thought alike require us to recognize the existence of others and our dependence upon them. Our most practical end is never definable in terms of material results but always and only in terms of a certain kind of community: a way of facing the uncertainties of life together. These are the conditions of our existence; rhetoric is the art by which they are addressed.

But the play does more even than this, for in its demonstration of what it means to treat another as an "end" or as a "means" it establishes standards by which we can judge particular conduct and speech, particular relations and communities. This literary demonstration in the text, as read or performed, has a clarity and force—a persuasiveness—that theoretical argument could never have, for it works by constituting the audience in a new way. The play addresses the whole reader, not just one capacity or faculty, and evokes an integrated response, in which pleasure, excitement, enjoyment, commitment, as well as learning, are engaged. It integrates the experience and the self, locating them in the conditions of uncertainty in which we must actually live. The audience is newly constituted by the play in a new position, from which the only imaginable attitude to take towards persuasion and community is that of recognition and integration, the only imaginable rhetoric is sincere and authentic (*peithō*, not *dolos*). It achieves this by creating a community with the audience that directly parallels the community created between Neoptolemus and Philoctetes: as we hear Philoctetes speak, we respond to him as Neoptolemus does; we respond to Neoptolemus as Philoctetes does; and so on.

The community the play creates with us in fact has an actuality the others lack: it exists in space and time, in our minds and responses, as on a hot morning in the theater we become something, collectively and individually, for which we earlier had only the potentiality. The true meaning of the play is our response to it, who we become in response to it. This is what is most real about it, and the experience teaches us how to live in the uncertain world it represents: what to value and cling to, what to disregard, where to direct our attention and our energy.

For the rest of us, lawyers especially, this means that we must ask what worlds, what communities, our expressions and writings and conversations create. In our hands, what kind of theater can the law be, or become? When we practice law we represent others, whose needs to some degree determine our "ends," and our task is to "succeed": does that mean that, despite this play, we must act like Odysseus or be false to our profession? Must we see the "bow of Heracles" simply as an object, or can we see it as having a meaning that is essentially social and rhetorical: as standing for the autonomy and maturity of persons whose voluntary cooperation, upon equal terms, is always to be sought; a symbol of the attainment of full personality, for which community is always necessary?

BIBLIOGRAPHIC NOTE

The reader interested in exploring further the meaning of this play may find useful the following works: A. W. H. Adkins, *Merit and Responsibility: A Study in Greek Values* (Oxford: Clarendon Press, 1960); R. G. A. Buxton, *Persuasion in Greek Tragedy: A Study of Peitho* (Cambridge and New York: Cambridge University Press, 1982), chap. 4; P. E. Easterling, "*Philoctetes* and Modern Criticism," *Illinois Classical Studies* 3 (1978): 27–39; Bernard Knox, *The Heroic Temper: Studies in Sophoclean Tragedy* (Berkeley: University of California Press, 1964), chap. 5; Martha Nussbaum, "Consequences and Character in Sophocles' *Philoctetes*," *Philosophy and Literature* 1 (1976): 25–51; Ruth Scodel, *Sophocles* (Boston: Twayne Publishers, 1984), chap. 7; Edmund Wilson, "*Philoctetes*: The Wound and the Bow," in *The Wound and the Bow: Seven Studies in Literature* (Boston: Houghton Mifflin, 1941), pp. 272–95.

In particular, Adkins is helpful on the ways in which the Greek language of value is disassembled by Odysseus (though I would disagree on some of the details); Nussbaum on Odysseus as a utilitarian, Neoptolemus as an exemplar of character ethics; Wilson on Philoctetes' love of his own injury.

There is a school that reads Odysseus' willingness to leave without Philoctetes not as a misreading of the prophecy but as a bluff. See A. E. Hinds, "The Prophecy of Helenus in Sophocles' *Philoctetes*," *Classical Quarterly* (new series) 17 (1967): 169–80, persuasively responded to by D. B. Robinson, "Topics in Sophocles' *Philoctetes*," *Classical Quarterly* (new series) 19 (1969): 45–56. See also Scodel, *Sophocles*, pp. 100–02.

It is true that at several points Odysseus speaks either to command Philoctetes to come or to explain the wish or expectation that he will come, and it would be possible to read these remarks as expressing a recognition that Philoctetes *must* come if his own mission is to succeed. (At lines 982–83 he says to Philoctetes, "You must go with them or they will take you by force"; at 993 he says, "You must go this road"; and at 1000–1004 he prevents Philoctetes from committing suicide—all this while Neoptolemus has the bow itself. And at the beginning, when Neoptolemus speaks of bringing the man to Troy [lines 90, 102, 112], Odysseus does not contradict him.) But this would, I think, be a misreading in light of the way Odysseus is said to respond when the prophecy is issued; his proposed plan to abandon Philoctetes; and the general focus of his expressed concern throughout, which is on the bow itself. It would be safer to bring Philoctetes than the bow alone, but he plainly thinks the bow alone is better than nothing; and in any event he completely misses the point that Philoctetes' cooperation must be wholly voluntary to have the meaning he wants for it.

Robinson also takes the view that the real ending of the play is the departure of Neoptolemus with Philoctetes; for him Heracles' intervention is simply forced upon Sophocles by tradition. Most readers would, I think, disagree with this point, but see A. J. Podlecki, "The Power of the Word in Sophocles' *Philoctetes*," *Greek, Roman, Byzantine Studies* 7 (1966): 233–50.

2 RHETORIC AND LAW

THE ARTS OF CULTURAL

AND COMMUNAL LIFE

In this essay I turn from the ethics of persuasion and community in the context of a Greek drama to an explicit consideration of the nature of modern law and rhetoric. I also shift modes of expression a bit, from analyzing a text to making a general argument of a somewhat abstract kind. My general idea is that while there are of course many useful and familiar ways to talk about law—say as a system of rules or a structure of institutions—it is most usefully and completely seen as a branch of rhetoric. But "rhetoric" also needs definition, and I think it should be seen not as a failed science nor as an ignoble art of persuasion (as it often is) but as the central art by which culture and community are established, maintained, and transformed. This kind of rhetoric—I call it "constitutive rhetoric"—has justice as its ultimate subject, and of it I think law can be seen as a species.

I do not mean to say that these are the only ways to understand law or rhetoric. There is a place in the world for institutional and policy studies, for taxonomies of persuasive devices, for the analysis of statistical patterns and distributive effects. But I think all of these activities will themselves be done better and criticized more intelligently if it is recognized that they too are rhetorical. As for law and rhetoric themselves, I think that to see them in the way I describe here—as continuous with the concerns of Sophocles' *Philoctetes*—is to make sense of them in a more complete way, especially from the point of view of the individual speaker, the individual hearer, and the individual judge.

1

When I say that we might regard law as a branch of rhetoric, I may seem to say only the obvious. Who ever could have thought it was anything else? The ancient rhetorician Gorgias (in Plato's dialogue of that name) defined rhetoric as the art of persuading the people about matters of justice and injustice in the public places of the state, and one could hardly imagine a more compendious statement of the art of the lawyer than that. A modern law school is, among other things, a school in those arts of persuasion about justice that are peculiar to, and peculiarly effective in, our legal culture. And the commitment of the rhetorician to the cause of his client presents him, in the ancient and the modern world alike, with serious (and similar) problems of intellectual and personal integrity. What do people think law is if it is not rhetoric, and why do they think so?

The answer lies I think in two traditions, one old, the other new. The older (primarily Judaic and Christian) tradition saw the law as a set of authoritative commands, entitled to respect partly from their antiquity, partly from their concordance with the law of nature and of God. On this view law is not rhetoric but authority. The newer tradition is that of institutional sociology, the object of which is to describe and analyze the structure and function of various social institutions, so far as possible from the point of view of "value-free" social science. These institutions may of course have certain kinds of political authority internal to the culture in which they can be found, but they are normally not seen as sources of true moral authority, as law once was. With the apparent death of the first tradition in most Western European (but not Islamic!) countries, we are left with the second, and tend to view law as a system of institutionally established and managed rules. As this conception has worked itself out in practice, it has led to a kind of substantive neutrality or emptiness that makes it natural once again to see a connection between modern law and ancient rhetoric, and to face—as Plato did in the *Gorgias*—the great question of what talk about justice can mean in a world as relativistic, adversarial, competitive, and uncertain as ours is and theirs was.

For these reasons the law is at present usually spoken of (by academics at least) as if it were a body of more or less determinate rules, or rules and principles, that are more or less perfectly intelligible to the trained reader. Law is in this sense objectified and made a structure. The question "What is law?" is answered by defining what its rules are, or by analyzing the kinds of rules that characterize it. The law is thus abstracted and conceptualized: H. L. A. Hart's major book on jurisprudence was appropriately entitled *The Concept of Law*. Sophisticated analysis of law from this point of view distinguishes among various kinds of legal rules and different sets or subsets of legal rules: substantive rules from procedural or remedial rules, or primary rules from secondary rules, or legal rules from more general principles.

This idea of law and legal science fits with, and is perhaps derived from, the contemporary conception of our public political world as a set of bureaucratic entities, which can be defined in Weberian terms as rationalized institutions functioning according to ends-means rationality. These institutions are defined by their goals, purposes, or aims, which they achieve more or less perfectly as they are structured and managed more or less well.

In this way the government, of which the law is a part (and in fact the entire bureaucratic system, private as well as public), tends to be regarded, especially by lawyers, managers, and other policy-makers, as a machine acting on the rest of the world; the rest of the world is in turn reduced to the object upon which the machine acts. Actors outside the bureaucratic world are made the objects of manipulation through a series of incentives or disincentives. Actors within the legal-bureaucratic structure are either reduced to "will-servers" (who regard their obligation as being to obey the will of a political superior), or they are "choice-makers" (who are in a position of political superiority, charged with the responsibility of making choices, usually thought of as "policy choices," that affect the lives of others). The choices themselves are likewise objectified: the items of choice are broken out of the flux of experience and the context of life so that they can be talked about in the bureaucratic-legal mode. This commits the system to what is thought to be measurable, especially to what is measurable in material ways; to short-term goals; and to a process of thought by calculation. The premises of cost-benefit analysis are integral to the bureaucracy as we normally imagine it. Whatever cannot be talked about in these bureaucratic ways is simply not talked about. Of course all systems of discourse have domains and boundaries, principles of exclusion and inclusion; but this kind of bureaucratic talk is unselfconscious about what it excludes. The world it sees is its whole world.

Law then becomes reducible to two features: policy choices and techniques of their implementation. Our questions are, "What do we want?" and "How do we get it?" In this way the conception of law as a set of rules merges with the conception of law as a set of institutions and processes. The overriding metaphor is that of the machine; the overriding value is that of efficiency, conceived of as the attainment of certain ends with the smallest possible costs.[1]

This is a necessarily crude sketch of certain ways in which law is commonly thought of. Later in this essay I shall propose, and in the rest of the book I shall elaborate, a different way of conceiving of law, which I think can be both more true to its actual nature as practiced and more valuable to us as critics.

2

I turn now to what is usually meant by "rhetoric." This term is in greater flux, and what I say must be somewhat less dogmatic. But it is my impression that rhetoric is at present usually talked about in either of two modes. The first of these is by comparison with science. The main claim of science is that it contributes to knowledge by informing us of what is knowable in the sense that it can be demonstrated. This is true both of deductive sciences, which establish propositions by demonstrating their entailment in certain premises, and of inductive sciences, which establish, but with less certainty, propositions that can be regarded as the most complete and economical accounts of the evidence available to us, and hence as presumptively true. From this point of view rhetoric is thought of as what we do when science doesn't work. Instead of dealing with what is "known," it deals with what is probably the case. Thus in Aristotle the enthymeme is defined as a syllogism based upon propositions that are not themselves true but probable. Rhetoric is the art of establishing the probable by arguing from our sense of the probable. It is always open to replacement by science when the truth or falsity of what is now merely probable is finally established.

The other heading under which rhetoric is frequently discussed is explicitly pejorative: rhetoric is defined as the ignoble art of persuasion. As I suggested above, this tradition has a history at least as old as the Platonic dialogues, in which rhetoric is attacked as a false art; and it is as contemporary as the standard modern condemnations of

---

1. This bureaucratic language is very deep in our ordinary culture as well: think of a conversation at a curriculum committee meeting where someone says, "Let us first state our educational goals and then determine how we can arrive at them." That is a dreadful way to talk about teaching, yet it is dominant in our world, and once the conversation has begun on those terms it is almost impossible to deflect it to address any true educational concerns.

propaganda in government and of advertising as practiced by the wizards of Madison Avenue. To the extent that law is today regarded as a kind of rhetoric, these two traditions establish the terms of analysis. In the courtroom the truth is never known, and each of the lawyers tries to persuade the jury not of the truth, but that his (or her) view is more probable than the other one or that the other side's case has not attained some requisite degree of probability. In doing so each employs untrustworthy arts of persuasion by which he seeks to make his own case, even if it is the weaker one, appear the stronger. Rhetoric, in short, is thought of either as a second-rate way of dealing with facts that cannot really be properly known or as a way of dealing with people instrumentally or manipulatively, in an attempt to get them to do something you want them to do.

The tendency to think of rhetoric as failed science is especially powerful in the present age, in which such determined attempts have been made to elevate, or to reduce, virtually every discipline to the status of true science. The idea of science as perfect knowledge has of course been recently subjected to considerable criticism, both internal and external. It is now a commonplace that scientific creativity is imaginative, almost poetic; that scientific knowlege is only presumptive, not certain; and that science is a culture that transforms itself by principles that are not themselves scientific. Yet the effort to make the language and conventions of science the ruling model of our age, our popular religion, lives on in the language and expectations of others, especially of those who are in fact not true scientists. Much of economic discourse, for example, is deformed by the false claims of the discipline to the status of perfect science, which leads to the embarrassing situation in which economic speakers representing different political attitudes couch their differences in scientific terms, each claiming that the other is no true economist. This not only confuses the observer but renders the field of economics less intelligible than it should be, even to its participants, and it reduces important political differences, which might be the topic of real conversation, to the status of primary assumptions.

3

In this essay I shall propose a somewhat different way of conceiving of law, and indeed of governmental processes generally: not as a bureaucratic but as a rhetorical process. In doing this I will also be suggesting a way to think about rhetoric as well, especially about that "constitutive" rhetoric of which law can I think be seen as a species.

I want to start by thinking of law not as an objective reality in an imagined social world, not as a part of a constructed cosmology, but from the point of view of those who actually engage in its processes, as something we do and something we teach. This is a way of looking at law as an activity, and specifically as a rhetorical activity.

In particular I want to direct attention to three aspects of the lawyer's work. The first is the fact that, like any rhetorician, the lawyer must always start by speaking the language of his or her audience, whatever it may be. This is just a version of the general truth that to persuade anyone you must in the first instance speak a language he or she regards as valid and intelligible. If you are a lawyer this means that you must speak either the technical language of the law—the rules, cases, statutes, maxims, and so forth that constitute the domain of your professional talk—or, if you are speaking to jurors or clients or the public at large, some version of the ordinary English of your time and place and culture. Law is in this sense always culture-specific. It always starts with an external, empirically discoverable set of cultural resources into which it is an intervention.

This suggests that one (somewhat circular) definition of the law might be as the particular set of resources made available by a culture for speech and argument on those occasions, and by those speakers, we think of as legal. These resources include rules, statutes, and judicial opinions, of course, but much more as well: maxims, general understandings, conventional wisdom, and all the other resources, technical and nontechnical, that a lawyer might use in defining his or her position and urging another to accept it.[2] To define "the law" in this way, as a set of resources for thought and argument, is an application of Aristotle's traditional definition of rhetoric, for the law in this sense is one set of those "means of persuasion" which he said it is the art of rhetoric to discover.

In the law (and I believe elsewhere as well) these means of persua-

---

2. In light of the current view of law as a set of rules, it is worth stressing that while much legal argument naturally takes the form of interpreting rules, or redefining them, and while some rules are of course superior in authority to others, the material as a whole is not structured as a set of rules with a hierarchical or other order, nor is it reducible to a set of rules. The rule is often the subject as well as the source of argument; its form and content and relation to other rules are in principle arguable. The best way to understand what a rule is, as it works in the legal world, is to think of it not as a command that is obeyed or disobeyed but as a topic of thought and argument—as one of many resources brought to bear by the lawyer and others both to define a question and to establish a way to approach it.

sion can be described with some degree of accuracy and completeness, so that most lawyers would agree that such-and-such a case or statute or principle is relevant, and another is not. But the agreement is always imperfect: one lawyer will see an analogy that another will deny, for example. And when attention shifts to the value or weight that different parts of the material should have, disagreement becomes widespread and deep. Ultimately the identity, the meaning, and the authority of the materials are always arguable, always uncertain. There is a sense in which the materials can be regarded in the first instance as objective, external to the self; but they are always remade in argument. Their discovery is an empirical process; their reformulation and use an inventive or creative one.

This suggests that the lawyer's work has a second essential element, the creative process to which I have just alluded. For in speaking the language of the law the lawyer must always be ready to try to change it: to add or to drop a distinction, to admit a new voice, to claim a new source of authority, and so on. One's performance is in this sense always argumentative, not only about the result one seeks to obtain but also about the version of the legal discourse that one uses—that one creates—in one's speech and writing. That is, the lawyer is always saying not only, "Here is how this case should be decided," but also "Here—in this language—is the way this case and similar cases should be talked about. The language I am speaking is the proper language of justice in our culture." The legal speaker always acts upon the language that he or she uses; in this sense legal rhetoric is always argumentatively constitutive of the language it employs.

The third aspect of legal rhetoric is what might be called its ethical or communal character, or its socially constitutive nature. Every time one speaks as a lawyer, one establishes for the moment a character—an ethical identity, or what the Greeks called an *ethos*—for oneself, for one's audience, and for those one talks about, and proposes a relationship among them. The lawyer's speech is thus always implicitly argumentative not only about the result—how should the case be decided?—and the language—in what terms should it be defined and talked about?—but about the rhetorical community of which one is at that moment a part. One is always establishing in performance a response to the question "What kind of community should we who are talking the language of the law establish with each other, with our clients, and with the rest of the world? What kind of conversation should the law constitute, should constitute the law?"

Each of the three aspects of the lawyer's rhetorical life can be analyzed and criticized: the discourse he is given by his culture to speak; his argumentative reconstitution of it; and his implicitly argumentative constitution of a rhetorical community in his text. The study of this process—of constitutive rhetoric—is the study of the ways we constitute ourselves as individuals, as communities, and as cultures, whenever we speak. To put this another way, the fact that the law may be understood as a comprehensibly organized method of argument, or what I call a rhetoric, means that it is at once a social activity—a way of acting with others—and a cultural activity, a way of acting with a certain set of materials found in the culture. It is always communal, both in the sense that it always takes place in a social context, and in the sense that it is always constitutive of the community by which it works. The law is an art of persuasion that creates the objects of its persuasion, for it constitutes both the community and the culture it commends.

This means that the process of law is at once creative and educative. Those who use this language are perpetually learning what can and cannot be said, what can and cannot be done with it, as they try—and fail or succeed—to reach new formulations of their positions. It also means that both the identity of the speakers and their wants are in perpetual transformation. If this is right, the law cannot be a technique, as the bureaucratic model assumes, by which "we" get what we "want," for both "we" and our "wants" are constantly remade in the rhetorical process. The idea of the legal actor as one who is either making policy choices himself (or herself) or obeying the choices made by others is inadequate, for he is a participant in the perpetual remaking of the language and culture that determines who he is and who we are. In this way we might come to see the law less as a bureaucracy or a set of rules than as a community of speakers of a certain kind; as a culture of argument, perpetually remade by its participants.

4

All this flows from the fact that the law is what I have called culture-specific, that is, that it always takes place in a cultural context into which it is always an intervention. But it is in a similar way socially specific: it always takes place in a particular social context, into which it is also an intervention. By this I mean nothing grand but simply that the lawyer responds to the felt needs of others, who come to him or her for assistance with an actual difficulty or problem. These felt needs may of course be partly the product of the law itself, and the very "intervention" of the law can create new possibilities for meaning, for motive, and for aspiration. From this point of view the law can be seen, as it is experienced, not as an independent system of meaning, but as a way of talking about real events and actual people in the world. At its heart it is a way of telling a story about what has happened in the world and claiming a meaning for it by writing an ending to it. The lawyer is repeatedly saying, or imagining himself or herself saying: "Here is 'what happened'; here is 'what it means'; and here is 'why it means what I claim.'" The process is at heart a narrative one because there cannot be a legal case without a real story about real people actually located in time and space and culture. Some actual person must go to a lawyer with an account of the experience upon which he or she wants the law to act, and that account will always be a narrative.

The client's narrative is not simply accepted by the lawyer but subjected to questioning and elaboration, as the lawyer sees first one set of legal relevances, then another. In the formal legal process that story is then retold, over and over, by the lawyer and by the client and by others, in developing and competing versions, until by judgment or agreement an authoritative version is achieved. (Think of the way that Neoptolemus recasts Philoctetes' story, with a different beginning and a different sense of causation, to give it a different meaning and to make a different ending seem possible, indeed inevitable and right.) This story will in the first instance be told in the language of its actors. That is where the law begins; in a sense this is also where it ends, for its object is to provide an ending to that story that will work in the world. And since the story both begins and ends in ordinary language and experience, the heart of the law is the process of translation by which it must work, from ordinary language to legal language and back again.

The language that the lawyer uses and remakes is a language of meaning in the fullest sense. It is a language in which our perceptions of the natural universe are constructed and related, in which our values and motives are defined, in which our methods of reasoning are elaborated and enacted; and it gives us our terms for constructing a social universe by defining roles and actors and by establishing expectations as to the propriety of speech and conduct. Law always operates through speakers located in particular times and places speaking to actual audiences about real people. Its language is continuous with ordinary language: it always operates by narrative; it is not conceptual in its structure; it is perpetually reaffirmed or rejected in a social process; and it contains a system of internal translation by which it can reach a range of hearers. All these things mark it as a literary and rhetorical system.

5

What I have said means something, I think, about what we can mean by "rhetoric" as well. What I have been describing is not merely an art of estimating probabilities or an art of persuasion, but an art of constituting culture and community. It is of rhetoric so understood that I think we can see the law as a branch.

Let me approach what I mean about rhetoric with a primitive example, meant to suggest that what I call "constitutive rhetoric" is actually the set of practices that most fully distinguish human beings from other animals. Imagine a bear, fishing for salmon in a river of the great Northwest. What is he doing? Fishing we say. Now imagine a man fishing in the same river for the same fish. What is he doing? Fishing, we say; but this time the answer has a different meaning and a new dimension, for it is now a question, as it was not before, what the fishing means to the actor himself. If a person does it, it has a meaning of a kind it cannot otherwise have. Today the meaning may well be that of sentimental escape to the wilderness by one sportily clad in his L. L. Bean outfit, demonstrating his place in a certain social class; but once—for a Native American say—it might have been a religious meaning.

Whenever two people fish (or hunt, or anything else), they necessarily share the question of the meaning of what they do. (Think of the conversations between Odysseus and Neoptolemus about the meaning of the methods of persuasion they might use, for example.) Their views may differ, and their differences may reach the meaning of their relationship as well as that of their common activity. There is, for example, the question of dominance or equality: is one person following the other, or are they in some sense together? Do their views of the meaning of what they do coincide, and if so how do they know? Or is there tension or disharmony between them, and if so what is to be done about that? How long will the terms upon which they are proceeding remain stable? The establishment of comprehensible relations and shared meanings, the making of the kind of community that enables people to say "we" about what they do and to claim consistent meanings for it—all this at the deepest level involves persuasion as well as education, and is the province of what I call constitutive rhetoric.

Let me expand my example a bit. Think of the kind of opposition that begins the _Iliad_, the opposition between two male human beings quarreling over a female. From one point of view this is just like two other male mammals doing the same thing, say two male bears or dogs. But from another point of view there is a completely new dimension added to the dispute: the question of what it means, from each point of view including that of the woman. It is from such a dispute, and from the claims of competing meanings for the events involved, that arose both the Trojan War (at least in Greek myth) and, from our point of view much more importantly, the _Iliad_ itself. Agamemnon and Achilles are engaged in a struggle. At some level the struggle is an animal one, with will opposed to will. It is also a human struggle, a struggle over what ought to be done, and why, and this is a struggle over meaning: what it means for Agamemnon to be deprived of a prize, or of this woman, or for Achilles to be deprived of a prize, or of this woman. At moments in this poem attention is directed to what it means from the point of view of the woman herself, as in the cases of Andromache, Helen, and at one moment Briseis herself.

Once the quarrel has begun, and Achilles has separated himself from the other Achaeans, the question shifts to what _that_ means, and, as time goes on, to how the quarrel might be made up. "Making up" a quarrel is a process in which the parties gradually, and often with great difficulty, come to share a common language for the description of their common past, present, and future, including an agreement as to what will be passed over in silence. In this process they reestablish themselves as a community with a culture of their own. In the _Iliad_, Agamemnon's attempts to make up the quarrel fail; community between them is never reestablished, even when Achilles returns to the battle, because that is done for a different reason, the death of Patroclus.

Or think of another great literary moment, the beginning of _Paradise Lost_, when Satan and the other rebellious angels try to establish a community of their own in Hell, based upon a new language of value and meaning. Their incredible attempts at self-creation and self-assertion have won them the admiration of many readers, from Shelley onwards; some even see Satan as the unacknowledged hero of the poem. ("The mind is its own place, and in itself / Can make a Heav'n of Hell, a Hell of Heav'n.") But the poem shows that no community can be built upon the language that they use, a language of selfishness and hatred—a language that in fact made a "Hell of Heav'n"—even by figures with such enormous capacities of imagination and will as Milton represents the angels to be. Compare with this the efforts of the participants at our own Constitutional Convention in the summer of 1787, who were also trying to find or make a language, and a set of relations, upon which a new community could be made, a new life proceed. Their arguments can be read as the gradual attempt to make a language of shared factual assumptions, shared values, shared senses of what need be said and what need not—of what could be said ambiguously, of what they could not resolve at all—resulting in a text that they could offer to others as the terms on which a new community might begin its tentative life.

What kind of community shall it be? How will it work? In what language shall it be formed? These are the great questions of rhetorical analysis. It always has justice and ethics—and politics, in the best sense of that term—as its ultimate subjects.

The domain of constitutive rhetoric as I think of it thus includes *all* language activity that goes into the constitution of actual human cultures and communities. Even the kind of persuasion Plato called dialectic, in which the speaker is himself willing, even eager, to be refuted, is in this sense a form of rhetoric, for it is the establishment of community and culture in language.

6

Like law, rhetoric invents, and like law it invents not out of nothing but out of something. It always starts in a particular place among particular people. There is always one speaker addressing others in a particular situation about concerns that are real and important to somebody, and always speaking a particular language. Rhetoric always takes place with given materials. One cannot idealize rhetoric and say: Here is how it should go on in general. As Aristotle saw—for his *Rhetoric* is for the most part a map of claims that are persuasive in his Greek world—rhetoric is always specific to its material. There is not an Archimedean point from which rhetoric can be viewed or practiced.

This means that the rhetorician—that is, each of us when we speak to persuade or to establish community in other ways—must accept the double fact that there are real and important differences between cultures and that one is in substantial part the product of one's own culture. The rhetorician, like the lawyer, is thus engaged in a process of meaning-making and community-building of which he or she is in part the subject. To do this requires him or her to face and to accept the condition of radical uncertainty in which we live: uncertainty as to the meaning of words, uncertainty as to their effect on others, uncertainty even as to our own motivations. The knowledge out of which the rhetorician ultimately functions will thus be not scientific or theoretical but practical, experiential, the sense that one knows how to do things with language and with others. This is in fact our earliest social and intellectual knowledge, the knowledge we acquire as we first begin to move and act in our social universe and learn to speak and understand. It is the knowledge by which language and social relations are made.

The rhetorician thus begins not with the imagined individual in imagined isolation, as political philosophers who think in terms of a social contract do, and not with the self isolated from all of its experience except that of cogitation, as metaphysicians in the Cartesian tradition do, but where Wittgenstein tells us to begin, with our abilities of language, gesture, and meaning. This knowledge is itself not reducible to rules, nor subject to expression in rules, though many analysts wish it were; rather it is the knowledge by which we learn to manage, evade, disappoint, surprise, and please each other, as we understand the expectations that others bring to what we say. This knowledge is not provable in the scientific sense, nor is it logically rigorous. For these reasons it is unsettling to the modern scientific and academic mind. But we cannot go beyond it, and it is a mistake to try. In this fluid world without turf or ground we cannot walk, but we can swim. And we need not be afraid to do this—to engage in the rhetorical process of life—notwithstanding our radical uncertainties, for all of us already know how to do it. By attending to our own experience, and that of others, we can learn to do it better if we try.

7

What would be the effects of thinking of law in this rhetorical way? If, as I think, it is more true to the experience of those engaged in the activity of law than the standard conceptual accounts, it should in the first place lead to richer and more accurate teaching and practice of law and to a greater sense of control over what we do. Law might come to be seen as something that lawyers themselves make all the time, whenever they act as lawyers, not as something that is made by a political sovereign. From this point of view the law can be seen as the culture that we remake whenever we speak as lawyers. To look at law this way is to direct one's attention to places that it perhaps normally does not rest: to the way in which we create new meanings, new possibilities for meaning, in what we say; to the way our literature can be regarded as a literature of value and motive and sentiment; to the way in which our enterprise is a radically ethical one, by which self and community are perpetually reconstituted; and to the limits that our nature or our culture, our circumstances and our imagination, place on our powers to remake our languages and communities in new forms.

To see law this way may also lead to a different way of reading and writing it. As I suggest above, the United States Constitution can be regarded as a rhetorical text: as establishing a set of speakers, roles, topics, and occasions for speech. So understood, many of its ambiguities and uncertainties become more comprehensible; we can see it as attempting to establish a conversation of a certain kind, and its ambiguities as ways of at once defining and leaving open the topics of the conversation. Similarly, a statute can be read not merely as a set of orders or directions or commands, but also as establishing a set of topics, a set of terms in which those topics can be discussed, and some general directions as to the process of thought and argument by which the statute is to be applied. To see the statute as a way of starting a conversation of a certain kind on a certain set of subjects might well assist both one's reading and one's writing of the form. Similarly, the judicial opinion, often thought to be the paradigmatic form of legal expression, might be far more accurately and richly understood if it were seen not as a bureaucratic expression of ends-means rationality but as a statement by an individual mind or a group of individual minds exercising their responsibility to decide a case as well as they can and to determine what it shall mean in the language of the culture. There might be another benefit as well, not irrelevant to the lawyer who has read *Philoctetes* and is worried by what it seems to mean: the view of law as constitutive rhetoric should define the lawyer's own work as far less manipulative, selfish, or goal-oriented than the usual models, and as far more creative, communal, and intellectually challenging.

From the point of view of the nonlawyer, this way of regarding law as rhetoric invites a certain kind of reading and of criticism, for it invites you to test the law in part by asking whether your own story, or the story of another in whom you have an interest, is properly told by these speakers, in a proper language. The basic premise of the hearing is that two stories will be told in opposition or competition and a choice made between them. It is the role of the jury to insist upon the ultimate translatability of law into the common language of the culture. You are entitled to have your story told in your language (or translated into it), or the law is failing. To ask, what place is there for me in this language, this text, this story, and to feel that you have a right to an answer, is a very different way of evaluating law from thinking of it as a mechanism for distributing social goods. The central idea is not that of goods, but of voices and relations: what voices does the law allow to be heard, what relations does it establish among them? With what voice, or voices, does the law itself speak? These are the questions with which rhetorical criticism would begin.

As I suggested above we can also see that the current habit of regarding law as the instrument by which "we" effectuate "our policies" and get what "we want" is wholly inadequate. It is the true nature of law to constitute a "we" and to establish a conversation by which that "we" can determine what our "wants" are and should be. Our motives and values are not on this view to be taken as exogenous to the system (as they are taken to be exogenous to an economic system) but are in fact its subject. The law should take as its most central question what kind of community we should be, with what values, motives, and aims; it is a process by which we make ourselves by making our language.

This means that one question constantly before us as lawyers is what kind of culture we shall have, as well as what kind of community we shall be. What shall be our language of approval and disapproval, praise and blame, admiration and contempt? What shall be the terms by which we identify and refine—by which we create—our motives and combine them into coherent wholes? This way of conceiving of law invites us to include in our zone of attention and field of discourse what others, operating under present suppositions, cut out, including both the uncertainty of life and the fact that we, and our resources, are constantly remade by our own collective activities. The pressure of bureaucratic discourse is always to think in terms of ends and means; in practice ends-means rationality is likely to undergo a reversal by which only those things can count as ends for which means of a certain kind exist. This often results in a reduction of the human to the material and the measurable—a reduction of the man to the bow—as though a good or just society were a function of the rate of individual consumption, not a community of a certain sort, a set of shared relations, attitudes, and meanings. To view law as rhetoric might enable us to attend to the spiritual or meaningful side of our collective life.[3]

Such a conception of law as I describe would lead to a rather different method of teaching it as well. It would at first require a rather old-fashioned training in the intellectual practices that are the things that lawyers do, from reading cases to drafting statutes and contracts. The rhetorician must always start with the materials of his or her language and culture, and we should continue to train our students to understand these materials, their resources and limits, and to learn to put them to work in the activities of narrative and analysis and argument that make up their professional lives.

But these activities would not merely be learned as crafts to be performed as efficiently as possible; they would be contrasted with other ways of doing similar things, both from ordinary life and from other disciplines. Learning how to argue in the law about the meaning of rules, or of fairness, or of blaming, can be informed by attending to the ways in which we already know how to do these things, in ordinary life, and by learning how they are done elsewhere. One focus would accordingly be upon the connection between legal language and ordinary language, legal life and ordinary life, as rhetoric connects them. Another focus would be upon other formal intellectual practices, in an interdisciplinary curriculum rather different from current models: not law *and* sociology or history or economics or literature, but law *as* each of these things. What kind of sociology or history or anthropology are we implicitly practicing in this legal rule, in that legal action or argument, in this judicial opinion? What can be said for and against our implied choices?

But the largest difference would be a shift in the conception of the triadic relation between the student, the teacher, and the subject. The law we teach would not be regarded as a set of institutions that "we" manipulate either to achieve "our policies," as governors, nor "our

3. As one example of what I mean by the difference between the material and the meaningful, consider the question of the invasion of privacy by officials. One way to try to compare different regimes would be to inquire how frequently, for example, police officers stopped individuals on the street, asked for their identification, and subjected them to pat-downs or searches. That would be a material mode of determining "how much" privacy existed in a particular culture. It could in principle be determined statistically. But far more important than that is the meaning of the described activities of the officers both to them and to the citizens. There are circumstances, war being the most obvious, in which almost everyone would agree that this kind of policing was important and valuable, and citizens would by and large not feel that their privacy was invaded, because they would feel that the officer was acting as their fellow worker in a common enterprise.

interests," as lawyers, but rather as a language and a community—a world, made partly by others and partly by ourselves, in which we and others shall live, and which will be tested less by its distributive effects than by the resources of meaning it creates and the community it constitutes: who we become to ourselves and to one another when we converse.[4] And our central question would become how to understand and to judge those things.

8

By this kind of conjunction with the law, rhetoric itself can perhaps be seen in a somewhat different light. No longer a substitute for science when science does not work, it can be seen as a science itself, at least in the eighteenth-century meaning of that term as an organized form of knowledge. It is the knowledge of who we make ourselves, as individuals and as communities, in the ways we speak to each other. Rhetorical knowledge is allied with artistic knowledge in that it is tacitly creative and acknowledges both its limits and the conditions of uncertainty under which it functions. Rhetorical analysis provides a way of addressing the central questions of collective existence in an organized and consistent, but not rule-bound, way. It directs our attention to the most significant questions of shared existence, which are wholly outside the self-determined bounds of science. Justice and ethics are its natural subject, art its natural method.

Rhetoric may also provide a set of questions and attitudes that will enable us to move from one academic and social field to another and in doing so to unite them. For at least tentative judgments of the kind rhetoric calls for can be made about the work of experts—in history say or psychology—without one's having to be an expert in the professional sense oneself. Not that one has not always something to learn—of course one has—but one can never know everything and ought not be barred from making important observations and judgments of one kind by a want of competence at making others. We can

4. I do not mean that distributive effects are irrelevant but that the context in which they are relevant, and from which they derive their meaning, is social and ethical. What does it mean about us that power and wealth are divided this way, or that? Or, more precisely—since power and wealth are at bottom social and cultural—what does it mean about us that we create these powers, these wealths, in this way? Without a social and ethical context, one has after all nothing but brute material—the bow—which has of itself no meaning at all, as wealth, power, or symbol.

say a lot about the kind of history written by Gibbon, for example—about the sort of community he establishes with us, about his language of value and judgment—without being able to make professional judgments about his use of certain inscriptions as evidence on a certain point.

Rhetoric in the highly expanded sense in which I speak of it might even become the central discipline for which we have been looking for so long—which "science" has proven not to be—by which the others can be defined and organized and judged. One reason rhetoric might be able to perform this role is its continuity with ordinary discourse and hence with real communities, real values, and real politics. It is at least contiguous to a ground that is common to us all. Rhetoric must deal with ordinary language because it is the art of speaking to people who already have a language, and it is their language you must speak to reach and to persuade them. This is the sense in which, as I suggested above, rhetoric is always culture-specific. You must take the language you are given and work with that.

One result of this affirmation of ordinary language is that it provides a ground for challenge and change, a place to stand from which to reformulate any more specialized language. It establishes a kind of structural openness. Another result is that it confirms our right and capacity to say what we think is really good about what is good in our world and what is really terrible about what is terrible. Rhetorical analysis invites us to talk about our conceptions of ourselves as individuals and as communities, and to define our values in living rather than conceptual ways. For example, consider what is good about America: our present public rhetoric seems to assume that what is good about it is its material productivity. But that is often wasteful, self-destructive, and ugly. I think what is really good about this country is its fundamental culture of self-government, independence, and generosity. These facts are all too often obscured or denied by the ways in which we habitually talk about our government and law.

How does rhetoric enable us to talk about these matters? It does so by giving us a set of very simple but fundamental questions to ask when someone speaks either to us or on our behalf, or when we ourselves speak. These questions focus on the three aspects of the lawyer's rhetorical situation I identified above.

1. *The inherited language.* What is the language or culture with which this speaker works? How does it represent natural and social facts, constitute human motives and values, and define those persua-

sive motions of the mind that we call reason? What does it leave out or deny? What does it overspecify? What is its actual or imagined relation to other systems of discourse?

2. *The art of the text.* How, by what art and with what effect, is this language remade by this speaker in this written or oral text? Is the text internally coherent, and if so by what standards of coherence? Is it externally coherent (that is, does it establish intelligible relations with its background), and if so, by what standards of coherence? How, that is, does this text reconstitute its discourse?

3. *The rhetorical community.* What kind of person is speaking here, and to what kind of person does he or she speak? What kind of response does this text invite, or permit? What place is there for me, and for others, in the universe defined by this discourse, in the community created by this text? What world does it assume, what world does it create?

Such questions may enable us to approach a set of texts as they are actually made, in widely varying cultures, languages, and human relations, and to establish connections among them across their contexts, above or behind their particularities. To ask them is of course not to answer them: but it may direct our attention to the proper place for thought to begin and suggest, by implication, appropriate modes of inquiry and judgment.

9

Consider, for example, the criticism of judicial opinions. It is common, and in a sense perfectly natural, for judicial critics to direct their attention primarily to the legal results reached by a particular court or judge. This kind of criticism argues the merits of the questions presented and resolved. You might thus criticize a judge, or a court, for being in your view insufficiently sensitive to the importance of free speech or to the rights of states to govern their own affairs; or you might argue that his (or her) method of statutory or constitutional interpretation, or his treatment of precedent, is unsatisfactory. In either case you can expect your argument to be met by others. The resulting conversations—let us call them political and professional—are important branches of judicial criticism. But there is I think another even more fundamental branch of judicial criticism, in which attention is focused less on results or methods than on a special kind of judicial ethics that is in large measure a matter of voice.

Of course one may properly argue against the results of particular cases and, more deeply, against a judge's institutional or political premises, and one may properly criticize technique as well. But any judge brings a set of basic values and orientations to his or her work, and it is hard to fault someone for having a different set from one's own. The law is meant to be a way in which people can live together in spite of their differences. Our most important concern is accordingly less with the original preferences and attitudes a judge brings to the bench, but with what he or she does with them; here we can imagine ourselves greatly admiring the work of a justice with whose substantive predispositions we disagreed, and having contempt for one who largely shared our own social and political attitudes. This is partly a matter of meeting what can be called professional standards—treating precedent in an appropriate way and knowing how, and how not, to use legislative history, for example. But what we admire cannot be reduced to such skills. The deepest judicial excellence is an excellence of attitude and character.

The ideal would be a judge who put his (or her) fundamental attitudes and methods to the test of sincere engagement with arguments the other way. We could ask, does this judge see the case before him as the occasion for printing out an ideology, for displaying technical skill, or as presenting a real difficulty, calling for real thought? The ideal judge would show that he had listened to the side he voted against and that he had felt the pull of the arguments both ways. The law that was made that way would comprise two opposing voices, those of the parties, in a work made by another, by the judge who had listened to both and had faced the conflict between them in an honest way. In this sense the judge's most important work is the definition of his own voice, the character he makes for himself as he works through a case.

Or take an example from substantive law: in evaluating the law that regulates the relations between police officials and citizens (which in our system is largely the law of the Fourth and Fifth Amendments to the Constitution), I think the important question to be asked is not whether it is "pro-police" or "pro-suspect" in result, nor even how it will work as a system of incentives and deterrents, but what room it makes for the officer and the citizen each to say what reasonably can be said, from his or her point of view, about the transaction—the street frisk, the airport search, the barroom arrest—that they share. Here too the central concern is with voices: whether the voice of the judge leaves room for the voices of the parties.

10

The practice and teaching of rhetoric is by its nature self-reflective, for the questions that one learns to ask of others can be asked of oneself as well. We have asked, for example, what kind of community and culture a speaker or writer makes when he or she engages in a particular kind of intellectual analysis, say cost-benefit analysis. Those communities and cultures, performed and tentatively offered to the world, can be analyzed and judged. But the same question can be asked of what we ourselves say and what we think. What kind of community do we make in our own writing and our own speech, what language of meaning do we create? What is the voice with which we speak? These are the first and hardest questions, and they can be asked of this book and of all of our expressions to each other. Whenever we speak or write, we should be prepared to ask ourselves what kind of community and culture we make, what kind of meaning they shall have. It is with these questions in mind that we turn now to the way law is learned, as a language and as an art.

BIBLIOGRAPHIC NOTE

For further analysis of what I call the rhetoric of the Fourth Amendment, which regulates and in part constitutes the relation between citizen and official in our culture, see my articles, "The Fourth Amendment as a Way of Talking About People: A Study of the *Robinson* and *Matlock* Cases," 1974 *Supreme Court Review* 165–232, and "Forgotten Arguments in the 'Exclusionary Rule' Debate," 81 *Michigan Law Review* 1273–84 (1983). For a fuller statement of the "rhetorical" view of the United States Constitution outlined here, see chapter 9 of *When Words Lose Their Meaning*. Another book that sees law as a way of making meaning in an uncertain world by reasoning through progressive analogies is Edward H. Levi's seminal *An Introduction to Legal Reasoning* (Chicago: University of Chicago Press, 1949). For a general view of rhetoric rather similar to my own, see Ernesto Grassi, *Rhetoric as Philosophy: The Humanist Tradition* (University Park: Pennsylvania State University Press, 1980).

3

THE STUDY OF LAW AS AN

INTELLECTUAL ACTIVITY

A TALK TO ENTERING STUDENTS

This essay is a talk I gave to a first-year law school class some years ago. It is included here as a partial definition of the intellectual and persuasive life of the lawyer. This is what law school (and the law) is like from the inside, or what it can become. As you read it I hope that you imagine (or remember) yourself beginning law school, wondering what it will all be like, and so on.

Here I begin to work out in a particular context the conception of law that is the central subject of this book, law as an intellectual and cultural activity—as something we do with words, with our minds, and with each other. Themes emerge that recur throughout the book: the life of law as a life of reading and writing (and talking); the conditions of radical uncertainty in which that process goes on; the responsibility for what one says, and who one becomes, that this uncertainty generates; and the dilemma of all cultural criticism, that we must find a way to analyze and judge what we ourselves are.

In this essay I speak about the "case method," and for the reader who is not a lawyer a word of explanation may be of some help. The case method is still, despite some criticism, the standard modern form of law teaching. It requires the student to read a series of opinions written by appellate judges, usually with very little by way of introduction, background, explanation, or evaluation. As you can imagine, the opacity of these texts, and one's uncertainty as to what to do with them, presents the new student with real difficulty. In this essay I say something about the reason for this method and suggest how it can best be understood and practiced.

Others have recently spoken to you about the social and psychological conditions of law school life, and no doubt conversations on those intriguing topics will command your attention for some time to come.

Law as an Intellectual Activity

Today I want to talk to you about a different subject. My concern is with what you will be doing in law school intellectually speaking, that is, with what we are asking you to do with your minds as you do the work of law school: reading your cases; preparing for class; asking and responding to questions in the classroom; and thinking and talking about legal questions with each other over coffee or lunch. The process may well seem new and strange to you, very different from what you have done in college, and I hope that I can make some remarks that will help to prepare you for it.

1

I don't want to attribute to any of you the sort of ignorance I once had, but it is possible that some of you think—as many nonlawyers do—that the law is at bottom very simple. I once thought that what the word "law" referred to was, obviously enough, the laws themselves. And I naturally expected that the laws were all written down somewhere to be looked up and applied to life. The rules, once found, were simple: the mystery of the law had to do with their location. What mainly distinguished me from the lawyer, I thought, was that he knew where to find the rules and how to be sure he had found all of them. What I conceived of as the "application" of the rules was easy. You move to a new state and you need to obtain a new driver's license and automobile registration. You send for or pick up the appropriate information and follow the directions until the process is completed. Or take traffic regulations: it is easy to understand that you should stop at a stop sign, yield at a yield sign, and the like. The rules are clear: you either follow or disobey them.

It is true that the law often works in this simple way, perhaps most of the time; for in many situations the law is sufficiently intelligible for people to use it easily and sufficiently fair to occasion no feeling that there is something deeply wrong that calls out for correction. What is more, strongly held values support this simple view of the law: to one raised in a democratic system it seems that this is how the law *must* work. The rules are for my guidance, after all, and they must be intelligible to me. I vote for candidates on the "issues," which are frequently stated in the form of proposed legislation or regulation; to be competent as a voter, which my political system no doubt rightly assumes I am, I must be able to understand the laws. If they are unclear, it is certainly not through any necessity but because they have been made so by lawyers, eager to maintain the profitable mysteries of their profession.

But this simple view does not account for all the ways in which the law works, and it omits entirely what is most interesting, difficult, and important in what we do. Think for a moment what would follow if it were true that the activity of law consisted of nothing more than memorizing certain clear rules and learning where to find the others. First, both law school and the practice of law would be intolerably boring. On the face of it, few things could be more dull than simply memorizing large numbers of rules or learning one's way about a bibliographical system. But the fact is that for many people the study and practice of law are both difficult and fascinating.

Second, since the rules that must be memorized are not invented at the law schools but exist outside them, generally available to the world at large, there would be no substantial or interesting difference between a good legal education and a poor one. (Indeed, it would not be plain under these circumstances why we should have law schools or formal legal training at all. We could publish lists of rules and examine students on their "knowledge" of them at a bar examination.) And if this view of the law were accurate, there would be little to distinguish a good lawyer from a poor one. But there is general agreement, among those who claim to know, that a good legal education is important and special, and very difficult to attain; that a good lawyer has capacities and powers the poor one lacks; and that in this field as in others excellence is rare and valuable.

The third consequence of this simple view of the law would be that the case method—"learning the law by reading cases"—would seem bizarre and perhaps sadistic. Why should one read these complicated and difficult cases simply to discover the general propositions for which they stand? But a great many lawyers regard their experience of learning how to read cases as a step of huge importance in their education as minds and as people, involving much more than learning to discover and repeat rules. Some, at least, would say that this training has helped them to find in the material of their daily professional existence a set of puzzles and difficulties that can interest them for life.

In my view, and I think in that of my colleagues here, the simple model of the law with which I began is right only in the sense that it describes how the law sometimes works in the world; it is wholly wrong as a conception of the field of study and practice with which you are about to become engaged. For it is in the main only when things seem or threaten not to work in such easy and direct ways that lawyers are called upon to act. Our primary field of concern is the problematic and complex in the law, not the simple and orderly. Let me suggest that you regard the law, not as a set of rules to be memorized, but as an *activity*, as something that people do with their minds and with each other as they act in relation both to a body of authoritative legal material and to the circumstances and events of the actual world. The law is a set of social and intellectual practices that defines a universe or culture in which you will learn to function. Like other important activities, law offers its practitioner the opportunity to make a life, to work out a character for himself or herself. What you will learn in law school, in this view, is not information in the usual sense, not a set of repeatable propositions, but how to do something. Our primary aim is not to transmit information to you but to help you learn how to do what it is that lawyers do with the problems that come to them. In the course of all this you must necessarily acquire a great deal of information, much of it essential to your training, and some of it will come from your teachers. But the acquisition of such information is incidental, not central. As a professor once said, "I am not a data bank; what I hope to be is a teacher."

Of course the law as an activity can and should be studied—and is studied at this law school—from the point of view of other disciplines. The operations of lawyers and of the legal system can be studied by the anthropologist, the economist, the historian, the literary or rhetorical critic, the psychiatrist, the philosopher, the social theorist, and many other specialists. But in studying the law in such ways one is functioning, not as a lawyer, but as an anthropologist, as a historian, and so forth. What is peculiar and central to your experience both in law school and beyond is that you learn how to participate in this activity, not as an academic, but as a legal mind.

It might help if you were to compare the process of learning law not so much with your other experiences of the classroom as with your experiences of learning in ordinary life: learning to swim, to sail, to ski, to fly-fish, to understand music or art, to play poker or bridge, or to carry on a conversation at a lunch counter or a cocktail party. How would you describe what learning to engage in such activities involved for you? To what extent does it make sense to say that what you did was to "acquire information" in the usual sense? What did you do beyond that?

Let me address one of these analogies. Suppose that you were asked to teach a person how to sail a boat, and that you proceeded by explaining the names of the parts of the boat, how the various parts operated, and the principles on which they functioned. Suppose your student learned to repeat perfectly what you had said. What would he or she know about *sailing*? One summer I tried to teach people to sail that way, and what I found was that even those who could repeat what I said did not understand it. When they got into a boat and felt it move and shift on the water, the sails shake and fill in the wind, they had no real idea of what to do. Of course the information I offered was useful to one who wished to sail, but it could only begin to be meaningful after he or she understood something about sailing. I am suggesting that knowing the rules of the law is like knowing the names for the parts of the boat; it is useful information that teaches little about the enterprise itself. Or consider fly-fishing, or a golf swing: what do you know when you can explain the structure of the equipment and the principles upon which it is used, when a cast or a swing has been described to you, but before you yourself have tried it? To learn law, one must do law. It is the function of our classes to help you learn how to do law.

A more complete analogy may be learning a language. One must of course learn the rules of grammar and the meaning of terms, but to know those things is not to know how to speak the language. That knowledge comes only with use. The real difficulties and pleasures lie, not in knowing the rules of French or of law, but in knowing how to speak the language, how to make sense of it, how to use it to serve your purposes in life. One's knowledge of a language, like one's knowledge of the law, is never complete. Again and again one hears new sentences and new terms; one sees, with surprise and pleasure, new operations and new moves. The speaker of ordinary competence constantly invents new ways to use the language. It is said that the most effective way to teach a language is to immerse students in the culture, to start them speaking and talking and reading the language before they "know" anything about it. Then it is always a language and not a scheme, not a subject, that they are learning. It is a similar perception that underlies the way we teach law.

In both language and law, learning has a double focus: if one is to live and act competently in a particular culture, one must learn how the language—or the law—is in fact spoken by others, by those whom one wishes to address, to persuade, to learn from, and to live with. But one also wishes to learn how to turn the language, or the law, to one's own purposes: to invent new sentences, to have new ideas, to do new things, perhaps to change the nature of the language itself. Your concern in law school is thus a double one: to learn as completely as you can how the legal culture functions; and to establish a place for yourself in relation to it from which you can attempt to use it in your own ways—in ways that increase your capacities and powers, ways that enable you to speak truthfully to the conditions of the world and to take positions (and offer them to others) that seem to you to be right. In doing all this you will subject your own views and inclinations to the discipline of the inherited culture and the conditions of the world. You will have a chance, sometimes, not only to maintain but to improve the culture of which you become a part.

What I have said may suggest an explanation of what we call the "case method" of learning law, that is, studying actual cases in which the law can be seen in action rather than memorizing general principles or rules. It is true that the cases you will read in your courses can usually be said to stand for one or more propositions of law, and cases are often referred to that way by a lawyer writing a brief or by a judge writing an opinion. But it is not primarily to learn those propositions of law (which may indeed be, in your view or that of others, erroneous) that you read those cases. Cases in your casebooks are offered to you as the occasion for individual and collective thought, as genuine problems for the mind and heart. Each opinion is the final stage of a complicated series of legal events. You are asked to reconstruct these events in your imagination so that you can participate in them at second hand—pretending now that you are the seller, now the buyer, now one of the lawyers, now the other, now a judge, now a legislator. "What would I have done here, and why?" is your constant question and test.

This experience can be regarded as an idealized apprenticeship, as an intellectual training in the experience of the law, and it has its roots in our traditions. As you may know, it was once the custom in this country for a lawyer to learn the law by doing it as a clerk or apprentice to an established lawyer. One can, of course, learn to do the law that way, and such a training has many merits for one who wishes to learn the language of the law. But the material that comes into any one lawyer's office is not selected or structured to train the student in a wide range of activities, and one is stuck with an early and necessarily untutored choice of a single instructor. The idealized or imaginary apprentice system that the case method entails thus has the advantages of coverage, structure, and—may it also be said—unreality. The mistakes you make as you first try to do law are, under this system, harmless ones.

Your apprenticeship is idealized in another, perhaps to you less attractive, way, for your teachers are not themselves primarily engaged in the busy life of clients and cases—though many of them once were—but are people who think about and participate in the law in a different way, as writers or scholars. We cannot, as a group, pretend to offer you what seasoned and experienced practitioners would, and perhaps it is appropriate to say something of what we think we can offer. What our position gives us is the chance to stand back from the world of detail and of practice and to try to see something in it, to find something to say about it, of a more general nature than would likely emerge from the press of life in practice. At this school it is widely felt that good teaching requires a critical and creative engagement with the subject taught, for it is only when the teacher can regard the material as meaning or exemplifying something, as a field for the operation of his or her independent intelligence, that it becomes in any but a mechanical way teachable. Our professional writing is, among other things, the record of our engagement with the law, an engagement of a more general and reflective kind than we enjoyed in practice. We hope that this engagement will deepen our engagement with you.

We do not purport to be able to teach you everything you want to know, as lawyers or as people. It is of course true that, if you apply yourself, there are many things you will be able to do and do well when you graduate. But our function cannot be to create maturely competent practicing lawyers, for no one has figured out how to do that in three years. Perhaps our object in this respect could be said to be to prepare you to make the most of your actual experience of the law at work in the world when the time comes, to see more and to learn more than you otherwise would. If you go into law practice in a firm after law school, you will find that the apprenticeship system continues, for a good law office puts a very high priority on teaching its young people, and a recent law graduate has a great deal to learn.

2

To return to your present situation: what does the conception of the process of law school I have outlined above mean for you? What should you do, for example, when you read a case? What sorts of questions should you expect your teacher to ask of you, and how should you prepare to respond to them?

The first thing to understand is that the judicial opinion that you read in your casebook is the last stage of a long and complicated process. This kind of literature, which will form the bulk of your first-year reading, is the cultural deposit or artifact left behind by weeks or months or years of work by actual people in the real world, from which it is your task to learn—to figure out—as much as you can about the activity of law. It is a little as if you were given the last chapter of a novel and asked to imagine what went before. A prodigious task.

In my view, the best way to proceed is chronologically. Begin by trying to reconstruct from the opinion, so far as you can, the facts that occurred in the real world before any lawyer was brought into play. Tell the story chronologically, without any terms of legal conclusion. You should try to create a movie of life, a story of the experience of ordinary people in the ordinary world. Reflect in your story how each of the participants would characterize the events in his or her ordinary language. This is the experience upon which the law will be asked to act in its peculiar and powerful ways and for which the various people of the law will claim particular—and competing—legal meanings.

You will probably discover that your knowledge of the facts is less than complete. Ask yourself what additional facts you would like to know, and why. Here you can pretend that you are a lawyer representing one of the clients: ask yourself what questions you would put to him about what happened. This is, after all, what a lawyer does when a client comes into the office and tells his (or her) story. The client believes he has told the whole thing. The lawyer examines and reexamines the story, asking questions and more questions until he (or she) is satisfied that he has "enough" to enable him to turn to his books; what he reads there will suggest new questions, to which the answers will suggest new lines of legal inquiry, and so it goes, a jostling between the facts and the law throughout the life of the case. You can at least begin this process with every case you read.

The next stage of reconstruction is to ask (so far as you can determine from the opinion that you read) what each lawyer did, why you think he did so, and what you would have done in his place. One lawyer, for example, initiated the judicial process by filing a complaint, which necessarily rests upon one or more legal theories. What were the legal theories? Are these the legal theories that you would have asserted? Is the case properly in this court rather than another, and why, if the lawyer had a choice of courts, did he choose this one? What relief does he seek and why? How else might you have acted on behalf of the plaintiff in the case? After the first lawyer acted, the second lawyer responded by filing an answer or motion in reponse to the complaint. How did the second lawyer respond? What would you have considered doing in her place, and why? Could the lawyers have anticipated their difficulties by sound planning or more skillful drafting? Is there a negotiated solution they seem to have overlooked? You are asked to put yourself in the place of each of the parties and each of the lawyers and ask yourself how you would have behaved, how you would have interpreted and responded to the events that underlie the case.

Almost all of the judicial opinions in your casebook are explanations of decisions reached in appellate proceedings. An appellate court is asked to approve or disapprove the decisions made by a judge at the trial of the case (or at some stage prior to trial). The evidence available to you on these matters is often skimpy, but you should try, so far as you can, to reconstruct the course of the proceeding whose result is in question on appeal. Can you figure out what each lawyer did? How would you have acted in his or her place? What actions of the trial court are claimed by the appellant to be erroneous, and why? Can you see other actions that you would have designated as error on appeal? On what theory would you have done so?

The appellant's designations of error usually define the issue or issues on appeal. Frequently the issues so defined will be stated by the court and the arguments of counsel summarized, explicitly or implicitly. At this stage ask yourself: What arguments would you have advanced for each side? Why? How do you evaluate the arguments you would make?

At the end you read an opinion that explains the judgment in the case, and here you face the hardest questions of all: How would you decide this case? How would you explain and defend your judgment? At this stage, the process of the law is no longer, if it ever was, a matter of argumentative skill and intellectual deftness. It is a matter of judging right and wrong, better and worse, of coming to terms with the necessity and difficulty of judgment. The simple question— "How should this case be decided?"—presents a puzzle and a challenge that can occupy a life.

You can take it, then, that part of your training in this school is a training in a special kind of reading: not "reading for the main idea," as you may have learned in high school, and certainly not reading for maximum content acquisition in the minimum time, but reading as a species of thought, with a reconstructive and critical imagination. What can you see here, we ask, and what can you make of it? What seems at first easy enough becomes, as you study it, perplexing; simplicity becomes complicated. This should not surprise you. A football game—or a single move in it, say a block or a tackle—is simple enough to the mere fan, complex indeed to the coach or scout; beauty in music is one thing to the ordinary listener, quite another to the critic or performer or composer. So it is with a case that is read not as an exemplification of a rule, but as a deposit of the processes of the world, in which experience continually frustrates expectation, in which facts and arguments seem inexhaustible and inconclusive. So it is with a statute or regulation, read not as the statement of a general idea, but with a critical and inventive eye for the problematic case that will expose uncertainty or incoherence in what may at first seem a plain and clear statement.

In your classes you can expect your teachers to ask you to describe as accurately as the materials permit what happened at each stage of the process by which a case was made, how the lawyers behaved, and what you would have done in their places. It is especially important for you to understand and to be able to state clearly the arguments made by each lawyer on appeal, and to see where each could be said to be defective.

The truth is that there are no experts in the law, in the sense that there are no persons upon whose judgment you may as a lawyer rely without understanding it. Each of us is responsible for what he thinks and says, and it is no discharge of your duty to repeat to your professor what she has told you she thinks. You must make your own way.

It may or may not be comforting to hear this, but the sense of inadequacy and isolation that you should have as you now contemplate this process will always, in one form or another, be with you. One never knows all the law; one never feels wholly confident about any step taken in the law. The lawyer lives in an uncertain and indeterminate world, and the task of his or her profession is to survive and flourish in it. To return to the sailing analogy, while you are sailing you can no longer plant your feet firmly on the ground and proceed by certain steps in a certain direction; but you can sail a boat on the water.

There is another way to put my point. The sense of isolation you now have is in large part the burden of acknowledged responsibility for what you do with the law. That sense of responsibility—which will be most acute when you find yourself making real decisions that actually affect the property, lives, and interests of other people—is central to the experience of the lawyer. I hope you feel it now. One way to state what I urge upon you is this: take the view that you have now spent the last day of your life as a "student of a subject" in the ordinary sense, as a student whose education is the responsibility of a school. Put your school days behind you. From this day on, you are a professional person, responsible alone for your own education, for the improvement of your mind, and for the judgments that you will make in the world you will inhabit. What this means in practical terms for you as a new law student is that you should work hard on your cases, in the way suggested above, rather than looking for answers elsewhere. You should participate in class, both directly and imaginatively; if you are not asked to respond to a question, pretend that you are. When another person speaks, ask yourself how you would respond to him or her. Don't be afraid to be foolish or to be wrong; when your concern is how you can function in the law, there is nothing to be gained by hiding what you are. When you talk with other students about the law outside of class, try to talk as colleagues, teaching each other outside class as you learn in it.

I would now like to make a general remark about the view of legal education I have offered you. On the one hand it is, as I have just suggested, a genuinely professional education, in which you are asked to function as a professional from the first day you begin. You are asked not only to do what a professional does but to have the attitude a professional has and to meet professional standards. In order to survive and to succeed in the world defined by what lawyers do, you must learn how to do those things well. In that sense, you are all asked to learn the same thing: the conventions of that branch of our culture that consists of the activity of law. But, as I have defined it, your legal education is not merely a professional education. It is also a liberal education in the deepest sense. Our ultimate concern is not with your competence at imitating what others do, at learning the moves the lawyer must know, but with the development of your own capacities, sensitivities, and styles, based on a just recognition of the powers and limits of the human mind. As you work through the material of the law, now and later, you make judgments and choices, you write and say sentences, in which you fashion a character for yourself out of your experience. You will learn both how to function in an inherited culture, as a member of it, and how to function at the same time as an individual. How you do this, as I have said, is your responsibility; our task is to offer you a world in which you can begin to work out your own double identity, as lawyer and as mind.

4

THE INVISIBLE DISCOURSE

OF THE LAW

REFLECTIONS ON LEGAL LITERACY

AND GENERAL EDUCATION

This essay was originally given as a talk to teachers of writing. I include it here because it defines certain features of legal discourse that give a distinctive quality and structure to the intellectual activity of the law, to legal reasoning and to legal expression. In it I also show some of the ways in which the conventions of legal language are like and unlike those of ordinary language; elaborate my claim that the law can be regarded as a branch of constitutive rhetoric; and raise an issue that is central in the *Philoctetes* and will concern us to the end of the book, the meaning and importance of "coherence" in a character or in a discourse.

My subject today is "legal literacy," but to put it that way requires immediate clarification, for that phrase has a wide range of possible meanings, with many of which we shall have nothing to do. At one end of its spectrum of significance, for example, "legal literacy" means full competence in legal discourse, both as reader and as writer. This kind of literacy is the object of a professional education, and it requires not only a period of formal schooling but years of practice as well. Indeed, as is also the case with other real languages, the ideal of perfect competence in legal language can never be attained. The practitioner is always learning about his or her language and about the world, is in a sense always remaking both, and these processes never come to an end. What this sort of professional literacy entails, and how it is to be talked about, are matters of interest to lawyers and law teachers, but are not my subject here. The other end of the spectrum of "legal literacy" is the capacity to recognize legal words and locutions as foreign to oneself, as part of the World of Law. A person literate in this minimal sense would know that there was a world of language and action called "law," but little more about it: certainly not enough to have any real access to it.

Between these extremes is another possible meaning of "legal literacy": that degree of competence in legal discourse required for meaningful and active life in our increasingly legalistic and litigious culture. The citizen who was ideally literate in this sense would not be expected to know how to draft deeds and wills or to try cases or to manage the bureaucratic maze, but would know when and how to call upon the specialists who can do these things. More important, in the rest of life such a person would be able to protect and advance his or her own interests: for example in dealing with a landlord or a tenant, or in interactions with the police, with the zoning commission, or with the Social Security Administration. He or she would be able not only to follow but to evaluate news reports and periodical literature dealing with legal matters, from Supreme Court decisions to House Committee Reports; and to function effectively in positions of responsibility and leadership (say as an elected member of a school board, or as chair of a neighborhood association, or as a member of a zoning board or police commission). The ideal is that of a fully competent and engaged citizen, and it is a wholly proper one to keep before us.

But this ideal is for our purposes far too inclusive, for however one defines "legal literacy," such a figure possesses a great deal in addition to that: he or she has a complete set of social, intellectual, and political relations and capacities. But perhaps we can meaningfully ask: what is the "legal literacy" that such an ideal figure would have? How could this sort of competence be taught? What seem to be the natural barriers to its acquisition? In the first part of this essay I deal with these questions, but in reverse order: I begin by identifying those features of legal discourse that make it peculiarly difficult for the nonlawyer to understand and to speak; I then suggest some ways in which those features might be made comprehensible and manageable, and their value and function appreciated. This in turn will constitute my answer to the first question, that is, what kind of legal literacy an ordinary citizen ought to have, and how it can contribute not only to the development of social competence but to a true education of the mind and self.

1

It is a common experience for a nonlawyer to feel that legal language is in a deep sense foreign: not only are its terms incomprehensible, but its speakers seem to have available to them a repertoire of moves that are denied the rest of us. We neither understand the force of their arguments nor know how to answer them. But the language is, if possible, worse than merely foreign: it is an unpredictable, exasperating, and shifting mixture of the foreign and the familiar. Much of what lawyers say and write is after all intelligible to the nonlawyer, who can sometimes speak in legally competent ways. But at any moment things can change without notice: the language slides into the incomprehensible, and the nonlawyer has no idea how or why the shift occurred. This is powerfully frustrating, to say the least.

But it is more than frustrating, for it entails an increasingly important disability, almost a disenfranchisement. At one time in our history it could perhaps have been assumed that a citizen did not need to have any specialized knowledge of law, for our law was a common law that reflected the customs and expectations of the people to such a degree that ordinary social competence was normally enough for effectiveness in the ordinary enterprises of life. No special legal training was required. But in our increasingly bureaucratic and legalistic world, this seems less and less the case: frustrated citizens are likely to feel that their lives are governed by language—in leases, in form contracts, or in federal or state regulations—that they cannot understand. Who, for example, can read and understand an insurance contract, or a pension plan? An OSHA or IRS regulation? Yet these govern our lives, and are even said in some sense to have the standing of our own acts: either directly, as in the case of contracts we sign, or indirectly, as in the case of laws promulgated by officials who represent us. In a democracy this unintelligibility is doubly intolerable, for "We the people" are supposed to be competent both as voters to elect the lawmakers, and as jurors to apply the laws, and we cannot do these things if we cannot understand the law.

What can explain this flickering pattern of intelligibility and unintelligibility, the stroboscopic alternation of the familiar with the strange? The most visible and frequently denounced culprits are the arcane vocabulary of the law and the complicated structure of its sentences and paragraphs. This leads some to ask: why can lawyers not be made to speak in words we recognize and in sentences we can understand? This would enable the ordinary citizen to become competent as a reader of law, and even as a legal speaker. Our political method of democracy and its moral premise of equality demand no less. It may be, indeed, that the only actual effect of this obfuscating legal jargon is to maintain the mystique of the legal profession, and if that mystique is destroyed so much better.

Impulses such as these have given rise to what is known as the Plain English Movement, which aims at a translation of legal language into comprehensible English. This movement has had practical effects. At the federal level, for example, one of President Carter's first actions was to order that all regulations be cast in language intelligible to the ordinary citizen, and New York and other states have passed laws requiring that state regulations and form contracts meet a similar standard.

If such directives were seriously regarded, they might indeed reduce needless verbosity and obscurity, and streamline unwieldy legal sentences. But even if they succeeded in these desirable goals, they would not solve the general problem they address, for, as I will try to show, the most serious obstacles to comprehensibility are not the vocabulary and sentence structure employed in the law, but the unstated conventions by which the language operates: what I call the "invisible discourse" of the law. Behind the words, that is, are expectations about the ways in which they will be used, expectations that do not find explicit expression anywhere but are part of the legal culture that the surface language simply assumes. These expectations are constantly at work, directing argument, shaping responses, determining the next move, and so on. Their effects are everywhere, but they themselves are invisible. It is these conventions, not the diction, that primarily determine the mysterious character of legal speech and literature—not the "vocabulary" of the law, but what might be called its "cultural syntax."

In what follows I will first identify those features of what I call the "cultural syntax" of legal language that seem most radically to differentiate it from ordinary speech. I will then outline some methods by which I think students can be taught to become at least somewhat literate in a language that works in these ways. Finally I will suggest that this kind of literacy not only entails an important increase in social competence, but itself contributes to the development of mind and attitude that is the object of a general education.

2

Many of the special difficulties of legal language derive from the fact that at the center of most legal conversations will be found a form we call the legal rule. Not so general as to be a mere maxim or platitude (though we have those in the law, too), nor so specific as to be a mere order or command (though there are legal versions of these), the legal rule is a directive of intermediate generality. It establishes relations among classes of objects, persons, and events: "All A are [or: shall be] B"; or, "If A, then B." Examples would include the following:

> Burglary consists of breaking and entering a dwelling house in the nighttime with intent to commit a felony therein. A person convicted of burglary shall be punished by imprisonment not to exceed 5 years.

> Unless otherwise ordered by the court or agreed by the parties, a former husband's obligation to pay alimony terminates upon the remarriage of his former wife.

Legal conversations about rules such as these have three characteristics that tend to mystify and confuse the nonlawyer. The first of these is that the form of the legal rule misleads the ordinary reader into expecting that once it is understood, its application will be very simple. The rules presented above, for example, have a plain and authoritative air and seem to contemplate no difficulty whatever in their application. (Notice that with the possible exception of the word "felony," there is nothing legalistic in their diction.) One will simply look at the facts and determine whether or not the specified conditions exist: if so, the consequence declared by the rule will follow; if not, it will not. "Did she remarry? Then the alimony stops." Nothing to it, the rule seems to say: just look at the world and do what we tell you. It calls for nothing more than a glance to check the name against the reality, followed by obedience to a plain directive.

In practice of course the rule does not work so simply, or not always. Is it "breaking and entering" if the person pushes open a screen door but has not yet entered the premises? Is a garage with a loft used as an apartment a "dwelling house"? Is dusk "nighttime"? Is a remarriage that is later annulled a "remarriage" for the purpose of terminating prior alimony? Or what if there is no formal remarriage but the ex-wife has a live-in boyfriend? These questions do not answer themselves but require thought and conversation of a complex kind, of which no hint is expressed in the rule itself.

Of course there will be some cases so clear that no one could reasonably argue about the meaning of the words, and in these cases the rule will work in a fairly simple and direct fashion. This is in fact our experience of making most rules work: we can find out what to do to get a passport, we know what the rules of the road require, we can figure out when we need a building permit, and so on. But these are occasions of rules-obedience for which no special social or intellectual competence is required.

One way to identify what is misleading about the form of a legal rule might be to say that it appears to be a language of description, which works by a simple process of comparison, but in cases of any difficulty it is actually a language of judgment, which works in ways that find no expression in the rule itself. In such cases the meaning of its terms is not obvious, as the rule seems to assume, but must be determined by a process of interpretation and judgment to which the rule gives no guidance whatever. The discourse by which it works is in this sense invisible.

The second mystifying feature of the legal rule is that its form is likely to mislead the reader into thinking that the kind of reasoning it requires (and makes possible) is deductive in character. A legal rule looks rather like a rule of geometry, and we naturally expect it to work like one. For example, when the meaning of a term in a rule is unclear—say "dwelling house" or "nighttime" in the burglary statute—we expect to find a stipulative definition somewhere else (perhaps in a special section of the statute) that will define it for us, just as Euclid tells us the meaning of his essential terms. Or if there is no explicit definition, we expect there to be some other rule, general in form, which when considered in connection with our rule will tell us what it must mean. But we look for such definitions and such rules often in vain, and when we find them they often prove to be of little help.

Suppose for example the question is whether a person who is caught breaking into a garage that has a small apartment in the loft can be convicted of burglary: does a statutory definition of "dwelling house" as "any residential premises" solve the problem? Or suppose one finds in the law dealing with mortgages a definition of "dwelling house" that plainly does (or does not) cover the garage with the loft: does that help? Upon reflection about the purpose of the burglary statute, which is to punish a certain kind of wrongdoing, perhaps "dwelling house" will suddenly be seen to have a subjective or moral dimension, and properly mean: "place where the actor knows that people are living" or, if that be thought too lenient, "place where he has reason to believe that people are living."

The Invisible Discourse of the Law

Or consider the annulment example. Suppose one finds a statutory statement that "an annulled marriage is a nullity at law." Does that mean that the duty to make alimony payments revives upon the annulment of the wife's second marriage? Even if the annulment takes place fifteen years after her second wedding? Or suppose that there is another statute, providing that "alimony may be awarded in an annulment proceeding to the same extent as in a divorce proceeding"? This would mean that the wife could get alimony from her second husband, and if the question is seen in terms of fairness among the parties, this opportunity would be highly relevant to whether or not her earlier right to alimony has expired.

The typical form of the legal rule thus seems to invite us to think that in reading it our main concern will be with the relations among propositions, as one rule is related to others by the logical rules of noncontradiction and the like, and that the end result of every intellectual operation will be determined by the rules of deduction.

In fact the situation could hardly be more different. Instead of each term having a meaning of the sort necessary for deductive operations to go on, each term in a legal rule has a range of possible meanings, among which choices will have to be made. There is no one right answer to the question whether this structure is a "dwelling house," or that relationship a "remarriage"; there are several linguistically and logically tolerable possibilities, and the intellectual process of law is one of arguing and reasoning about which of them is to be preferred. Of course the desirability of internal consistency is a factor (though we shall soon see that the law tolerates a remarkable degree of internal contradiction), and of course in some cases some issues will be too plain for argument. But the operations that lawyers and judges engage in with respect to legal rules are very different from what we might expect from the form of the rule itself: they derive their substance and their shape from the whole world of legal culture, and draw upon the most diverse materials, ranging from general maxims to particular cases and regulations. The discourse of the law is far less technical, far more purposive and sensible, than the non-laywer is likely to think. Argument about the meaning of words in the burglary statute, for example, would include argument about the reasons for having such a statute, about the kind of harm it is meant to prevent or redress, and about the degree and kind of blameworthiness it should therefore require. Legal discourse is continuous at some points with moral or philosophic discourse, at others with history or anthropology or sociology; and in its tension between the particular and the general, in its essentially metaphorical character, it has much in common with poetry itself.

These characteristics of legal language convert what looks like a discourse connected with the world by the easy process of naming, and rendered internally coherent by the process of deduction, into a much more complex linguistic and cultural system. The legal rule seems to foreclose certain questions of fact and value, and of course in the clear cases it does so. But in the uncertain cases, which are those that cause trouble, it can better be said to open than to close a set of questions: it gives them definition, connection with other questions, and a place in a rhetorical universe, and this permits their elaboration and resolution in a far more rich and complex way than could otherwise be the case. Except in the plainest cases the function of the ordinary meanings of the terms used in legal rules is not to determine a necessary result but to establish the uncertain boundaries of permissible decision; the function of logic is not to require a particular result by deductive force, but to limit the range of possibilities by prohibiting (or making difficult) contradictory uses of the same terms in the same sentences.

But you have perhaps noticed an odd evasion in that last sentence, and may be wondering: does not the law prohibit inconsistent uses of the same terms in the same rules? Indeed it does not, or not always, and this is the last of the three mystifying features of legal discourse about which I wish to speak.

I have thus far suggested that while the legal rule appears to operate by a very simple process of looking at the world to see whether a named object can be found (the "dwelling house" or the "remarriage"), this appearance is highly misleading, for in fact the world often does not present events in packages that are plainly within the meaning of a legal label. Behind the application of the label is a complex world of reasoning which is in fact the real life of the law, but to which the rule makes no overt allusion, and for which it gives no guidance, or, more precisely, gives guidance that is misleading. For the form of the rule often suggests that it should be interpreted and applied by the use of deductive reasoning, an expectation that is seriously incomplete. The real discourse of the law is invisible.

This may seem bad enough, but in practice things are even worse, and for two reasons. First, however sophisticated and complex one's reasoning may in fact be, at the end of the process the legal speaker is required after all to express his or her judgment in the most simple binary terms: either the label in the rule fits or it does not. No third possibility is admitted. All the richness and complexity of legal life seems to be denied by the kind of act in which the law requires it to be expressed. For example, while we do not know precisely how the "dwelling house" or "remarriage" questions would in fact be argued out, we can see that the process would be complex and challenging, with room both for uncertainty and for invention. But at the end of the process the judge or jury will have to make a choice between two alternatives, and express it by the application (or nonapplication) of the label in question: this is, or is not, a "dwelling house." In this way the legal actors are required to act as if the legal world really were as simple as the rule misleadingly pretends it is. Everything is reduced to a binary choice after all.

Second, it seems that the force of this extreme reductionism cannot be evaded by giving the terms of legal rules slightly different meanings in different contexts, for the rudiments of logic and fairness alike require that the term be given the same meaning each time it is used, or the system collapses into incoherence and injustice. The most basic rule of logic (the rule of noncontradiction) and the most basic rule of justice (like results in like cases) both require consistency of meaning.

A familiar example demonstrating the requirement of internal consistency in systematic talk about the world is this: "However you define 'raining,' the term must be used for the purposes of your system such that it is always true that it either is or is not 'raining.'" Any other principle would lead to internal incoherence and would destroy the regularity of the discourse as a way of talking about the world. To put the principle in terms of the legal example we have been using: however one defines "dwelling house" for purposes of the burglary statute, it must be used in such a manner that everything in the world either is or is not a "dwelling house"; and because the law is a system for organizing experience coherently across time and space, it must be given the same meaning every time it is used. Logic and fairness alike require no less.

You will notice that these principles of discourse are very different from those employed in ordinary conversation. Who in real life would ever take the view that it must be the case that it either is or is not "raining"? Suppose it is just foggy and wet? If someone in ordinary life asked you whether it was raining out, you would not expect that person to insist upon an answer cast in categorical terms, let alone in categorical terms that were consistent over a set of conversations. The answer to the question would depend upon the reason it was asked: does your questioner want to know whether to wear a raincoat? Whether to water the garden? To call off a picnic? To take a sunbath? In each case the answer will be different, and the speaker will in no case feel required to limit his or her response to an affirmation or negation of the condition "raining." One will speak to the situation as a whole, employing all of one's resources. And one will not worry much about how the word "raining" has been used in other conversations, on other occasions, for the convention of ordinary speech is that critical terms are defined anew each time for the purposes of a particular conversation, not as part of a larger system.

What is distinctive about conversations about the meaning of rules is thus their systematic character: terms are defined not for the purposes of a particular conversation, but for a class of conversations, and the principle of consistency applies across the class. And this class of conversations has a peculiar form. In the operation of the rule all experience is reduced to a single set of questions—say whether the elements of burglary exist in this case—each of which must be answered yes or no. We are denied what would be the most common response in our ordinary life, which would be to say that the label fits in this way and not in that, or that it depends on why you ask. The complex process of argument and judgment that is involved in understanding a legal rule and relating it to the facts of a particular case is at the end forced into a simple statement of "application" or "nonapplication" of a label.

But there is another layer to the difficulty. We may talk about the requirement of consistency as a matter of logic or justice, but how is it to be achieved? Can we, for example, ensure that "dwelling house" will be used exactly the same way in every burglary case? Obviously we cannot, for a number of reasons. We know that different triers of fact will resolve conflicts of testimony in different ways—one judge or jury would believe one side, a second the other—and this builds inconsistency into the process at the most basic level, that of descriptive fact. Also, while the judge may be required to give the same instruction to the jury in every case, the statement of that instruction will be cast in general terms and to some extent admit a fair variation of interpretation, even where the historical facts are settled. (For example, a definition of "dwelling house" as "premises employed as a regular residence by those entitled to possession thereof.") And if the instruction includes, as well it might, a subjective element (such as something to the effect that the important question is whether the defendant *knew* he or she was breaking into a place where people were living), there will be an even larger variation in the application of what is on the surface the same language.

In short, the very generality of legal language, which constitutes for us an important part of its character as rational and as fair, means that some real variation in application must be tolerated. As the language becomes more general, the delegation of authority to the applier of the language, and hence the toleration of inconsistency in result, becomes greater. As the language becomes more specific, this delegation is reduced, and with it the potential inconsistency. But increasing specificity has its costs, and they too can be stated in terms of consistency. Consider a sentencing statute, for example, that authorizes the punishment of burglars by sentences ranging from probation to five years in prison. This delegation of sentencing authority (usually to a judge) seems to tolerate a wide variation in result. But it depends upon how the variation is measured. For to insist that all burglars receive the same sentence, say three years in jail, is to treat the hardened repeater and the impressionable novice as if they were identical. That treatment is "consistent" on one measure (burglars treated alike), "inconsistent" on another (an obvious difference among offenders not recognized).

For our purposes the point is this: the two requirements (1) that terms be defined not for a single conversation but for the class of conversation established by the rule in question, and (2) that the meaning given words be consistent through the system, are in practice seriously undercut by a wide toleration of inconsistency in result and in meaning. I do not mean to suggest, however, that either the requirement of consistency or its qualifications are inappropriate. Quite the reverse: it seems to me that we have here a dilemma central to the life of any discourse that purports to be systematic, rational, and just. My purpose has simply been to identify a structural tension in legal discourse that differentiates it sharply from most ordinary speech.

3

Legal literature is radically distinguished from ordinary language in another way: by its procedural character. That is, in working with a rule as a lawyer one must not only articulate the substantive questions it is the purpose of the legal rule to define—is dusk "nighttime"? is a bicycle a "vehicle"? etc.—but one must also ask a set of related procedural questions, of which very little recognition is usually to be found in the rule itself. For every question of interpretation necessarily involves these procedural questions as well: who shall decide what this language means? Under what conditions or circumstances, and subject to what limits or controls? Why? In what body of discourse are these procedural questions themselves to be thought about, argued out, and decided?

Suppose for example the question is what the word "nighttime" should mean in the burglary statute; or, to begin not with a rule but with a difficulty in ordinary life, whether the development of a shopping center should be permitted on Brown's farm. It is the professional habit of the lawyer to think not only about the substantive merits of the question, and how he or she would argue it, but also about (1) the person or agency who ought to decide it, and (2) the procedure by which it ought to be decided. Is the shopping center question a proper one for the zoning commission, for the neighbors, for the city as a whole, or for the county court? Is the "nighttime" question one for the judge to decide, for the jury, or—if you think what matters is the defendant's intent in that respect—in part for the defendant himself or herself? Every legal rule, however purely substantive in form, is also by implication a procedural and institutional statement as well, and the lawyers who read it will realize this and start to argue about its meaning in this dimension too. The function of the rule is thus to define not only substantive topics but procedures of argument and debate, questions about the definition and allocation of competencies to act. The rule does this either expressly or by implication, but in either event it calls upon a discourse that is largely invisible to the ordinary reader.

To sum up my point in a phrase, what characterizes legal discourse is that it is in a double sense (both substantively and procedurally) constitutive in nature: it creates a set of questions that reciprocally define and depend upon a world of thought and action; it creates a set of roles and voices by which meanings will be established and shared. In creating both a set of topics and a set of occasions and methods for public speech it does much to constitute us as a community and as a polity. In all of this it has its own ways of working, which are to be found not in the rules that seem to be at the center of the structure, but in the culture that determines how these rules are to be read and talked about.

I have identified some of the special ways of thinking and talking that characterize legal discourse. Far more than any technical vocabulary, it is these conventions that are responsible for the foreignness of legal speech. To put it slightly differently, there is a sense in which one creates technical vocabulary whenever one creates a rule of the legal kind, for the operation of the rule in a procedural system itself necessarily involves an artificial way of giving meaning both to words and to events. These characteristics of legal discourse mean that the success of any movement to translate legal speech into Plain English will be severely limited. For if one replaces a Legal Word with an Ordinary English Word, the sense of increased normalcy will be momentary at best: the legal culture will go immediately to work, and the Ordinary Word will begin to lose its shape, its resiliency, and its familiarity, and become, despite all the efforts of the writer, a Legal Word after all. The reason for this is that the word will work as part of the legal language, and it is the way this language works that determines the meaning of its terms. This is what I meant when I said that it is not the vocabulary of the legal language that is responsible for its obscurity and mysteriousness, but its "cultural syntax," the invisible expectations governing the way the words are to be used.

4

Thus far I have been speaking as a lawyer to nonlawyers, describing those features of legal discourse that most mark it off from ordinary speech and make it difficult to understand. Now I wish to speak differently, as one teacher to another, and ask what kind of knowledge of this language can best be the object of a writing course, in high school or college. What kind of legal literacy is it possible to help a nonprofessional attain? How can this best be done?

As I have made clear above, I start with the idea that literacy is not merely the capacity to understand the conceptual content of writings and utterances, but the ability to participate fully in a set of social and intellectual practices. It is not passive but active; not imitative but creative, for participation in the speaking and writing of language is participation in the activities it makes possible. Indeed literacy involves a perpetual remaking both of language and of practice.

To attain full legal literacy would accordingly require that one master both the resources by which legal topics can be defined and argued and the set of procedural possibilities for argument established by the law, from the administrative agency to the jury, from the motion to strike to the writ of mandamus. Literacy of this sort is the object of a professional education and requires full-time immersion in the legal culture. It obviously cannot be attained in a high school or college course.

But this does not mean that nothing can be done to reduce the gap between the specialized language of the law and the ordinarily literate person. While one cannot make nonlawyers legally literate in the sense of having a full and active competence at law, one can do much to teach them about the kind of language law is and the kind of literature it produces. I think a student can come to understand, that is, something of what it means to speak a discourse that is constitutive and procedural in character and founded upon the form we call the rule. The successful student will not be able to practice law, nor even follow the lawyer in all of her moves, but he will have some knowledge, both tacit and explicit, of the kind of expectations the lawyer brings to a conversation, the kinds of needs and resources she has, and the kinds of moves she is likely to make. If what is at first invisible can be seen and understood, legal discourse will lose some of its power to frighten and to mystify. One will of course still experience a lack of comprehension, but these experiences will more often occur at expected moments and be of expected kinds. This means that one will be more confident about what one does comprehend and more certain about the moments at which one is entitled to insist upon clarification, or upon being heard. All this can come from an understanding of the legal system as a constitutive rhetoric based upon the rule.

But how is such an understanding to be stimulated? An explicit analysis of the sort I have sketched above will be of little assistance to most students, for it proceeds largely at the conceptual level and literacy involves knowledge of a very different kind. (A student could learn to repeat sentences describing the rhetoric of the law, for example, without ever having any real sense of what these sentences mean.) Of almost equally limited value for our purposes are the standard courses in government, for here once again students often learn to repeat what they hear without any sense of what it means (think of the cliches about "checks and balances," for example, or the "imperial presidency"). Courses that attempt to teach students legal substance are often not much better, for knowledge of the rules does little good unless the student understands something of what it means to read and write a discourse based on rules. Besides, it frequently happens that the topics chosen are those of current popular interest, like abortion or the death penalty, where legal discourse (at least at the Supreme Court level) is not very sharply distinguished from ordinary political and journalistic talk.

More promising than the foregoing, or useful perhaps as a possible supplement to them, would be a course that asked students to write not about the law, but about analogues to the law in their own lives.

The idea would be that they would become more competent not at law itself, but at law-like writing, and that this would teach them much not only about the law, but about themselves and their world.

What I have in mind is something like the following. Suppose students were asked to write a series of assignments about an aspect of their own lives that was regulated by rules—say their athletic team, or the school itself, or their apartment house, or their part-time jobs. These rules could be examined from several different perspectives. First, for example, students might be asked simply to reproduce the rules governing such parts of their lives. Without overtly burdening the students with the knowledge, this assignment would raise very sophisticated and interesting questions about the nature of rules in their social context (for example about the relation between written and unwritten rules, and the relation between rules and practice). One might ask the students: "In what form do these rules appear in the world? Are they written and published, and if so where? How do you know that these rules apply to you? Are they all the rules that do apply, and if so how do you know that? If the rules are not written and published, how do you even know what the rules are? Why do you suppose they are not written and published?" Or: "What exceptions are there to these rules, and how do you know?" And so on. Similar questions could be raised about the relationship between rules and authority: "Who promulgated these rules, and upon what authority? How do you know? What does it mean to have authority to promulgate rules of this kind?" And so on.

The students could then be asked to talk about the ways in which questions arising under their rules should be resolved. What problems of meaning do these rules present? How should they be resolved, and by whom, acting under what procedures? Perhaps here a teacher could reproduce one or two sets of rules the students had provided, and think up imagined situations where their application would be problematic. (After one or two such assignments, the students could be asked to do it themselves.) This would present the students with the difficulty of thinking in terms of a system meant to operate with constant or consistent—or at least apparently consistent—definitions over time, for they can be led to see that the way they resolve the meaning of the rules in one case will have consequences for others. This involves an extension of both imaginative and sympathetic capacities, and a complication of the idea of fairness. It might also begin to teach them that in difficult cases the meaning of the rules cannot be seen in the rules themselves but must be found elsewhere: in the resources and equipment one brings to thought and argument about the questions. What is more, since these resources are partly of our own invention, it is right to ask how they can be improved. Finally, depending on the particular system of rules, this method may lead the students to think in terms of procedures and competences: why the judgment whether a particular player is "trying hard" (as required by a rule) is a matter for the coach, not for the players (or vice versa); why the umpire's decision that a pitch is a strike or a ball must (or must not) be final; and so on. Or one might consider rules governing life in a cooperative apartment, and the procedures by which decisions should be made when there are real differences of opinion about the necessity of roof repair, the costs of heating, and so on.

Finally, students could be asked to draft rules of their own devising, whether regulations or contractual provisions, and submit them to collective criticism. This could be a real lesson in the limits both of language and of the mind, as the students come to realize how little power they actually have to determine how their words will be given meaning by others, and how little they can imagine the future that their rules are intended to regulate.

All of this could be done with materials from the student's own life, without the use of legal terms or technicalities. It need not even be done in Standard English: the student's writing (or talking, if these assignments were done orally) should indeed reflect the way people actually speak in his or her own world. One important lesson for us all might be the discovery that it is not only in the law, or only in the language of the white middle class, that community is constituted, or that argument about justice proceeds.

To do this with material from the student's own lives would tend to make the process seem natural and immediate, within their ordinary competence. But in the process they should be introduced to questions of extraordinary depth and sophistication: about the construction of social reality through language (as they define roles, voices, and characters in the dramas they report); about the definition of value (as they find themselves talking about privacy or integrity or truthfulness or cooperation); about the nature of reasoning (as they put forward one or another argument with the expectation that it cannot be answered, as they try to meet the argument of another, and so on); and about the necessarily cooperative nature of society (as they realize that whatever rules they promulgate can work only with the assistance of others and must work equally for all people and all cases); and so on. They might learn something of what it means that the law seeks always to limit the authority it creates. They might even come to see that the question "what is fair?" should often include the qualification "under this set of rules, under these procedures, and under these particular circumstances." If I am right in my expectations, after working on rules in their own lives the students would find this material more complex, more interesting, and more comprehensible—also perhaps more difficult—than before. This would itself be an important demonstration of legal literacy, and a direct manifestation of the student's increasing competence as an educated citizen. This kind of legal literacy can I think be a true part of general education.

5

READING LAW AND

READING LITERATURE

LAW AS LANGUAGE

This essay was originally published as part of a symposium on interpretation in law and literature, and it naturally proceeds from a comparison between the lawyer and the literary critic as readers of texts. But, as you will not be surprised to learn, the conception of "reading" I work out here is a conception of writing as well.

The general position elaborated here is that the law is a language, a set of resources for expression and social action, and that, accordingly, the life of the lawyer is at its heart a literary one—a life both of reading the compositions of others (especially those authoritative compositions that declare the law) and of making compositions of one's own. The language in which we do these things is itself a literary one, for these activities take place on conditions of radical uncertainty. Our knowledge of the world, our sense of the meaning of events, our confidence in our own capacities must all have their roots within us, in our competence as users of ordinary language, not in any claims we can make as scientists to observe and measure the external world.

As for "interpretation," I shall say below that for me the most valuable way to talk about the "meaning" of a text is to ask, among other things, what version of himself or herself it invites its reader to become: that is, to focus attention upon what I call its "ideal reader." I hope my own reader can see connections here with the way in which we saw Philoctetes persuade Neoptolemus, by stimulating him to become a better version of himself, and also with the way in which Sophocles' play itself teaches us, its audience, by what we become in response to it. Or to take the reading of the soothsayer's prophecy in that play, Neoptolemus' ultimate reading of it can be taken as a model of the "good legal reading" I recommend here, Odysseus' impossible literalism as an example of the opposite.

To some people the approach I shall describe may seem to depoliticize the law or to work as a mere apology for the status quo. For me, however, it gets us closer to the true political nature of the law, as a way of establishing community and giving meaning to experience; and, as I say more fully in "The Judicial Opinion and the Poem" (Chapter 6), it implies general standards of political and cultural judgment that, while deeply rooted in certain strains in our tradition and culture, are very far indeed from defending present power arrangements under the bureaucratic state.

The lawyer and the literary critic are both readers of texts, and as such they face difficulties, and enjoy opportunities, that are far more alike than may seem at first to be the case. In a deep sense, indeed, I believe they are the same.

1

The lawyer must read the statutes, cases, and other documents that it is his (or her) task to understand, to interpret, and to make real in the world. This is essential to his work. Of course, he is not only a reader but a writer as well; his kind of reading completes itself only in the process of speech and writing by which he argues for one result or another, shapes his client's legal arrangements to avoid a particular hazard, or otherwise acts verbally in the world. His reading is by nature a communal activity, and he must always be alert to the readings that may be proposed by others. Indeed, as we shall see, reading a legal text is often not so much reading for a single meaning as reading for a range of possible meanings. Law is in a full sense a language, for it is a way of reading and writing and speaking, and, in doing these things, it is a way of maintaining a culture, largely a culture of argument, that has a character of its own.

This is all rather like some current views of reading literature. Literary critics have come to focus on the fact that reading literature (like reading law) is not merely a process of observing and receiving, but an activity of the mind and imagination, a process that requires constant judgment and creation. Like law, literature is inherently communal: one learns to read a particular text in part from other readers, and one helps others to read it. In this shared process readers maintain what might be called a culture of reading, a set of understandings and conceptions by which the process can go on. This is an interpretive culture rather like the culture of argument established by lawyers. The basic idea of those critics who place great emphasis on the creative and active aspects of reading is to claim for the reader of literature a life with demands and opportunities and responsibilities of its own—a life in fact of writing. Like lawyers, literary readers are also members of communities defined by their shared interest in a set of texts, and whether they know it or not, both groups are always asking and answering the central question: what kind of community shall we be?

One issue upon which current critical and philosophical attention has recently focused is this: can texts have determinable and objective meanings, or is what we call their "meaning" in fact created by a community of interpreters? Some assert the possibility of objective meaning of this kind, and some deny it. The question as stated seems central to the disciplines both of law and of literature: if it is true that the text has no fixed meaning, the basis of both enterprises seems to change its character radically, perhaps to disappear. Why are we reading Shakespeare's plays, or these old opinions, if they mean only whatever we want them to mean? At its extreme, this view leads to a radical solipsism or nihilism. On the other hand, those who assert that texts can have objective meanings are faced with a series of questions that seem unanswerable: where is this meaning to be found, and how can its existence be demonstrated to the doubtful? If meaning is a matter of intention, how do you discover what the writer's intention was, and how do you establish any connection between that subjective condition and the document in question? If meaning is not a matter of intention, what is it? And what do you do about differences of opinion among readers: do you declare some right and some wrong, and if so, from what position, how defined, do you presume to do that?

Despite its apparent importance, I think that the question of determinable meanings in both law and literature is actually a false one. By this I mean that it states alternatives neither of which is possible, alone or in combination with each other, and does so because it reflects fundamental misconceptions about the activities of reading and writing. It is the purpose of the rest of this essay to explain what I mean, but it will perhaps be helpful if I first summarize my position now.

To begin with, there are in both legal and nonlegal texts enough real ambiguities and uncertainties to make it seem to me absurd to speak as if the meaning of a text were always simply there to be observed and demonstrated in some quasi-scientific way. What is more,

Reading Law and Reading Literature

these ambiguities and uncertainties are not in my view lapses from an ideal of perfection, or defects of the sort to be expected in any practical enterprise, but structural. They are a necessary part of what we mean both by law and by literature and are in fact essential to the highest achievements of both of these forms of expression. It is not only necessary but right that there be serious argument and disagreement about the meaning of such texts. Indeed the establishment of such arguments, and the management of the terms in which they proceed, is one of the major purposes both of literary and of legal texts.

On the other hand, I think it equally absurd to say that the uncertainties inherent in any text, or the fact of unresolvable disagreement, show that there is no meaning in the text itself, or that "meaning" is simply a word for what we in our wisdom happen to agree about at the moment. The view that the community of readers creates the text by determining its meaning stands things on their head: for me the text does more to create the community than the other way around. It is with the text that reading starts, or should start; and different texts can be shown to create markedly different communities, both immediately, with their individual readers, and more extensively, among those readers, both at a single historical point and over time.[1] What is more, texts of the important kinds with which we are most concerned almost always have an intelligibility, as well as a greatness, that is radically superior to what is achieved in most interpretations of them. With all my uncertainties about their meaning, I think I understand the texts of John Milton and John Marshall better than I understand most of what is written about them.

For me, then, the meaning of a text is not to be found in it like a stone and help up for display; nor do I think that texts as such are inherently unintelligible. One can neither disregard the independent force of the text nor assume that all one's questions are unambiguously answered within it. To ask "Does it or does it not have a determinate and objective meaning?" is thus to ask a false question; a bit

---

1. One of my discoveries in working on *When Words Lose Their Meaning* was that the different texts I studied generated very different interpretive communities. While there are of course individual exceptions, Homer seems to have stimulated in his readers a generosity of spirit, a kind of cheerful love of life, that is largely missing from the more dark, somber, and aggressive world of Thucydidean scholarship. Or to take examples from English literature, those who write about Jane Austen often seem to be struggling to become better persons, perhaps to earn her imagined approval, a quality not usually dominant in those who write about Swift, who all too often reduce his texts to a set of satiric "devices" by which "fools" and "knaves" are "exposed."

like asking whether you follow the "spirit" or the "letter" of the law, or prefer form to substance, or are guided by reason rather than feeling, or believe in regulating life solely (or never) by the calculation of costs and benefits. Despite its form such a question does not really state a choice, for neither alternative is really possible. At best the question defines a topic of inquiry and argument, a field of concern marked by a tension between extremes.

A closely related but somewhat more specific example of a false question is this: in interpreting a text (legal or nonlegal) do you regard the intention of the writer as ultimately irrelevant to, or as determinative of, your reading? This is a current topic especially in the interpretation of the United States Constitution, where it takes the following form: do you favor following the intention of the Framers of the Constitution, or do you hold that we should disregard their original intention in light of the traditions we have since established? As I shall explain below, it seems to me that one can do neither to the exclusion of the other. Indeed, as the question is elaborated, its alternatives become increasingly crazy. If you say that you favor "following" the intention of the Framers, for example, you will immediately be asked a set of questions such as these. Who are "the Framers"? The participants at the Constitutional Convention, the spokesmen for the Constitution, the authors of the *Federalist Papers*, the state representatives at the conventions who ratified it, the people who elected the representatives, or someone else? (How about all those who have refrained from acting to amend it?) How do you answer these questions and justify your choices? Second, even if you can figure out who the Framers are, how do you "know" what their "intentions" were? Do you look to private letters and diaries, for example, or speeches made in the legislature or on the stump? And what do you do when one Framer's intentions are demonstrably different from another's? And in what special sense are you using the term "intention" when discussing language as vague as, for example, that of the due process clause? And even supposing that the problems of collective authorship and of knowledge of another's mind somehow disappeared, and you had a single writer about whom you knew everything, how would you define his relevant intention? Intention can, after all, be stated with generality or particularity, as a matter of motive or a matter of aim; and we are always subject to conflicts in our intentions, many of which are to some degree unconscious and out of our control. To try to follow the intention of the writer seems an inherently unstable procedure, leading to a radical conceptual collapse.

But if you favor "disregarding" the intention of the Framers, on the ground that there is no such thing or that it cannot be found, you will be asked: "Doesn't that method destroy the written Constitution and with it the authority upon which our government is based? And what will you do after you have 'disregarded the original intention': whatever seems best to you at the time? And anyway, how can you possibly justify claiming to be unintelligible the plain meaning of provisions such as those governing the age of Senators?"

Similar questions about the relationship between the intention of a writer and the meaning of his or her work are of course common in literary criticism as well. In this field, it has been strenuously argued, on one side, that the subjective intention, indeed all of the author's subjective experience, is irrelevant to the interpretation of texts, each of which is to be read as if it were a separate object dropped from the sky, and, on the other, that the sole point of the enterprise is to establish an understanding of what the particular author actually meant by what he or she wrote when the work was written.

In both contexts, the questions about determinable meanings and intention are I think false ones. I believe that it is possible to read both legal and literary texts in such a way as to establish confidently shared understandings of what they mean, what they do not mean, and what they are unclear about; and in my view one may properly call the meanings so established objective, though not in any simple or extreme sense. These meanings are not simply items of information as plainly on the page as a pebble is in the hand, nor are they the creations of a community of readers, as that phrase is usually meant. They are something different from either, as it will be my object to try to explain. As for intention, I think we need to attend in a new way to what we can sensibly mean when we speak of the "intention" of a writer.

2

I will speak first about literary texts, but I hope also to show that what I say is true, in a somewhat modified form, of legal texts as well.

For me the first step in working out a way to talk about these matters is to recognize that the activity of reading, like the activity of writing with which it is inseparably connected in the life of the reader—and like other human activities, such as dancing, quarreling, playing football, telling a story, even sleeping—is not susceptible to complete reduction to descriptive or analytic terms. Each of these activities engages parts of the self that do not function in explicitly verbal ways, and behind all of our attempts to describe or direct them remains an experience that is by its nature inexpressible. No one can fully explain what a person does when he or she writes a sentence, or even holds out a hand in a signal to stop. More specifically, writing is never merely the transfer of information, whether factual or conceptual, from one mind to another, as much of our talk about it assumes, but is always a way of acting both upon one's language, which the writer perpetually reconstitutes in his or her use of it, and upon the reader. Action of this kind can never be wholly explained, and our talk about reading and writing should reflect this fact.

A second point is this: to begin to understand the kind of meaning a literary text can have—and this can be said of a legal text as well—it is necessary to abandon the expectation that if its meaning is to deserve the label "objective," it must be reducible to a unitary and completely restatable message. A literary text of any real value has far too complex a structure, and offers far too rich an experience, to be restated once and for all in a single sentence or paraphrase or book. If the message were the meaning, the writer could after all have saved himself or herself and the reader a lot of trouble by simply stating it, and letting the play or poem or novel go. It is indeed something of a critical truism that the meaning of a literary work is not in its message but in the experience it offers its reader.

Much could of course be said in explanation and elaboration of this truism. For example, one could point to the metaphoric nature of language, to the implications of the kind of narrative that any text contains, or to the ways in which form gives meaning to a text. One could identify the double meanings and surprises that good writing seems necessarily to entail, whether by way of ambiguity, irony, or paradox. Or one could analyze the tension that exists between the claim to a kind of fixed reality that is almost always made by the surface of a text and the unknown processes of choice and creation and uncertainty that lie behind it. And of course the truism can never be wholly explicated, in any of these ways or in all of them together. But on the understanding that what I say is meant to be suggestive rather than exhaustive, I wish to make two rather simple points about the ways in which the meanings of both legal and literary texts resist restatement.

In the first place, a text often acts directly upon its language in such a way as to give its words a significance within it that they would otherwise lack in the discourse of the writer and the reader. This necessarily weakens any secondary statement of meaning immeasurably, often reducing it to the level of cliche or banality. As applied to poetry this observation is a commonplace: we have long been trained to see the poem, among other things, as a pattern of images and words that acquire unique significance through their association, operating in several planes or dimensions at once. But what is true of poetry can be true of prose as well, and even of "expository" prose.

Consider for example the definition of religious "toleration" achieved in the following passage from Burke's *Reflections on the Revolution in France*:

> We hear these new teachers continually boasting of their spirit of toleration. That those persons should tolerate all opinions, who think none to be of estimation, is a matter of small merit. Equal neglect is not impartial kindness. The species of benevolence, which arises from contempt, is no true charity. There are in England abundance of men who tolerate in the true spirit of toleration. They think the dogmas of religion, though in different degrees, are all of moment; that amongst them there is, as amongst all things of value, a just ground of preference. They favour, therefore, and they tolerate. They tolerate, not because they despise opinions, but because they respect justice.

This definition of "toleration" is not substitutive in character, asserting as a dictionary often does an equivalence between one word and some other word or words, but performative. It works by using the key word in combination with other important words in sentences that establish contrast, connection, and hierarchy, and this makes all of these words available in a new way. To say that toleration is not a species of contempt, but of justice, is to define not one but all three terms, especially when it is observed that "justice" is at work on both sides of the equation: the preference is "just," as is the toleration. This is a complex and important achievement. But this passage and its key word "toleration" acquire additional significance from other passages in the text as a whole: from, for example, the famous early paragraph on liberty, in which Burke says that he "must suspend . . .[his] congratulations on the new liberty of France," until he has been informed how it has been combined with all the other things that a country needs (government, public force, revenue, morality, religion, property, civil peace and order, and so on); or the passage in which he mocks Dr. Price's "curious" zeal, "not for the propagation of his own opinions, but of any opinions. . . . Let the noble teachers but dissent, it is no matter from whom or from what." In these passages, as in many others, Burke insists upon making a language that distinguishes and then combines into order what his opponents only confuse and merge into a kind of chaos. Burke makes a language more adequate to what he calls the *"difficulty"* of real thought about politics, which his opponents constantly aim to reduce to an impossible simplicity. His text thus exemplifies in its language an "excellence in composition" of the sort that the British Constitution he intends to define and celebrate exemplifies in the political world. In this way, his definition of "toleration" becomes a part of a definition of an idea that is even more complex, even less restatable—that of the British Constitution itself.

It is possible for a writer to give "toleration" quite a different meaning, as Gibbon shows in these sentences: "The various modes of worship, which prevailed in the Roman world, were all considered by the people, as equally true; by the philosopher, as equally false; and by the magistrate as equally useful. And thus toleration introduced not only mutual indulgence, but even religious concord." In this passage the value of "toleration" is not elevated to a high virtue, to a species of justice and charity, as in Burke, but reduced to mere "mutual indulgence." The enormously powerful term of value, "religious concord," is rendered trivial. To do these things to these words is indeed the point of the passage.[2] And this passage, like Burke's, derives additional meaning from its larger context. To go no farther than one example, there is here an echo of Gibbon's earlier well-known sentence about the Roman Republic, the form of which, balancing one item against another, imitates the form of the Republic itself: "The principal conquests of the Romans were achieved under the

---

2. Compare what Gibbon does in chapter 16 to "faith," perhaps the central word of protestant Christianity: "The primitive Christians perpetually trod on mystic ground, and their minds were exercised by the habits of believing the most extraordinary events. They felt, or they fancied, that on every side they were incessantly assaulted by daemons, comforted by visions, instructed by prophecy, and surprisingly delivered from danger, sickness, and from death itself, by the supplications of the church. The real or imaginary prodigies, of which they so frequently conceived themselves to be the objects, the instruments, or the spectators, very happily disposed them to adopt with the same ease, but with far greater justice, the authentic wonders of the evangelic history; and thus miracles that exceeded not the measure of their own experience, inspired them with the most lively assurance of mysteries which were acknowledged to surpass the limits of their understanding. It is this deep impression of supernatural truths, which has been so much celebrated under the name of faith; a state of mind described as the surest pledge of the divine favour and of future felicity, and recommended as the first or perhaps the only merit of a Christian."

Republic; and the emperors, for the most part, were satisfied with preserving those dominions that had been acquired by the policy of the senate, the active emulation of the consuls, and the martial enthusiasm of the people."[3] In the sentence on religious concord we have as it were a negative republic, made of parts that do not interact but ignore each other, united not by shared energies but by mutual indifference. Gibbon in this way says that the best kind of community it is possible to have with respect to religion is community of disdainful indifference.[4]

Or consider the way Jane Austen gives a special range and weight of meaning to the word "principles" in *Mansfield Park*. By this term she means to point not only to the common truisms of Christian morality and practice, which can of course be stated as "principles," but to an aspect of character: the organized strength of self that enables one to act properly in adversity. Related to "principles" in this text is the word "manners," which is used in deliberately inconsistent ways: first, in contrast to "principles," when it is used to mean the skills merely of pleasing or manipulating others; second, as an essential part of "principles," when it is used to mean proper moral conduct. (Edmund Bertram, describing the way in which he means to claim that a clergyman has charge of the "manners" of his congregation, says: "The *manners* I speak of, might rather be called *conduct*, perhaps, the result of good principles.") The ambiguity in the term is deliberate; it catches—and forces upon the reader—the radically problematic fact of our moral life that the self is dependent upon its culture.

3. This sentence is analyzed in some detail in Chapter 7, p. 144.

4. Another example of a text giving a meaning of its own to toleration is Tom Paine's response to Burke in *Rights of Man*, page 74 (London, 1791):

> "Toleration is not the *opposite* of Intolerance, but is the *counterfeit* of it. Both are despotisms. The one assumes to itself the right of with-holding Liberty of Conscience, and the other of granting it. The one is the pope, armed with fire and faggot, and the other is the pope selling or granting indulgences. The former is church and state, and the latter is church and traffic.
>
> "But toleration may be viewed in a much stronger light. Man worships not himself, but his Maker; and the liberty of conscience which he claims, is not for the service of himself, but of his God. In this case, therefore, we must necessarily have the associated idea of two beings; the *mortal* who renders the worship, and the IMMORTAL BEING who is worshipped. Toleration, therefore, places itself, not between man and man, nor between church and church, nor between one denomination of religion and another, but between God and man; between the being who worships, and the BEING who is worshipped; and by the same act of assumed authority by which it tolerates man to pay his worship, it presumptuously and blasphemously sets itself up to tolerate the Almighty to receive it."

One reason we cannot simply restate the meaning of such texts as these in any language otherwise available to us is that much of their meaning lies in the language they have remade, and this language exists in the text and not in the world. This is not solely a matter of new or complicated definition of terms, for a central part of the meaning of these passages is the very process by which the writer acts upon his or her language. It is in the intellectual activity by which "toleration" is redefined that Burke exemplifies the constitutive processes he celebrates. Much the same can be said both of Gibbon's "republican" sentence and of his "civilized" reduction of religion to superstition, hypocrisy, and manipulation. And Jane Austen's fullest definition both of manners and of principles lies in her own performance as a writer, in the way she acts upon her language and with her reader.

Does anything like this textual redefinition of terms exist in legal texts? Of course it does, and all the time, though perhaps rarely in the self-conscious and artful way of the texts just discussed. Our central common-law terms acquire their meaning from their gradual redefinition, over time, as cases are decided in a wide variety of factual circumstances. In reading a legal instrument, whether a contract or a will or a statute, we know that words are defined not only through explicit statements of "definition" but also by their use in combination with other terms. It is for example a powerful argument in favor of the rather soft reading given by Chief Justice Marshall in *McCulloch v. Maryland* to the word "necessary" (in the necessary and proper clause) that in the same instrument, in connection with state imposts, "necessary" is qualified by "absolutely." Of course there are also classic redefinitions of key terms in single opinions, such as Brandeis's redefinition of "privacy" in *Olmstead v. United States,* or McReynolds's of "liberty" in *Meyer v. Nebraska.* And to return to *McCulloch*, Marshall defines "necessary" not only in the way suggested above, but by reference to its usage in ordinary language, a reference that is given force—a kind of "necessity" of its own—by virtue of the fact that the usage upon which Marshall relies is rhetorically connected to "the people," upon whom he has earlier told us the authority of the Constitution itself depends. Similarly, Marshall's definition of the central constitutional term "power" is to be found not only in his explicit discussion of it in terms of "ends" and "means," but also in such things as his account of the origins of the Constitution in the people ("It is the government of all; its powers are delegated by all; it represents all, and acts for all"); in his poetic representation of America as a kind of Paul Bunyan among nations ("this vast republic, from the

St. Croix to the Gulph of Mexico, from the Atlantic to the Pacific"); and, perhaps most of all, in the authority and power of his own voice: "Let the end be legitimate, let it be within the scope of the constitution, and all means which are appropriate, which are plainly adapted to that end, which are not prohibited, but consist with the letter and spirit of the constitution, are constitutional." Like Burke, Marshall gives us at once a new language and a new conception of what a constitution can be.

The textual redefinition of our words is, of course, not confined to legal or literary texts, but is a universal aspect of language use. In every conversation our words are to some degree ambiguous, and we undertake to use them in ways that are intelligible to our interlocutor, to let him or her know something of the special senses in which we mean them, and these meanings will often be to some degree new. What is distinctive about legal and literary texts is that they seek to speak to a range of readers, not just one, and to operate across a spectrum of contexts. They seek to establish the meaning of terms not merely for one conversation, for the present moment, but for a class of conversations across time. Every legal and literary text implies a reader who will use it in circumstances that cannot now be known.

This suggests a second reason why it is a mistake to speak as if the meaning of legal and literary texts could simply be restated in other terms. Texts of both kinds have, and are from the beginning known to have, a shifting relation to the cultural context upon which much of their meaning necessarily depends. Even the text that is truly ephemeral, meant to die with the present conversation, is not wholly self-explanatory. It more or less unconsciously assumes in its reader a specific set of cultural competences that will render it intelligible. Since these competences define the very context of expression and action, they can never be wholly known or exhaustively identified. When things change we are surprised to discover what we have earlier assumed.

Whenever a writer intends that his or her text be read by others on other occasions, both reader and writer face the problems and opportunities of changing cultural context. The writer wants the text to be taken out of its present context and read in another, and this means that it is intended to be read by someone who is to this degree unknown and unknowable—structurally an alien. This is what it means to hope that one's text will have a life of its own. As for the reader, he or she knows that over time words change their meaning and values shift, that expectations as to form evolve. All of this is bound to have an effect on the reading of the text. For example, in an age so atheistic, or at least so determinedly pluralistic as this one—I write for the moment, and to a small segment of our world—we may have difficulty in responding to Burke's talk about religious toleration, or Austen's about religious principles. This is not merely a theoretical matter. There is a sense in which *The Merchant of Venice* is for us unreadable, so different is the meaning of "Jew" to Shakespeare and to us. And think how recently one's own use of the word "gay" has been made problematic.

There is another aspect to the process of cultural change. As our language changes, we acquire the material for asking new questions. To these new questions, the text will yield new answers; in this sense it gains a new meaning. Thus the Marxist can complain about, or celebrate, Jane Austen's attitude towards class in ways that her original reader could not have done; the Freudian can analyze the incestuousness of her characters' erotic relations (Fanny marries an emotional brother, Emma an emotional father); and so on. Or, to take an example from the law, consider the Fourth Amendment to the United States Constitution, which prohibits "unreasonable searches and seizures." This seems originally to have been a constitutionalization of the main lines of trespass law, the function of which was to define and protect the liberty and property of the citizen. It comes from a world in which "trespass" and "property" and "liberty" were associated with every civil right, and indeed did much to define the constitutional relations between citizen and state. In England property law controlled the Crown, and in the early years of our national existence, when government was thought to derive its power from the governed, one's "property" was what one had not yielded to the state. But in an era in which "property" has degenerated into wealth, and the language of rights into a calculus of the interests that serve the general welfare—in which the Supreme Court has interpreted the language of the amendment to protect not "property" but "privacy"—the context of the constitutional language has changed the network of associations that gives it much of its meaning.

3

So far I have suggested some reasons why literary and legal texts do not have, and cannot have, objective and determinate meanings in the simple sense that would permit these meanings to be accurately and exhaustively restated in other terms. This is perhaps obvious in any case. But I think that such texts do have objective meanings in another sense, notwithstanding the uncertainties I have just described. Indeed the very uncertainties they contain, and the arguments they accordingly give rise to, are a central part of their meaning. These uncertainties are in fact essential to what we mean by literature and by law.

I can perhaps best suggest the kind of complexity and coherence of meaning that I think literary texts can have by an analogy. For me, learning to live with such a text—say, the *Iliad*—is a bit like learning to live in a new city. The experience is of necessity somewhat different for everyone who does it. This is in part because the complexities of detail and relation can never be wholly mastered, and are thus in fact somewhat different for each observer, in part because the individual always sees from a particular point of view and functions from a particular set of concerns. But there are, nonetheless, accounts of the *Iliad*, just as there are accounts of Paris or Chicago, that are illuminating and accounts that cannot be right.

In the process of coming to know a text, readers can assist one another. With such an aim I once wrote an article on the *Iliad*. If you read it, I know that it will not make your *Iliad* identical with mine, and it is not my object that it do so. What I do hope is that the process by which you check what I say against the text, both as you remember it and as you reread it, will help you establish a better understanding of it and a deeper relation with it. That relation will of course be yours, not mine. What is to be sought among readings of a text, whether readings by different people or successive readings by oneself, is not identity—there can never be that—but consistency and mutual instructiveness.

To speak less analogically, reading literature is an interaction between mind and text that is like an interaction between people—it is in fact a species of that—and the expectations we bring to a text should be similar to those we bring to people we know in our lives. Just as a person does not have a fixed and unchanging identity for every other person, even for every friend—even for the same friend—so a work as rich and varied as the *Iliad* cannot have identical and fixed meanings for every reader, or every good reader, or even for the same reader all his or her life. But this is not to say that either the person or the text has no stable identity of its own, or has only such an identity as some group decides it should have. Both have real identities, but they are too complex ever to be completely known, let alone restated, and too alive to be fixed in a single interpretation forever.

The reader, both of texts and of people, changes as he or she reads: one is always learning to see more clearly what is there and to respond to it more fully—or at least differently—and in the process one is always changing in relation to text or to friend. It is in this process of learning and changing that much of the meaning of a text or of a friendship resides; the text is in fact partly about the ways in which its reader will change in reading it.

To carry this way of talking one step further, one might say of any literary text that it defines an ideal reader whom it asks its audience to become, for the moment at least and in some sense forever. In this view, the reading of a text is guided by two central questions: first, what possibilities for perception and response, for judgment and feeling, does this text seek to realize in me? (Think here of the person that Philoctetes invites Neoptolemus to become, for example, or the very different version of himself to which Odysseus would reduce him.) Second, what do I think of such a prospect? In other words, as one works through a text one is always asking who the "ideal reader" of this text is, and deciding whether one wishes to become one's own version of such a person even for the moment.

When I speak of the reader "becoming" someone in the process of reading, I mean to speak literally, not metaphorically. Think, for example, of what happens when a person opposed to racism is told a successful racist joke: he (or she) laughs and hates himself for laughing; he feels degraded, and properly so, because the object of the enterprise is to degrade. He need not feel ashamed that he has aggressive feelings, nor that they can be stimulated by racist humor, for something like that is true of anyone. Nor should he be ashamed that these possibilities for being are realized in him against his will. A great work of literature might evoke such possibilities against the will of the reader to help him understand and correct them, and this would be an act of the deepest friendship. Rather, the reader is ashamed of having this happen at the instigation of one who wishes to use those possibilities as the basis for ridicule or contempt. He is ashamed of the person he has become in this relationship with this speaker.

This is a negative ideal, of course, but if the text—in this case the racist joke—is successful it makes that ideal real. Literary texts can likewise stimulate aggressive or destructive impulses in the reader, not in order to subject them to understanding and to integration with a larger context of impulses and values, but in order to give them free rein. This would be a momentary and uncorrected disintegration of the reader's character—compare what Odysseus does to Neoptolemus—and no act of friendship.

But in other cases the central achievement of a great text can be said to be the ideal reader it defines—the version of oneself it calls into existence and addresses. One could say of such a work as Jane Austen's *Pride and Prejudice*, for example, that it is meant to teach one how to read one's way into becoming a member of the audience it defines—into becoming a person who understands each shift of tone, who shares the perceptions and judgments the text invites one to make, and who feels the sentiments proper to the circumstances. Both for its characters and its readers, this novel is in a sense about reading and what reading means. When in chapter 13, for example, we read Mr. Collins's unctuous letter announcing his intentions to visit the Bennets, to make some "amends" for his being heir to their property, and to be of perpetual service to Lady Catherine de Bourgh in whatever capacity she should desire, we know exactly how to take it. In rightly perceiving his character defined in his writing we acquire for the moment a character of our own as readers, defined by the activities of perception and judgment in which we have been led to engage. This character of ours is then contrasted with the character that each of the Bennets exhibits in his or her reading of it: Mrs. Bennet can see it only in the light of a possible marriage for one of her daughters, and completely misses its vulgarity; Mr. Bennet sees it only as the occasion for laughing at the ridiculous—"there is a mixture of servility and self-importance in his letter, which promises well"; Mary sees it only as the opportunity to utter pompous commonplaces—"'In point of composition, . . . his letter does not seem defective.'" Jane is here, as always, too kind in her constructions: "'Though it is difficult . . . to guess in what way he can mean to make us the atonement he thinks our due, the wish is certainly to his credit.'" (In her career as a whole this indeed proves a serious fault, for it is at last to luck, and to the activity of others, that Jane owes her happiness.) Elizabeth alone reads well—"There is something very pompous in his stile.—And what can he mean by apologizing for being next in the entail?—We cannot suppose he would help it if he could."[5]

Elizabeth's judgment, however, is not always so sound. For under-

---

5. Compare Elizabeth's implicit conception of a true "apology" with Burke's definition of true "toleration."

standable reasons, relating both to his rudeness to her and to her own feelings of attraction towards him, she is too harsh—too "prej-udiced"—in her reading of Darcy. This leads her into a dangerous credulity in her reading of Wickham, a mistake the reader is led to share. Like Elizabeth, we later remember the scene in which Wick-ham first tests her attitude towards Darcy, makes his false case against him, then says he "can never . . . expose him"—though that is exactly what he has just done—with mortification at our having missed what was going on. Like Elizabeth and Darcy, who look back on their entire history with clear eyes at the end, good readers at last, we too, if the book has done its work, have become at the end better readers, and for Jane Austen this means better people as well. This novel is a moral fiction not because it teaches us that vice is punished, or anything like that, but by reason of the capacities for perception and being that it realizes in us.

Of course no one is an ideal reader the first time through a book like this, and, as I suggested above, that is part of the point: move-ment towards that condition is what the text offers. In one sense, this movement takes place in ordinary time, as the reader engages with the text over and over. But it also occurs in what might be called ideal time: in seeking to understand the text, the reader constructs or re-members a reading of it that is not interrupted, as actual readings are, by answering the phone and making dinner and so on—a read-ing that exists in an ideal world. This reading produces a sense of the text working on its reader, on oneself, that is different from any way it actually could work in the real world on any person. One imagines a series of surprises and confirmations, for example, as they would occur in textual sequence; but actually as one perceived them they took place in altogether different readings.

Pride and Prejudice may be thought a slightly unfair example, be-cause it is itself so explicitly about reading, and because Jane Austen so consciously connects excellence in reading with excellence in char-acter. But the passage from Burke quoted above lends itself to a sim-ilar kind of analysis. That paragraph defines its reader as one to whom the activity of forming "just preferences" is an essential part of life: to give it up in favor of universal indifference would be to lose a central aspect of the self. Its ideal reader is also one who recognizes the claims of others, in qualification of those very preferences, and can thus make a real claim to the virtues of toleration and of justice. And the ideal reader of this passage will not only acquire this char-acter in reading it, but will carry it into the rest of life, as he or she speaks the language learned here.

The reader's engagement with such a text is always tentative. While responding to the text he (or she) is always asking how he responds, who he is becoming, and checking that against his other wishes and aspects. Sometimes he is fooled: the racist joke may make him a momentary and chagrined racist, or Hemingway may turn him briefly into a sentimentalist. Sometimes—and this is the central point—he is educated, for reading is a process in which the reader himself, through a process of assimilation and rejection, response and judgment, becomes more fully one set of the things that it is possible for him to be. Reading works by a perpetual interchange between the person that a text asks you to become and the other things you are.

The capacities for being and acting that a particular text realizes in its readers will in some ways be similar for all competent readers: I have just suggested something of what I think the experience of reading Burke's *Reflections* and Austen's *Pride and Prejudice* should mean for everyone. But in other respects, and important ones, there will be great variations and differences, for different readers are different people and are located in different cultural contexts. It is always one's own version of the ideal reader that one at last becomes, or resists becoming.

The mistake that underlies the false question about meaning is really a hope: a hope for a kind of restatable and provable message that a literary text cannot by its nature have. When that hope is disappointed, one kind of reader declares, in a kind of rage, that the text has no objective and determinable meaning at all. Thus to give up in despair when rationality of a certain kind runs out is understandable enough: the disconcerting discovery that the conceptual and logical apparatus of quasi-scientific rationality will not do for the understanding of life or of literature—or of law—seems naturally to lead to the conclusion that we therefore exist in an elemental flux, a perpetual collapse of meaning. But to say this is to proceed under an image of human life diminished by the metaphor of science, as if the only knowledge worthy of the name must be wholly restatable in other terms and provable by the operations of deductive logic or inductive demonstration. As we have seen, legal and literary texts alike have a life and complexity that is not reducible to statements of "meaning" of this restatable, exhaustible, and scientifically verifiable kind. But to say that there is no meaning of one kind is not to say that there are no meanings of other kinds. In our lives we show, all the time, that we know how to read—and to live with—texts and other people, and to do so with considerable confidence. This, as I suggested in "Rhetoric and Law" (Chapter 2), is the heart of our competence at ordinary language and ordinary life. But we must accept the terms upon which this competence is given us—that is, the radical uncertainty in which we in fact know how to make our way. When we discover that we have in this world no earth or rock to stand and walk upon, but only shifting sea and sky and wind, the mature response is not to lament the loss of fixity, but to learn to sail. With respect to talk about meaning, this requires us to recognize that the question, "What does this text mean?"—when properly understood—starts a conversation of a kind we know how to participate in and benefit from. The meaning of a text is not its informational content, nor those statements that any rational person can be forced by logic and fact to make about it, but the cooperative experience it offers its readers. It is impossible to describe or analyze this experience completely, but it is not impossible to say something intelligible about it.

4

To turn now to reading law, this is at heart just one version of the process I have described, but it does have some particular features of its own. For example, a legal text is authoritative in a different way from a literary text, and this means that the kind of tentativeness it requires (or permits) is different. Whether one likes it or not, as reader of the statute or contract or trust or judicial opinion one is in the first instance its servant, seeking to make real what it directs. But its authority is not unquestioned. As the text is being understood, it is checked, not only against the other parts of the reader's being—other standards and sentiments and wishes—but against other parts of the literature of the law. How does this text, so read, fit within the larger legal culture? We look to the statute to see if the regulation is valid, to the Constitution to see if the statute is valid, to other opinions to see how the implications of this one fit with them, and so on.

Another difference is that the textual community that a legal text establishes with its individual reader is also a way of making another community, a community among its readers. In this sense, law is structurally ulterior in character, for it is always meant to affect what you say and do in relation to others, as you obey the command of the statute, for example, or correctly employ the argument underlying a judicial opinion. The law is literally and deliberately constitutive: it creates roles and relations, places and occasions on which one may speak; it gives to the parties a set of things that they may say, and prohibits them from saying other things; it makes a real social world. A literary text does not do these things, or not in such direct ways. Two other differences seem obvious as well: first, that individual texts in the literature of the law seldom achieve greatness on any scale, let alone that established by the *Iliad* or the plays of Shakespeare; second, that the canon of authoritative legal texts is somewhat less subject to individual selection than the canon of literary texts. If the law is to be great, it is perhaps more obviously the case than with literature that we must make it so.

Yet these points should not be overstated. There is a sense in which no text is great except as it is made so by those readers who perceive its possibilities; literary critics may sometimes feel that they are trapped by an authoritative canon of texts no less rigid than the lawyers' canon; and literary texts, like legal texts, are also in the first instance authoritative and seek both to establish community and to affect behavior. The differences are largely in emphasis and in the degree of explicitness with which these things are done.

Accordingly, I think that to focus attention upon the "ideal reader" may be a helpful way of thinking about what happens when we read legal texts as well as literary ones, and helpful too in thinking about how we do it well and badly. Instead of asking what a statute or opinion or constitutional provision "means," that is, as if we expected a one-sentence response, we can ask what it means in a different way: how would the ideal reader contemplated by this document, indeed constituted by it, understand its bearing in the present circumstances? This requires an understanding of the text in its cultural and political context, in light of the accepted meanings of words, and with an understanding of the major purposes of the text, of its types and examples. It thus requires one to become an expert reader of the culture itself. Once a particular text is understood in this way, it must be fitted together with other texts and with the rest of the culture to make what we call a field or body of law. The lawyer becomes the ideal reader not only of one text, but of a collection of texts in the very selection of which he or she participates.[6]

Is the ideal reader of the law different every time, as the ideal

---

6. To say that the culture is read not only to interpret but to check the text means that the lawyer is engaged in a continuous argument the terms of which are always changing, in an interaction between the particular document and its larger world. The lawyer's work thus contributes to a process of collective or cultural education that is in structure analogous to that experienced by the single reader of the literary text.

reader of literature is? If so, how can we square the fact with our view of the rule of law, which assumes universal intelligibility of those rules and standards that enable us to achieve "like results in like cases"? It follows from what I have said that the ideal reader of a legal text cannot be the same every time, partly because of differences among people (or differences among various stages in the development of one person) and partly because of shifts in the cultural context in which words will have to work. But while ideal readers cannot be identical, any more than your *Iliad* and mine can be identical, in this case as in the other there can be either coherence and consistency among readers or the opposite of these things. The goal is not identity, but something like what Wittgenstein calls a family resemblance. In law, as in literature, I cannot state the meaning of a text in some other form and insist upon that as the full equivalent of the original statement: the meaning is in the experience of the original statement and nowhere else. But this is not to say that solid judgments cannot be made about the meaning of particular texts, or that meaning is wholly subjective and indeterminate, or merely the function of our political or literary preferences.

It has been the genius of our law to recognize these things and to profit from them. It is not a defect but a merit of our system that judges are acknowledged to have discretion, that legal questions are seen as open and difficult, that juries can decide within a wide range. To pretend that all cases, all questions, could be made to fit within some preexisting categorical scheme would be to pretend the impossible, and to hide unjustified judgments behind a fiction. It is the aim of our law not to obliterate individual judicial judgments in favor of a scheme, but to structure and discipline them, to render them public and accountable. This is true of the lawyer as well as the judge, and the client knows it; he or she pays not for skill in determining mechanical consequences, but for highly complex individual judgments. Reading is always writing, always done by an individual mind. The reconstitution of our legal culture and its language must always be done, if it is to be done at all, by individual minds, and that means with individual differences. These differences, when properly publicized and disciplined, are not to be lamented but celebrated.

The view that the legal text ought to have a clear and restatable meaning, and the subsequent collapse into nihilism or "legal realism" upon the discovery that it does not, arises from a mistaken attitude towards law that resembles the mistaken attitude underlying the similar response among readers of literature. The error in law is to conceive of the legal system simply as a system of rules, substantive and procedural. This positivist tradition insists upon conceiving of laws as commands, delivered by a superior to an inferior, or as rules determining who shall be authorized to make such commands and under what circumstances. In its most extreme form it assumes that these commands and rules have invariable and plain meanings. But the law can more properly be seen not as a set of commands or rules (even with a set of restatable principles or values behind them) but as the culture of argument and interpretation through the operations of which the rules acquire their life and ultimate meaning. A rule is not self-interpreting, after all, and will always leave open certain aspects of its significance, especially when it is brought to bear in circumstances no one ever thought of. Except in the clear and by definition nonproblematic case, the rule can be thought of as establishing not a single necessary result but a range of culturally possible results, among which choices will have to be made by lawyers and by judges. It is the processes of thought and conversation by which these choices are made, the culture of legal argument, that is the law itself.

The law is a way of creating a rhetorical community over time: it works by establishing roles and relations and voices, positions from which one may speak, and giving us as speakers the materials and methods of a discourse. It is this discourse working within the social context of its own creation, this *language* in the fullest sense of the term, that is the law. It is a culture that makes us members of a common world. This culture is not reducible to rules, but it is objective, in the sense that it can be found and mastered and in the sense as well that it cannot be disregarded or unilaterally changed. Like the text produced by a single mind, the text produced by the culture has a genuine force and reality notwithstanding its irreducibility to rules or to scientific "knowledge."

This view of law accords with the way in which we teach it in our law schools, as I observed in "The Study of Law as an Intellectual Activity" (Chapter 3). In most courses the "rules" the student must learn to repeat are very few in number—they could perhaps be put on a page or two—but the mastery of the appropriate arguments that may be made for or against a particular result, especially in a new kind of case, is complex and difficult. There lies the heart of legal teaching and legal learning. Students seek out good teaching to learn not the rules but the culture, for the rules are everywhere the same.

The law can thus be regarded as working by a conversational process that has, as I said above, two main subjects: first, what the "ideal reader" of the text in question would know and think and say; and second, how that result fits with the rest of the material in this part of the legal field. In a simple sense, the contemporary community is "authoritative" because it is always this community that decides what the text means. But this is the same simple sense in which John Chipman Gray once maintained that the judges are the true lawmakers, for it is they who give final effect to every legal rule or direction. But the judge recognizes the legislature's authority, and conceives of himself or herself as serving its will; similarly, legal argument of the kind I describe takes as its subject, not what we prefer, but what the text means.

The trouble with saying, as some do, that all meaning is the function of community is that one version of the statement is wrong, another meaningless. It is wrong if it means that the nature and life of the community of readers are not affected by the particular text they are engaged in reading. In reading Milton and Dylan Thomas we read different poets, of different quality and different meaning; no one would confuse the Fifth Amendment to the United States Constitution with the Public Utility Holding Company Act of 1935; and so on. Indeed, the very idea of community among readers requires that there be intelligibility among us, the readers. And if among us, why not between us and Milton, say, or Homer?

In its other version, the idea that meaning is a function of community rests upon the fact that any person so disposed can refuse to acknowledge the validity of any interpretation of any text and still (almost always) make some claim to reason. Indeed he or she may even be able to attract adherents and start a school. Of course it is true that our shared understandings of texts are what might be called rhetorical rather than scientific, in that they rest upon the capacity of one person to make clear to another his or her reasons for reading a text in a certain way. This presupposes, as rhetoric always does, the freedom of the other to turn and walk away. (Neither Neoptolemus nor Philoctetes can be *compelled* to agreement, nor to keep to a course agreed upon.) On the surface at least this is different from science, which proceeds by the twin compulsions of logic and factual demonstration (though how different science is in fact is another question). While this second version of the view that meaning derives from community is of course true enough in its way, it destroys a valuable distinction among different kinds of communities: the community that counts itself free to do whatever it will with its own, such as a group starting a business, founding a college, or planning a clambake, and one that conceives of itself as bound by external fidelities or authorities: by the meaning of corporate documents or university statutes, for example, or of the customs regulating certain ritual observances, or of a literary text.

To say that the enterprises of law and literature are rhetorical in the way described is useful as a way of explaining to someone who thinks that his or her refusal to be persuaded proves something important when it does not. But to use such a statement to obliterate the valuable distinction between the two kinds of communities I have described would be irrational and pernicious.[7] We have the power to disregard the meaning of the Constitution, but that does not mean we have the right to do so. Of course, our readings of our texts are in some sense communally determined; but the texts themselves are external to the community, not mere wish fulfillments of it.

5

I would like now to suggest a way of dealing with the problem of the writer's intention referred to earlier. The central difficulty, in both literature and law, lies I think in the tendency to confuse "intention" with meaning, to talk as though what a statute or a poem means, and what its author intended, were obviously the same thing. But I think this is simply a mistake.

To take an old example, suppose that a state has a law saying that "all voters are eligible for jury service," passed at a time before women had the vote. One hundred years later, women are given the vote in state and federal elections, and the question arises: What reading should the old jury statute be given with respect to the eligibility of women for jury service today? It is inconceivable that the legislators thought they were making women eligible for jury service. Yet one can state their intention more generally, and say that they did intend that the exercise of the franchise and jury duty should go hand in hand; therefore, they did intend that women should serve on juries. The trouble with shifting the level of generality in this fashion is that it pretty nearly strips "intention" of all meaning: "they

7. Compare the similar, and similarly pernicious, statements that deny the existence of "free will" or attribute every human action to "self-interest." While perhaps in some unprovable way "true," these generalizations destroy the important moral resource of distinguishing between circumstances in which an actor is ordinarily "free" and those in which he or she is extraordinarily constrained, and between "serving one's own interest" at the expense of others and doing so through generosity, or even through self-sacrifice.

wanted the world to be a safer and happier place, didn't they? Well this result—against the express meaning of their words—will have that effect; therefore they intended it." And, as I suggested earlier, beyond such difficulties as these are those that arise whenever one speaks of human motivation: there are subconscious intentions as well as conscious ones; conflicts of intention; proper and improper intentions. Suppose you could show that a swing vote was bought by bribery? By a promise from the president of political reward? Also, in the very nature of the case, all human intentions about the future are imperfect and rooted in ignorance. (You say you want to be a lawyer? But what that will mean you can have little idea.)

I think the difficulty with talk about intention in both law and literature arises from a confusion about what is meant when one says of another's text, "What the writer intended by this set of expressions is . . ." (or indeed when the same kind of statement is made about one's own text—i.e., "What I intended is . . ."). Since the meaning of what one says is never wholly restatable in other terms, especially when the text is written to be read in contexts beyond the immediate one, statements of intention are always second-order statements, reductive and interpretive. They involve selection and highlighting, a reordering of the meaning of the language as originally uttered. Any purported statement of a writer's intention can be met with the question: "If that is what he meant, why didn't he say it?" What the writer actually meant to say was what he in fact did say through the language in the contract or the statute or the poem. Problems of mistake aside, statements of intention are not substitutes for interpretation, but are themselves a species of interpretation, and, like other interpretations, they are inexhaustible: one can continue to state the intention at different levels, in different imagined circumstances, forever.

The proper question is accordingly not "what the writer intended," as this question is usually meant—as if its answer were something other than an interpretation—but "what this language by this speaker in this context means." This is to some degree an objective and determinable question, for what the language means is the way it modifies our cultural situation.

The meaning of a legal or a literary text is thus partly indeterminate when viewed from the point at which it is composed; I know my words may be read by others in circumstances unimaginably different from my own. But this is different from saying that the meaning of the same words, read from the point of view of the readers of them, is indeterminate, in the sense that they can fairly mean whatever we wish them to—except in the sense that one "can" say that the sun comes up in the west. The relevant intention is the intention to produce the text in question. The legislature intended to make that statute a part of the law, or the judge intended to make this language part of his or her opinion. What the language means is a function of its placement in a larger culture, and must be determined by us. But this is not to say that it has no meaning; and it is always the meaning of the document, not our wishes or preferences, that we are determining.

To call upon something called "intention" as a substitute for reading the text, or to support a reading different from that otherwise justified, therefore seems to me an inappropriate and not wholly intelligible procedure. Of course I do not think that a text ought to be read out of context, as though it necessarily told you all by itself all you needed to know. Evidence about what the writer knew and cared about, about the cultural background that the text assumes, about what the words meant in the world in which it was written, and so on, is of course properly to be taken into account by the reader. But this is to be done as part of the process of determining the meaning of the text, not as a way of discovering something that is to substitute for that meaning.

To return to the questions about determinable meanings and the intention of the Framers with which we began, I can summarize my position this way. I think texts do have determinable meanings, of the complex kind I have tried to describe; that it is a mistake to confuse these meanings with something called the intention of the authors (though of course some evidence bearing on the intention will also bear on meaning); that the "intention of the Framers" is in this sense not binding upon us—indeed, that the search for it is mistaken and impossible; but that the meaning of the constitutional text *is* binding upon us, and binding by the force of law.

6

What this means in the context of the current debate about interpreting the Constitution is this. To say, as some do, that "we" ought to regard ourselves as "free" from the constraints of meaning and authority, free to make "our" Constitution what "we" want it to be, is in fact to propose the destruction of an existing community, established by our laws and Constitution, extending from "we" who are alive to those who have given us these materials of our cultural world, and to substitute for it another, the identity of which is most uncertain indeed. In place of the constituted "we" that it is the achievement of our past to have given us, we are offered an unconstituted "we," or a "we" constituted on the pages of law journals. One can properly ask of such a person, and mean it literally, "Who are you to speak as you do? Who is the 'we' of whom you speak?" To answer that the new "we" is defined not by the Constitution we have, but by the Constitution we wish we had, is no answer at all, for who is the "we" doing the wishing? In the new world, who shall be king?

Perhaps the basic mistake that underlies the claim that we should feel free to disregard the meaning of the language of the Constitution is to think that because the people who drafted and adopted the Constitution are dead, we can have no binding relations with them, nor they with us. This is a version of the mistake that lies at the heart of all legal realism, which is to assume that, because our constructed and constituted relations are artificial (in the sense that they are made and maintained by men and women), they are artificial in another sense: that they are unreal and can thus be dispensed with in the interests of truth. Actually, of course, as with other aspects of culture, the expectations and sentiments and understandings that underlie these relations, and give them meaning, are as real as anything can be—surely as real as an unconstituted "we" talking about its preferences in a political vacuum; more "real," as Odysseus discovered, even than a material weapon.

Among the consequences for the law, and for literature, of my position, the first is attitudinal: a sharpened sense of respect for the cultural inheritance which constitutes "us," and from which we learn. In the law this means caution in abandoning inherited concepts and terms and procedures in favor of some substitute that seems for the moment superior, and an acknowledgment that what is jettisoned may never be recovered. In literature it means recognizing the true importance to us of the achievements of certain writers, and their difference from us. In both contexts, the attitude is one of cultural humility. This is connected with a second point: a conception of law and of cultural life generally as a way in which the community educates itself over time, a way of giving usable present meaning to past experience. The traditional conception of the judiciary as working from case to case (rather than legislatively) can be seen as a method by which the past is regularly tested against the present, the inherited language against the demands of actual circumstance, and intelligent change made possible.

Reading Law and Reading Literature

This view of legal process does not of course necessarily lead to the choice of one substantive result over another in any particular case. But I hope it does suggest how such questions can be defined and talked about by judges and lawyers. It is a form of that sort of judicial criticism that focuses more on method and process than on result, and praises or condemns less for the decision in a case than for the way in which the decision is reached and expressed. There is a sense, then, in which what I say is not novel but very old indeed, familiar to the lawyer almost as a matter of second nature, for what I seek to understand and celebrate is an aspect of the tradition that has made us what we are. Much of what I say about interpretation, for example, is already built into the ways lawyers have for centuries used their own special word for reading statutes and wills and constitutions: "construction." From this point of view, my aim has simply been to make somewhat more conscious what we already know about what we do and who we are, so that these things can be more completely understood and, if appropriate, defended. Verification of what I say is to be found not in a quantitative analysis but in an empirical test of another and more old-fashioned kind, in the legal reader's own experience of the activities that define his or her professional life.

To conceive of the law as a rhetorical and social system, as a way in which we use an inherited language to talk to each other and to maintain a community, suggests in a new way that the heart of law is what we always knew it was: the open hearing in which one point of view, one construction of language and reality, is tested against another. The multiplicity of readings that the law permits is not its weakness, but its strength, for it is this that makes room for different voices, and gives a purchase by which culture may be modified in response to the demands of circumstance. It is a method at once for the recognition of others, for the acknowledgment of ignorance, and for cultural change. So too is that literary fiction which gives a voice to the voiceless. Both law and literature have as their essential object then, in George Eliot's phrase, "the extension of [our] sympathies." They surprise us into "that attention to what is apart from [our]selves, which," as she says, "may be called the raw material of moral sentiment."

BIBLIOGRAPHIC NOTE

For proponents of the two views about meaning contrasted at the outset of this paper, see the work of Stanley Fish, especially *Is There a Text in This Class?: The Authority of Interpretive Communities* (Cambridge: Harvard University Press, 1980), pp. 13–17 (arguing that the reader and interpretive communities determine meaning), and E. D. Hirsch, *The Aims of Interpretation* (Chicago: University of Chicago Press, 1976), pp. 24–30 (arguing that the author's meaning is paramount), and *Validity in Interpretation* (New Haven: Yale University Press, 1967) (defending the stable determinacy of meaning).

For an approach to reading closer to my own, see Wolfgang Iser, *The Implied Reader: Patterns of Communication in Prose Fiction from Bunyan to Beckett* (Baltimore: Johns Hopkins University Press, 1974), pp. 272–97, where he summarizes and elaborates what he calls a phenomenological approach to reading, in which among other things he compares reading a text to looking at stars: the stars are fixed in the sky, but a "constellation" is a pattern made by the observer.

For further reading on these questions, see Jonathan Culler, *Structuralist Poetics: Structuralism, Linguistics, and the Study of Literature* (Ithaca: Cornell University Press, 1975); Steven Mailloux, *Interpretative Conventions: The Reader in the Study of American Fiction* (Ithaca: Cornell University Press, 1982); and Jane P. Tompkins, *Reader-Response Criticism: From Formalism to Post-Structuralism* (Baltimore: Johns Hopkins University Press, 1980).

The proper role of original intention in legal interpretation is currently a topic of considerable discussion. See, for example, Paul Brest, "The Misconceived Quest for the Original Understanding," 60 *Boston University Law Review* 204 (1980); Ronald Dworkin, "The Forum of Principle," 56 *New York University Law Review* 469 (1981), especially good on the difficulties inherent in using "intent" as the ultimate test of significance; Henry Monaghan, "Our Perfect Constitution," 56 *New York University Law Review* 353 (1981); Terrance Sandalow, "Constitutional Interpretation," 79 *Michigan Law Review* 1033 (1981). The classic work is Jacobus tenBroek, "Admissibility and Use by the United States Supreme Court of Extrinsic Aids in Constitutional Construction"(pts. 1–5), 26 *California Law Review* 287, 437, 664 (1938); 27 *California Law Review* 157, 399 (1939).

On the conception of the meaning of a text as the experience of reading it, see, for example, Cleanth Brooks, "The Heresy of Paraphrase," in *The Well-Wrought Urn: Studies in the Structure of Poetry* (New York: Reynal & Hitchcock, 1947), p. 194: "The poem, if it be a true poem [,] is a simulacrum of reality—in this sense, at least, it is an imitation—by *being* an experience rather than any mere statement about experience or any mere abstraction from experience." The poets have of course always known this. Keats, for example, knew that the meaning of a poem was not its message, which especially in the best poems would often be deeply familiar, but what he called its "surprise" for the reader. "I think poetry should surprise by fine excess, and not by singularity; it should strike the reader as a wording of his own highest thoughts, and appear almost a remembrance." (Letter from John Keats to John Taylor, Feb. 27, 1818.) Compare Robert Frost, "The Figure a Poem Makes," in *Selected Prose*, ed. Hyde Cox and Edward Latham (New York: Holt, Rinehart & Winston, 1966), p. 17: "No surprise for the writer, no surprise for the reader." And critics have always known it too. See, for example, Aris-

Reading Law and Reading Literature

totle's talk (in the *Poetics* 13–14) about the way tragedy arouses pity and fear in the audience and Longinus' analysis of the way literature gives rise to the sense of elevation and grandeur (*On the Sublime*, passim). More recently, the work of the New Critics assumed an interactive relation between text and reader. Here, for example, is F. R. Leavis speaking of Swift's irony: "[It is] essentially a matter of surprise and negation; its function is to defeat habit, to intimidate and to demoralize." ("The Irony of Swift," *Scrutiny* 2 [1934]: 366–67.) For an analysis of the potentially poetic or nonconceptual character of our "prose" language, see Owen Barfield, *Poetic Diction: A Study in Meaning* (London: Faber & Gwyer, 1928).

The following works are quoted in the text. The passages from Burke can be found in *Reflections on the Revolution in France, and on the Proceedings in Certain Societies in London Relative to That Event*, ed. Conor Cruise O'Brien (Harmondsworth, Eng.: Penguin Books, 1969), at pp. 258 ("toleration"), 90 ("liberty"), 95 ("dissent"), 278–79 ("difficulty"), 282 ("composition"). The passage from Gibbon on "toleration" is in chap. 2 of *The Decline and Fall of the Roman Empire*.

On "manners" and "principles" in *Mansfield Park* see David Lodge, "The Vocabulary of *Mansfield Park*," in *Language of Fiction: Essays in Criticism and Verbal Analysis of the English Novel* (London: Routledge and K. Paul; New York: Columbia University Press, 1966), pp. 94, 99–102, and, more generally, Stuart Tave, *Some Words of Jane Austen* (Chicago: University of Chicago Press, 1973).

Citations for the Supreme Court Cases referred to are as follows: *McCulloch v. Maryland* 17 U.S. (4 Wheat.) 316 (1819), pp. 411–16, 405, 408, 421; *Olmstead v. United States*, 277 U.S. 438, 478 (1927) (Brandeis, J., dissenting); *Meyer v. Nebraska*, 262 U.S. 390, 399 (1923). The problem about voter's rights and juror's duties is taken from Henry Hart and Albert M. Sacks, *The Legal Process* (Tentative ed., Cambridge: Harvard University, 1958), p. 1203.

The remark by George Eliot can be found in "The Natural History of German Life," in *Essays* (Edinburgh: W. Blackwood, 1884), p. 235.

The discussion of Burke, Marshall, and "the ideal reader" to some degree uses or draws on material from chaps. 1, 9, and 10 of *When Words Lose Their Meaning*. For a fuller statement of my views of the conception of "property" and "trespass" at work in the Fourth Amendment see my article "Forgotten Arguments in the 'Exclusionary Rule' Debate," 81 *Michigan Law Review* 1273–84 (1983).

6 THE JUDICIAL OPINION AND

THE POEM

WAYS OF READING, WAYS OF LIFE

This is an essay in what I call the poetics of the law. I begin with a (largely autobiographical) account of legal and literary education, describing what seems to me a striking similarity in the ways in which poetry and law were once taught—and to some degree still are taught, though less comfortably so. I then suggest and elaborate some connections: between these two kinds of thought and expression; between the ways in which we are habituated to read texts of each sort; and between the dilemmas that confront readers and critics in each field. In doing this I am both trying to establish relations between two branches of our culture that are often thought to have little to do with each other and claiming that these relations teach us something about the way each branch can and should proceed.

This is of course one expression of my view that law can be best understood as a set of literary practices that at once create new possibilities for meaning and action in life and constitute human communities in distinctive ways. But my ultimate hope reaches beyond law, even beyond poetry: it is to work out some ways in which we who are engaged in the processes of cultural and communal life, lawyers and poets and critics among the rest, might better come to understand and to judge both our cultural situations and our own activities.

In fact I think that a proper ground for judgment is implicit in an understanding of law and literature alike as compositional activities. To attend wholeheartedly to the central rhetorical and ethical questions—who we make ourselves in our speech and writing, what relations we establish with our language and with other people—is, I believe, to attend to the first questions of justice. If we address these questions well, good answers will emerge to the secondary questions too, for implicit in any tolerable response to them are standards of justice—attitudes towards ourselves and others—that will inform what we say and do far better than any *a priori* theory or empirical science could do. If we can get our voice and sense of audience and language right, everything else we care about, or should care about, will follow. Or such at least is my hope.

In this essay I shall speak for the most part of my own education, on the assumption that it is to some degree typical of the experience of others whose training also took place in the immediate postwar decades. I should also say that for obvious reasons of space and emphasis my accounts of literary and of legal education will be somewhat schematized and idealized.

In my own experience at least, the same central method was at work in both legal and literary education, for both to a remarkable degree proceeded by drawing the student's attention to a series of discrete texts, one after another, and holding it there. In law the text was typically the judicial opinion; in literary studies usually, though not always, the poem. In both fields the emphasis was on the text as a self-justifying, self-explaining, self-authenticating object. The primary method of analysis was to focus on the text's language and form, rather than, for example, on its social or economic or other context. There is a sense in which my own literary education could almost be reduced to "how to read a poem," and my legal education to "how to read a judicial opinion." This emphasis, at one time widely predominant, is of course still a part of what we do; but in both fields it is also under increasing attack from many directions.

In English studies we did read things other than poems, of course, from novels and plays to histories and letters. But we were trained to read these things almost as if they were poems, or as if they aspired to become poems. Hence, for example, the paper assignments on the imagery of a Shakespearean play or of a Conrad novel, or the books we read on the imagery of Shakespeare's work more generally, or Sophocles', as if all of a writer's work could be read as one grand poem. Hence also the talk about the "movement" and "turning point" of a novel as though it had to have a moment of confusion and clarification, like that of the typical metaphysical poem; hence the analysis of Burke's prose style, or Samuel Johnson's, in terms of its metaphors and images. Even a history could be read as an imaginative design, with an eye to its shape and its metaphorical structure. Reading poems is what we knew how to do, or thought we did, and we assimilated our other literary experience to that model. It was all that we could do; but it was enough.

In law school our reading was not wholly confined to the judicial opinion, but the judicial opinion provided the context in which other things were read, if they were read at all, and it was the model by which we measured everything else. If we could understand the judicial opinion, we would also learn how to perform our own roles as lawyers, for we thought our central task, which controlled all the others, was to learn to argue to a judge. There was of course some study of statutes, of constitutional provisions, of procedural rules, and of regulations, but for the most part only as these came up in the course of reading judicial opinions. Sometimes these were studied independently as well, but—and in this we were perhaps unlike our continental contemporaries—we did not then, and if I may say so, do not now, know very well how to read a statute, a constitution, a scheme of regulations, or a contract as a whole, let alone how to teach our students to do so. Every once in a while we would look at legislative history, social science studies, or lawyers' briefs, but almost always from the perspective of the judicial process. In law school, what we knew how to do, or thought we did, was to read judicial opinions, and we assimilated our other experience to that model. It was all that we could do; but it was enough.

In both fields our education thus proceeded by reading a series of central texts. These texts were privileged both in the sense that they were made the centerpieces of an education and in the sense that one could always retreat to them as the testing grounds for ideas raised in other sorts of conversation. ("But how could that be recast as an argument for one side or another in an actual case?" Or: "I see what you mean: the terms 'nature' and 'civilization' are given by Gibbon a complexity of a kind we see in poetry.")

I suppose one reason why the poems and opinions were studied as they were is that they were small enough to be grasped all at once, to be held in the mind as wholes; they could thus serve both as manageable examples of a kind of thought and as material for a certain kind of criticism.[1] But, whatever the reason, we felt that mastery of

1. There is a kind of text the very meaning of which is tied to the fact that it cannot be grasped at once or read at a sitting. When Proust's *Remembrance* or Gibbon's *History*, towards the end, looks back on a "past" of which it has told, the reader likewise has a past, in his (or her) life with the text, that reaches back not hours but months, or even years, to a time when his own life outside the text as well as within it was in important ways different from what it is now. Part of the meaning of both texts lies in the way they evoke and act upon this sense of a past that is partly shared with the text, partly independent of it.

these forms implied mastery of all, and we gave our attention for the most part to the particular texts, the particular expressions, and did not wonder much—did it matter?—how the particular texts were chosen or in what sense the "series" they made corresponded to anything outside itself.

1

How did such an education in reading actually work, in each of the contexts?

I will start with law school. The original idea of the case method (which is another term for what I have been describing) was simple-mindedly scientific: cases were studied as if they were plants or butterflies in order to discover the laws of regularity by which they could be classified; those regularities in turn constituted "the law." By the time I was in law school the emphasis had shifted. Now cases were seen as problems, as pieces of law-life, to be taken apart and put together, to be imaginatively participated in. As I said in "The Study of Law as an Intellectual Activity" (chapter 3), the idea of this kind of education is like that of the apprenticeship system it supplanted: one learns law by doing law. Law school is thus a kind of language school, working by total immersion, that uses the "case" as its archetypal occasion for speech, and the judicial opinion deciding the case as its archetypal form. In reading a series of judicial opinions one imagines oneself arguing the cases on each side, or deciding them, and does so in combination with others similarly engaged. In this way one learns the practices that define the community of which one is to become a part.

This remarkable emphasis on the judicial opinion actually makes more sense than it may at first seem to do, for the reason that almost all legal disputes can end in judicial cases, even if they are in fact earlier settled by negotiation. Our sense of how the case might be argued and decided therefore does much to inform our other activities of negotiation, advising, and so on. And a set of judicial opinions naturally picks up or reflects much of the rest of legal life. Whatever is problematic in a contract, a statute, a regulation, or an administrative decision—indeed whatever is problematic in our collective life—is likely to end up in a judicial opinion. If it is not in principle or practice reflected in a judicial opinion, some would say, it is not the law. It is for such reasons as these that the judicial opinion has been thought to be a proper model of legal thought and expression.

Law school asked of course an additional question: how do the judicial opinions we read fit together? For in law school (and in our world more generally) it was assumed or claimed that they did fit together to form a more or less coherent whole, a whole with a shape and a history. The shape was that of a field of law; the history, we were told, a movement from "conceptual jurisprudence" to "interest analysis" or "policy science." In my own law school days, at least, this movement was characterized as progress. Today there is much less shared confidence about the meaning of the changes that we see. But even now it is an assumption of legal education that to read one judicial opinion well will lead you to others, which, when read well, will define the cluster of opinions that count, and will mark out among them some that count with special force. Each item implies the series of which it is a part. In this sense at least the individual judicial opinion is thought to define a field, by reference, by example, and by implicit connection. Indeed, it may even be thought to define the whole of law.

In our literary education, poems were read for deeply analogous purposes: in part as apprenticeship pieces, upon which to train the eye, the sensibility, to see what the educated reader should see; in part to train the tongue, to say what an educated reader might say; and in part as a constituent item of what we now call the canon, the collectivity of texts that count. Taken together the poems of the canon were said to form a whole, a central segment of our high culture, perhaps its highest segment. This had its history too, reflected in the sequence of authors and of periods in which it was talked and thought about, and it was sometimes thought to be a history of progress. Once again each item was seen to be intimately connected to the rest of the series: T. S. Eliot could say, for example, that the poet should feel "that the whole of the literature of Europe from Homer and within it the whole of the literature of his own country has a simultaneous existence and composes a simultaneous order."

In both law and poetry, as I was taught them, there was a conception, culturally defined and reinforced, of what a "good lawyer" or "educated reader" would see and say and do. The texts were taken to define a cultural ideal to which it was part of the students' task to assimilate themselves. The especially creative student would also modify that ideal, or perhaps ultimately reject it, but he had to respond to it somehow, and respond intelligibly, if he was to succeed at his courses and the profession for which they prepared him.

In both law and literature the field was defined by the texts we read, and it had a structure of its own, a structure that perhaps reflected a structure in the world, or defined a safe and imaginary place away from it, or expressed a goal to strive for.

2

How were these poems and cases actually read? In both instances the heart of the process was attention to language and to form of a kind that engaged the reader in an imaginative reconstruction of the process by which the text was made. In this kind of reading one learned to see each text as a composition, made by a series of choices of word and phrase and image and issue, each of which could be exposed by asking: What else could have been said here? What is this expression *instead of?* (In *McCulloch v. Maryland,* Chief Justice Marshall said in a famous phrase, emphasizing the key terms, "we must never forget, that it is *a constitution* we are expounding." This kind of teaching says: "we must never forget, that it is *a composition* we are reading.") When it is seen as a composition, from the point of view of the composer, a text no longer seems simply necessary, as its presence in type on the page of a book seems to announce, but contingent or artificial; it is an artifact made by another mind, with a meaning of its own.[2]

Among other things, this kind of reading leads us to see that the text can make its own language of meaning, its own internal discourse, out of the larger materials the writer has inherited. One function of a text in both fields is in fact to give special and related meanings to sets of words that carry with them in ordinary usage a wide and uncertain range of possible significances and to make these new meanings available to others. For the most part the text gives these meanings to its terms not by stipulative definitions but, as we saw with respect to Burke's definition of "toleration" in Chapter 5, by the way it uses them: by association and contrast with other terms, by location in a larger imaginative and purposive design, and by the tensions it establishes among them and among their various uses. It is a commonplace about poetry that the terms and images by which it works interact to create new patterns of association and contrast.

2. For a contemporary statement, see Helen Vendler in her well-known *The Odes of John Keats* (Cambridge: Harvard University Press, 1983), p. 3. "I know no greater help to understanding a poem than writing it out in longhand with the illusion that one is composing it—deciding on this word rather than another, this arrangement of its masses rather than another, this prolonging, this digression, this cluster of sentences, this closure."

(Thus Wordsworth's poem "Upon Westminster Bridge" celebrates the "city" by seeing it as a part of "nature"; thus "Rome" and "Egypt" are given new and contrasting meanings in *Antony and Cleopatra;* and so on.) But this is true in law as well: freedom of "speech" is defined in part by contrast with "conduct," and both terms derive their significance in part from their exemplification in the cases. The associations upon which a text draws are not only internal but external. In this sense the language it remakes is the common language that defines the audience of the text—the associations, allusions, and references that make us what we are.

Two brief examples. When Walt Whitman wishes to write a poem about the source of his poetic art, his muse, he naturally enough ("naturally" for one in his culture, that is) sings about a bird, and in doing so acknowledges his place in a tradition that includes odes to skylarks and nightingales (and later, thrushes): but being an American, and Whitman, the bird he sings about is not of the usual poetic variety, but a mockingbird—a mockingbird defined in part by the implicit allusion to other ornithological images of the muse, in part by his American transfiguration of that tradition, and in part by the way the poem itself is made: by the story of loneliness and desertion and song that gives this bird and its cry a special sort of pathos. (The poem is "Out of the Cradle Endlessly Rocking.") In *Katz v. United States,* the police place an electronic "bug" on the top of a phone booth, without a warrant, and seek to use the overheard conversation in evidence. The Supreme Court holds that the evidence should be excluded as the fruit of an unreasonable "search"—even though there is no trespassory invasion, as the word "search" was once thought to imply. In so doing the Court transforms a precedent—the muse is not a nightingale but a mockingbird—and gives new meaning to its key term: a search is an interference not with a possessory interest but with a reasonable expectation of privacy.

To look at the way the poem or the opinion is made, and at the ways it makes and remakes its language, as this kind of education requires, is to conceive of oneself, whether teacher or student, as a maker of compositions too, as one who also remakes language and reconstitutes form. This kind of training thus at once both informs and confirms one's own capacities for composition and language-making—for making expressions of one's own, a language of one's own, that will work in the world in new ways. It affirms the power of the individual imagination: the possibility of an originality that can work a change in our cultural circumstances. The task of the law student is not simply to understand and describe the law, but to make it and remake it in practice; the work of the critical reader is not merely to understand and to describe the poem but to give it new meaning and a new place in his or her own world. The sort of education of which I speak, in law and in literature, constantly tells us to recognize that we are makers of texts and remakers of culture. This is in fact its major lesson.

3

I have so far been speaking about attention to language, but, as I said above, in both fields our attention was directed to form as well. How did this work, and what did it mean?

In the reading of poetry, at least in my own training, the idea of form seems to have been that of organic design. The proper poem formed a complex and organic whole in which all parts belonged, nothing was missing, and everything counted somehow—preferably, everything counted in a comprehensibly hierarchical manner. To have a piece that doesn't fit or doesn't count the right way is to be, so far, defective. This has been an idea for us not only of literature, of course, but of painting and music and architecture as well: wholeness, harmony, and shape.

The central standard of poetic judgment was related to, perhaps derived from, this conception of an organic whole: it is that of complexity controlled or contraries comprehended. The poem comprises, brings together in one place and within one form, voices or feelings or languages (or facts or ideas or attitudes or wishes) that are normally not placed together and among which severe tensions or contradictions can be found. Much of the life of the poem—of its drama—lies in the reader's uncertainty whether the contraries will in fact be comprehended within a larger form or, rather, refuse to be contained and tear the form to pieces. From this point of view the model of the poem was naturally enough the "metaphysical poem," in which, in Samuel Johnson's famously disparaging phrase, "[t]he most heterogeneous ideas are yoked by violence together" (though we would deny the "violence" and celebrate the daring). A more approving statement of this aesthetic can be found in Coleridge's definition of the imagination of the poet as revealing itself "in the balance or reconciliation of opposite or discordant qualities."

The conception of excellence as the comprehension of contrariety or contradiction is an idea that leads out of poetry, as the idea of organic form does too, but perhaps less in the direction of art and architecture and music than that of drama, history, psychiatry, anthropology, and law. In each of these fields it is a commonplace that the most significant truth is a simultaneous statement of opposing truths. It is the very function of certain kinds of drama, for example, to present within one world implacable oppositions that are in the very act of representation comprehended within a single order: in *Antigone,* for example, the opposition between Antigone and Creon, or perhaps more profoundly still, the opposition between the self-righteous and legalistic way of thinking that those two share and the openness to human reality that characterizes the ways of thinking and feeling we see in Ismene and Haimon. Or in *Richard II* consider the opposition between King Richard and Henry Bolingbroke, and the wholly different conceptions of kingship and authority—of the purpose and nature of government—that they represent, an opposition that deeply characterizes the English public world of Shakespeare's day and (in transmuted form) of our own, for it is about what it means for a governor or a government to give up its claim to an authority external to itself. The play thus gives a common place to two things that are in their own terms implacably opposed. It comprehends them. When the oppositions cannot be comprehended into one larger thing, with a form of its own, as is perhaps the case with *Troilus and Cressida,* the play is said to fail.

Similarly, the good historian does not present a single view of the past as though that was all there was to it, but tries to make sense of competing views; the psychiatrist brings to the surface where they can be recognized (and, as it were, made a drama of—both pulls felt at the same time) certain conflicts in the patient that are too deep and significant to be comprehended without that aid; the anthropologist studies the cultural systems by which oppositions are at once defined and contained; and the law, as we shall see below, is an institution that at its center works by the practice of the open hearing, in which two opposed parties tell their opposed stories, make their opposed claims, in a common language that is, in the very process of disagreement, agreed to by both sides and thus made to comprehend their opposition.

In the language of poetic criticism, the principle of "contraries comprehended" can be found, for example, in the claim of Cleanth Brooks that the center of poetic experience is the paradox: a way of comprising into one thing elements that seem of necessity to belong apart. Others have made analogous claims for other tropes—irony, ambiguity, and metaphor—and the radical idea of all of them is the same, the uniting in one order of what seem, when regarded alone, to be impossibly contrastive differences: different voices, different languages, different points of view. This is the explicit idea, for example, of Robert Frost's essay, "The Constant Symbol," which defines poetry as metaphor—as "simply made of metaphor"—and defines metaphor as "saying one thing and meaning another, saying one thing in terms of another." Likewise it is the implicit idea of Empson's ambiguity and of Leavis's irony. It perhaps has been given most complete philosophic form in Bakhtin's conception of "heteroglossia," which roots all education, all cultural competence, all sound criticism, and all cultural change in "many-voicedness." I have myself, in another context, claimed to define good writing as "writing two ways at once."

The standards by which we learned to judge judicial opinions are remarkably similar to those I have just described, at a certain level of generality at least, and are also related to a similar conception of form. The opinion must in the first place be a coherent whole. All the parts must belong, all work together, and none be missing. As with a poem, a judicial opinion can be taught by asking how it would be different if this part, or that, were absent, or changed. The idea of "comprehending contraries" is if anything even more plainly essential to the judicial opinion, for the very idea of the legal hearing and of legal argument (of which the judicial opinion is intended to be a resolution) is that it works by opposition. Each party tells his (or her) story from his point of view, and in doing so reconstructs the facts and redefines the law so as to give the story a particular meaning. The hearing places these meanings in contrast; it is a measure of the excellence of a judicial opinion how far it recognizes what is valid or valuable in each side and includes that within itself. (An opinion that simply adopted one side's brief would not be worthy of the name.)

Of course it is not always possible to include in a coherent structure points that are diametrically opposed, and something must be left out at last. But here and elsewhere in the history of thought it is a measure of achievement how much of what seems ineradicably opposed can be comprehended within a larger order.

This means that the opinion can be criticized for failing to comprehend its contraries in two distinct ways: it can fail to place them in a coherent structure; or—perhaps more common—it can fail to include an element that belongs, or can fail to give it the force it deserves. The same is true of the poem. It may disintegrate under the forces it includes, or may wrongly exclude a part of the truth it touches on or speaks to. (One version of this vice, in literature as well as politics, is sentimentality.) In both cases, the conception of form as comprising contraries relates to the earlier point that one function of the text is to remake its language. For in both poetry and law (as well as in other forms of expression, including drama and history) the conjunction of two contraries is seen to give both a new meaning.

4

It is therefore never enough to read a poem or an opinion for its main idea, which is often, when simply stated, simply trite or meaningless. (I must die; I am in love; I constantly fool myself; life is tragic but basically good; and so on. Or: the police may interfere with liberty when the needs of the public outweigh the interest of the citizen; free speech may be interfered with only in cases of manifest necessity; and so on.) In both cases the interesting question is not what the main idea is but how it is given meaning by the text, and given meaning in particular by the oppositions that are its life. It is not the restatable message that is the most important meaning of the poem or the judicial opinion, but the reader's experience of the life of the text itself.

This is a commonplace about poetry but perhaps a word would be useful about the way it works in law. First and most obviously, a series of cases elaborating the tensions implicit in a central statement of value—say that of freedom of the press—gradually gives to its key terms a kind of richness and complexity and clarity, a location in our experience, that they could not otherwise have. The world often presents cases no mind could anticipate, in circumstances no one could wholly foresee, and in such instances the meaning the law gives to its governing words must be new (however the case is decided), for the meaning is in large part derived from a context that is new. And the meaning given by the law to its central terms has a deeply performative aspect as well. It is one thing, for example, to utter unchallenged pieties about freedom of speech in times of peace; it is quite another, as a matter of courage and self-confidence, to protect speech that one loathes or fears. The most important message is the one the judge performs, not the one he states.

There is another, perhaps less obvious, sense in which the meaning of an opinion lies more in its performance than in its message, suggested by the fact that our practices of judicial criticism often focus less upon the result of an opinion (its "message") than upon something that happens in the text, which we see as its more important meaning. The judicial critic of the sort I was trained to become learns to ask not only, "Do I agree with this result in this case?"—this affirmance or this reversal—but also "What do I think of this opinion *as an opinion,* as a piece of law-making?" The first question, however important, is "merely substantive," and on it legitimate opinions can vary widely; the second is our uniquely professional question. "Within the widest range judges are entitled to vote as their conscience directs," says the critic; "my kind of criticism is not about their vote, but about their performance as judges." This is a claim to neutrality on political issues, to professionalism, and to a special kind of knowledge. In order to focus students' attention on this aspect of judicial criticism, I have sometimes asked them to explain, in writing, what it is that they admire in a particular opinion the result of which they would vote against; and what they condemn in a particular opinion that "comes out" in a way they approve. This is a way of defining excellence not in terms of votes or "results" but in terms of the composition: what the case is made to mean; how the judge defines himself or herself as a judge; what possibilities for argument and life the opinion holds out to the future; and so on.

To look at the opinion this way is to open up a set of questions about "excellence" in the judicial opinion as a form of thought and life, on such topics as fidelity to facts and to law; openness to the contraries in the case, and hence to what can fairly be said against one's own result; the processes of reasoning by which the past is interpreted and brought to bear on the present; the degree to which the court recognizes the legitimacy and humanity of the litigant (especially the losing litigant) and fairly judges the legitimacy of his or her point of view; the way the court defines the legislature, the lower court, the jury, and the lawyer, and the sort of relations it establishes among them; and so on. From this point of view, as I suggested in "Rhetoric and Law" (Chapter 2), the most important "result" in an opinion is not the judgment it reaches on a particular issue but the character the court gives itself in its writing and the opportunities for thought and community that it creates. The truest meaning of the opinion is not its message, but the experience of mind it holds out as a model of legal thought: the language it makes as it places one item next to another, the community it makes with its several audiences.

The kinds of contraries or tensions at work in poetry and law are, at a certain level of generality, strikingly similar. In each, there is a tension between the restatable idea—the message, the result—and the enacted experience; between the language of the world and the language remade in the text; between form and substance; between the text's discrete design and the text in its larger context; and between the individual mind and the cultural inheritance, or what Eliot called "tradition and the individual talent." Both poetry and law unite the particular and the general, the image and the idea, the general principle and the particular case. (Each is, by Sidney's famous test, for this reason equally superior to mere philosophy or mere history.) Each has movement or shape: it starts out one place, ends up another, and between these points, if there is any life at all, is a surprise, a new clarification, or a series of them.

In each there is also a radical tension between these assumptions of the form and the recognition, or the fear, of the formlessness of life itself. Each is, in Frost's phrase, "a momentary stay against confusion." Each form thus defines a place that is a part of, yet cut off from, the rest of its world: a place in which its inherited resources for claiming meaning—its language—can be reconstituted in a text that is itself a hopeful but tentative claim of coherence; a text from which the rest of the culture, and its various possibilities for expression and action, can be viewed. Each is open to the possibility of shifts in language and perception; more than that, each seeks to achieve such shifts. Each has hopes of permanence: of being reread, even memorized, and being collected. Each has hopes of becoming one of the central texts by which the rest of us will define our own world.

There are, of course, differences between these two forms of expression and between the forms of life they entail, and these differences are worthy of attention. But for the present my attention is directed to what they share: to the more general activity of which each is a species and to the kind of education, the kind of reading, of which each has been the occasion.

5

This sort of reading and education obviously has its limits and defects. Some would say that the practices of criticism and judgment I describe are insufficiently theoretical in character. That is in my view very far from being a defect, as I shall say at greater length below. But I do think that in both law and poetry this kind of reading includes a bias towards the complex that renders us inadequately receptive to the occasional text that states a simple but important and integrated truth. ("All men are created equal.") Of course a simple but powerful statement of this kind is "simple" only on the surface. It works as it does in large part because it forcefully evokes a rich and shared knowledge of language and culture. (Thus in the quoted sentence the word "men," once perhaps thought simple enough, today presents us with special complexity and difficulty.) Also, speech that is apparently simple—as in the American plain-talk tradition at its best—often expresses a rare and living awareness of the limits of language. It can be a sophisticated way of respecting the autonomy and experience at once of one's auditor and of oneself. A simple voice may in fact be very far indeed from simplistic or simple-minded (or what I earlier called sentimental). And even where the voice is in every sense simple, a human cry of pain or loss or despair, its very simplicity should give it a sort of standing to which we are too often deaf. It need not be interesting to be important when it expresses another's deepest needs.

Consider in this context a child's unbelieving horror at being told about war, and how suddenly empty seem our accounts of the justifications that engage our grown-up world so completely; or how lamely one explains to such an audience why some of our neighbors are without adequate medical care or schooling. What the child feels at such times is the fundamental equality and value of all people. For the moment he or she identifies with others, especially other children, acknowledging the importance of their experience. Of course this impulse is not all, in the child or the adult, and in the child it is not integrated into a mature personality. This capacity for complete, if momentary, identification with others will to some degree be left behind as the child grows up. But in all of us the memory at least should remain of a simple voice stating, a simple self hearing, a central truth.

In all of these senses there are in our world simple voices saying simple things that ought to be heard and attended to in ways for which the training I describe does not adequately prepare us. We require our complexity to be explicit, spelled out, and we call it an aesthetic value and a test of truth. But in its own way this can itself be a kind of simplemindedness—an avoidance of the complexity that underlies and is evoked by some simple texts, or a denial of the importance of what simply matters most. This tendency has obvious political consequences, for it closes our ears to kinds of speech, and kinds of speakers, that do not meet our criteria of explicit complexity, and can thus be a way of drawing our attention away from inexcusable injustice, ugliness, and stupidity, and of unconsciously defending them.

I also think that each of these two educations has a kind of high-culture blindness. It is assumed as a premise of the reading that sooner or later everything that really counts will be brought within the poems or the judicial opinions that we read, especially within the very best of them. There is much to support this view, for in fact the really great text can reflect its context in remarkably rich and self-challenging ways. (Here one thinks of tiny things: the fact that Fanny, in Jane Austen's *Mansfield Park*, asked Sir Thomas "a question about the slave trade": what question we do not know, but we know Fanny, and it cannot have been a question reflecting a view of the world with which that trade, or that institution, was consistent, even though the house and community of Mansfield Park, the ideal form of which is a true ideal of the novel, is implicitly acknowledged to be dependent upon slavery.) And in the law what is *not* to be talked about is in fact often given a presence within the discourse, in an explicit refusal to talk. The denial of standing, which silences a particular voice; the adoption of a rule excluding certain evidence or denying a particular jury instruction, which renders a claim unsayable; the denial of a cause of action—all these are speech acts that incorporate for the moment what they will exclude. But not everything is proposed for inclusion, and in both cases there is a world that is ultimately beyond the text and its discourse, and what about *it*? What relation should exist between the privileged world defined by the legal or literary canon and the other world of expression and action that lies outside it? (One thinks here of the recent interest in slave narratives, which may move them from one class to another; but beyond even those narratives is an unnarrated life, and what about *that*?) One great merit of reading texts as compositions, made by composers, is that we affirm that we are composers too; one consequence of that is that we affirm our essential equality with the composer whose work we are reading; and as a consequence of *that* we affirm our equality with all composers—that is with all people—and their equality with us. What, then, of the voices we do not hear in the texts that we read, what of the composers to whom we do not attend?

A final difficulty has to do with the ground or standard upon which we make critical judgments of merit and demerit about the poems and judicial opinions that we read. The test of "comprehending contraries" has an appealing neutrality, but this is also, from one point of view, its weakness. The danger is that one will avoid substantive questions about the elements comprehended in the form, or excluded from it, and focus only on the relation that it gives them. Or, even more seriously, our argument about inclusion and exclusion may itself be incomplete because it will begin and stop with our sense of what belongs as that sense is formed by the text itself, or by other similar texts. This method seems to afford no reliable way for talking about what is left out or for criticizing the cultural context in which these forms occur: their unstated premises, their enacted but implicit values, their relation to their larger world, the nature of that larger world itself, and so on.

What is needed here is not a "demystification" of a usual kind—which simply replaces one set of complex fictions with another simpler set of even more impossible fictions (about the fact that the judge functions out of prejudice, for example, or the poet out of class interest, as though nothing else need be said)—but a responsible way of paying attention to what is before us: to the social and cultural context of the text, in as much fullness and detail as we can manage; to the "unsaid" that can render a simple statement complex, or a superficially complex one foolish; to the nature, in short, of the relation between text and world. What is needed is cultural or ideological criticism of the sort that anthropologists dance around but refuse to engage in (on the ground that it is incompatible with their claims to be scientists): a criticism of the merits and demerits of different civilizations, different stages of civilization, and so on. This project is resisted, perhaps because it threatens a return to a Whig view of history or to an imperialistic view of cultural difference, and we have worked hard to distance ourselves from these things; or it is embraced by ideologies committed to simplistic versions of experience that themselves do not meet our standards of comprehending contraries, or including what should be included. But without some attention to such topics, our conversations about poems and opinions, poetry and law, one author and another, are incomplete. Can we get to this kind of conversation from the kind of reading I describe—from a New Critical base? Or is something else entirely called for?

6

As a way of working my way towards these questions I want now to say something about the merits of the way of reading I have been describing, beginning with the law. One way to define the kind of reading I have described would be to say that it is reading law as a kind of literature (as opposed, for example, to reading law as a kind of policy science or economics or social process). For me, as you can tell from what I have said, this is not a metaphorical claim: there is an important sense in which the law *is* literature, and can properly be understood and taught and practiced only when that fact is fully recognized.

To read the legal text as a composition made by one mind speaking to another, constructed out of innumerable choices of word and phrase—as a text whose author decides what belongs within it, and what shall be left out, and how its elements shall be characterized and related—is, as I suggested earlier, to read not merely as a reader, but as a writer or composer. It is to acknowledge that the life of the law we practice, and to which we wish to introduce our students, is at its heart a life of composition: a life of making meaning with words about the world. To see the text as made in this way is to see the writer as a maker of his or her language, and that language therefore as made in part by him or her; this in turn is to break down the conceptual, mechanical, and theoretical views of language and the mind that form such powerful forces in our own intellectual world. The way of reading I describe is in this sense profoundly *antitheoretical*.

The language of the law, in hands trained this way, can be at its heart what Owen Barfield calls a poetic language, not a theoretical one—a language that works by association and connotation, by allusion and reference, by the way words are put together to make a whole. In this way it can maintain connections with the terms and processes of ordinary life and ordinary language. This in fact is a source of much of its political authority and significance: since it must ultimately make sense to a jury, it must ultimately make sense to us, and can therefore remain our law, not the possession of a bureaucracy or a cult.

In this sense, the kind of reading I describe is profoundly *antibureaucratic*. It rejects the idea, for example, that the judge can properly make himself (or herself) merely an analyzer of costs and benefits, or merely a voice of authority, or merely a comparer of one case with another, or merely a policy-maker or problem-solver. The judge is always a *person* deciding a case the story of which can be characterized in a rich range of ways; and he (or she) is always responsible both for his choice of characterization and for his decision. He is always responsible as a composer for the composition that he makes. One great vice of theory in the law is that it disguises the true power that the judge actually has, which it is his true task to exercise and to justify, under a pretense that the result is compelled by one or another intellectual system. Our way of reading takes aim at those pretenses, and seeks to destroy them, by defining the work of the law as the work of individual minds, for which individuals are themselves responsible.

The acknowledgment of inconsistency and tension, the openness to ambiguity and uncertainty, that are essential to good writing under this standard define the individual mind as aware of its limits and in need of instruction, from the past and from others, and as tentative in its own claims to assurance and to vision. It makes the speaker doubt the adequacy of any language, and seek to be aware of the limits of her own forms of thought and understanding. In committing her to an acknowledgment of the various ways in which stories can be told, claims made, and values characterized, it commits her to what can be called "many-voicedness": it is profoundly against monotonal thought and speech, against the single voice, the single aspect of the self or culture dominating the rest. In forcing us to the limits of expression and of our minds, it is a commitment to openness, to the recognition of mystery, to the value of what no one has yet found the words to say or to do. In all of this we must perpetually acknowledge that we have something to learn. This kind of reading thus forces the attention inward as well as outward: one learns in part from what happens as one tries to make an order and fails. This sort of reading is an engine of introspection, and self-criticism, and hence of education. It is a way of recognizing that the law can and should be regarded—and practiced—as one of the humanities.

To look at law this way, as I suggested above, is to affirm the equality of all legal actors, and by implication the radical equality of all people, for in a life of composition and reading each of us is at least potentially present as an individual mind ready to speak and ready to listen; and between such minds, recognized as such, equality is the only possible relation. As composers of texts that are addressed to those who will read what we write not as commands or declarations but as compositions, and as readers who insist upon reading in that way, we create for the moment a world together in which our common circumstances, and with them our common humanity, are confirmed.

7

But how does this help us with the questions raised above, about how we are to talk about what the poem or opinion "leaves out," about the meaning of a text in its larger context, and about that context itself—the political background and ideological basis of the text? (For only when we understand these things can we understand what the text really means as a contribution to that context and to the people who inhabit and constitute it.) I do not have a simple or programmatic answer to these questions, but implicit in what I have said are certain things that bear upon it, and it may be worthwhile to bring them to the surface.

In the first place, it would be inconsistent with everything I have said to expect or hope to work out a kind of cultural criticism that was conceptual or theoretical in character; that was mechanically rational (or bureaucratic) in operation (so that the granting of general premises entailed a concession of particular conclusions); that was not open to the discovery of its own limits and thus to the possibility of its reformulation; that was a program rather than a process. In other words, just as I argued above that the law should be true to its humanistic character and should be practiced on that model rather than the model of social science, of policy studies, or of analytic philosophy, so—and for the same reasons—we should seek a cultural criticism that is literary rather than theoretical in character. It should take place in the space between abstract theoretical argument on the one hand and particularized judgments of individual texts or actions on the other. Like the ideal of law, it should be tentative and poetic, recognizing the limits of its own terms and open to possible shifts in perception and in the very language in which it is constituted. But also—again like both law and literature—it should be responsive and responsible to the tradition of which it is a part, to the larger cultural community in which it takes place. It should acknowledge that it has much to learn from the past and should seek to be neither idiosyncratic nor wholly novel but publicly sharable in a meaningful way. We should expect our generalizations to be presumptive or incomplete and to derive their full meaning not from stipulative definitions but from the way they are put to work in the process of judgment as that is reflected in our compositions.

The trouble with what I call theoretical or conceptual discourse is that it makes seriously wrong assumptions about language, about knowledge, and about the reader. The wrong assumption about language (shared by some linguists) is that the way words work is by carrying bits of meaning, or information, from the speaker to the audience; usually one bit to a word, but sometimes multiple bits (and then the writer must take care to see that only the right bits are carried by the word). The image is of the word carrying something, like a raft carrying a passenger across a river or a container on a conveyer belt carrying sand or gravel. The object is to get "it" and nothing else "across." Good writing is writing that achieves this end. It is "clear." This sort of talk about language often assumes that ideas can be represented in single terms, or sets of terms, which can in turn be pushed about on the page, or in the mind, in varying patterns of equivalence and disequivalence, and that this kind of rudimentary mathematics is the proper model for all human thought. In formal terms, this sort of writing turns everything it can into a noun, reducing the verb to a copula (or perhaps words for "increasing" and "decreasing"). It objectifies the world by nominalizing it; once nominalization has taken place, quantification naturally follows as the obvious, or only, way to establish and describe relations among the objects the language has created.

The wrong assumption about knowledge made by what I call theoretical discourse is that the readers of a text need know nothing (except the English language, here reduced to a code) to read it, and that it will teach them, directly or by reference, all they need to know to get its meaning. Knowledge will in this way be acquired from the text: it can of course be checked against other texts, and against experience, but if it is not in this way falsified, it is in the text itself and by it made equally available to all other readers. As for the readers, they are reduced to the functions of cognition and ratiocination; and the world is reduced to what can be talked about in these terms. The political community created by such a text is necessarily bureaucratic and authoritarian, for there is no way in which this kind of language can recognize the autonomy and difference of others.

How might we proceed differently? First, we should conceive of language not as an apparatus for conceptual elaboration or information exchange but as the living material from which meaning is made in our individual and collective lives. Language is the center of that part of our life that is concerned with the meaning of events and the quality of relations, past and prospective. Information exchange is only a tiny part of what it is about, and even that part does not work in the machinelike way described above. In one direction language is continuous with culture, for it provides the terms of social and factual description, of motive and value, that make our culture what it is. (Think, for example, of the degree to which the heroic culture of the _Iliad_ is embedded in its language.) In another direction language is continuous with the mind and with the self, for language is the material of our thought and the register of our experience. We are ourselves to some degree formed by the languages that we use, for they imply criteria of selection, grounds of motivation, dispositions of mind and feeling, ways of telling the stories of our individual and collective lives, and so on, all of which become part of ourselves. When we learn our language, as children, we participate in practices that have meanings far beyond our conceptions of them; we learn more than we know, and in this way, among others, we are formed by what we learn. What distinguish us from each other, both as cultures and as individuals within cultures, are our languages: our ways of claiming meaning for experience and of giving ourselves experience to claim meaning for. But language is also the ground on which we meet; since it exists before and after us, it gives us a sense of participation in the immortal.

Our language of criticism should not be theoretical or conceptual but what I have called poetic or literary, that is, rooted in the sense that meaning is complex, not unitary; that meaning is acquired partly from the language, partly from the text; and that meaning is not restatable in other terms—"for purposes of discussion"—but must be reestablished whenever we talk. The declarative proposition cannot be the center of this sort of discourse, as it is of conceptual talk, for we know that our words and our thoughts cannot be reduced to the sort of unitary meaning, nor the world be reduced to the sort of fixed and knowable categories, required by that kind of thought. The meaning of our words, and of our world, is always shifting, always incomplete; we not only acknowledge but embrace that fact and the possibilities it entails.

Unlike conceptual language, literary language relies heavily upon the verb, or more precisely upon the relation between actor and action that the normal English sentence expects. The verb, with its noun, invokes a sense of action, usually of human and social action— it is itself action of both these kinds—and thus engages us in a world of action and activates the kind of knowledge proper to that world. By reference and by performance it incorporates a world of practice.

This set of understandings about language says something as well about the kind of knowledge we shall assume our readers to have. We shall not assume our reader to be a *tabula rasa* (except for the capacity to decode an utterance) but will assume, what is true of all of our readers, that he or she has a full competence at the social and linguistic practices by which our world is defined. It is thus on our knowledge of language as practice and art, on our shared social and linguistic competence, that we will most rely; this is not infirmity, but strength, for this is the knowledge we most securely have.

Another way to put this is to say that we shall undo two mistakes often made in modern philosophy: to think of the individual as primary, the social as secondary (made by individuals interacting with each other); and, within the individual, to think of cognition and logic as primary, the emotive, associative, and imaginative as secondary (to be replaced if possible by the superior primary modes). Actually our earliest experience is social, not individual (the conception of self as distinct from family and community comes rather late in life); and our earliest and deepest knowledge is not in the usual sense cognitive or logical but expressive and social. It is knowledge about the meaning of words and gestures; knowledge of the languages by which community is established and managed. The fact that this knowledge is not explicitly translatable into conceptual terms does not affect its reality or its importance. It is with this, our most certain knowledge, that we shall start: not with the imagined isolation of the self, as Locke or Hobbes are said to do; not with the *cogito* of Descartes; but with our knowledge of our own competence at language and the management of social relations through language. Not "I think," then, but "I speak." But speaking always implies an audience and hence a kind of social action: so "I speak, and I hear and I respond." But there must be room for you, too: so not "I think," or even "I speak"; but "we talk," or "we compose," making our world and our selves and our language together.

This is all a way of saying that while we cannot have the certainties we yearn for, we ought not on that account be afraid, for we have in fact always lived, and can only live, with radical uncertainty. We make the best sense we can of things, the best judgments we can make, always checking our account against experience, against our sense of our own dispositions to err, against the suggestions and imaginations of others. We are always tentative or presumptive, always revising; in all of this we are always making and remaking our culture. This is what we know how to do.

This means, of course, that we will abandon the metaphors of language as code or machine, of meaning as bits of information, and of reader as receptacle. Rather we shall seek to speak in our own voices to others, whom we address as knowing what we know they know. We shall not merely inform, but invite, surprise, tease, affront, offer, and so forth. We shall speak to our readers as we know they are, and we are too: in a world in which language is always bounded by the inexpressible; in which language is uncertain, always remade; in which we are always making and remaking our own characters and our communities.

All of this is implicit in the practices of reading I have described. To read in these ways is in fact to enact a certain kind of politics: not bureaucratic but personal; not hierarchical but egalitarian; not dominating but liberating. To speak to another as one who is surrounded by a sea of language, which he or she must use, and in using remake, is to create a political world in which there are others, beyond any simply authoritarian voice we might claim—others with their own lives to lead, their own meanings to make, their own capacity to join us in creating a community that deserves the name.

8

Can more be said about the method by which we should proceed? It will not have escaped you that in this essay I have done what I earlier said literary people are inclined to do: I have assimilated the legal experience to the literary experience, the judicial opinion to the poem. But in talking about the politics of composition and of reading have I not in a sense begun as well to assimilate the poem, and other literary forms, to the judicial opinion? Is it indeed perhaps possible to find a way to analyze both forms at once that will reflect what is common in their nature, as the similarities in reading described above seem to imply? Here let me propose two points upon which in such an effort we might focus our attention, two points that are somewhat different from "language" and "form" as I described those terms above.

The first point of attention I mean is the relation between the text and its cultural context. As a judicial opinion more or less explicitly reads, criticizes, accepts, and modifies earlier judicial opinions and other sources of the law, and reconstitutes them by giving these items a new order, in a new text, so also does the poem or novel act on its tradition: its culture, its language. It employs the expectations established by other works, and modifies them; it incorporates by allusion or imitation, and in doing so it modifies what it refers to. In both cases the text can be seen as a kind of argument with its culture, or, better, as an argumentative reconstitution of it, for what I have called "the culture" never exists in fixed and certain form, but only in performances each of which involves both reaffirmation and transformation (at least the kind of transformation implicit in repetition). What this means for our purposes is that in looking at the relation between text and culture our emphasis will be on the modification, not the continuity. We shall regard it as of little interest to say, "see, here he reproduces his ideology in this respect or that, unthinkingly or unaware"; instead, our interest will be given to the criticisms and transformations and modifications: the directions in which the resources of the culture are shifted by the text. For this is where the art is, the gift, of the text.

This focus of attention provides a basis for comparing not cultures themselves, which are in a practical sense incomparables—no one culture can turn itself into another, however much its members might think they wish to do so—but comparing responses to the cultures: ways in which the patterned resources of meaning that define all cultures, and their limits, are remade. These *are* comparable, for all of us share the problem that our language and the culture it defines are inadequate to the purposes, experiences, and actions we can sense in ourselves. To look here is to touch a universal characteristic of human experience.

The process of examination should in the first instance at least be comparative and integrated, calling upon the kind of thought that works not by argument from general premise to conclusion, but by a process of analogy and disanalogy, perceived similarities and differences. This process of thought, while alien to certain disciplines, is wholly familiar to the common lawyer, who has always proceeded in an uncertain world in which he or she is comparing one case, defined one way, with an array of other cases, defined another way; in which the definition of both items is always arguable; and in which, moreover, these definitions themselves determine the class of items on both sides that will be relevant. An impossible task, viewed mathematically; perfectly possible, viewed practically. And of course analogical reasoning runs deeper in our experience than that. It is how we first organize the world and our language. The conditions of uncertainty that so distress our academic selves are in fact not strange or anomalous and should not be regarded as threatening. They are familiar, natural, and should be felt to be comfortable. Actually, as I suggested above, to be confident in our capacity to work on such conditions is to be confident in what we know most deeply.

A second focus for attention, when we look at poems and opinions through the same lenses, is suggested by what might be called the rhetorical character of judicial opinions and of legal discourse more generally. What I mean by that remark is that legal literature is always produced by actual speakers in actual social contexts, addressing actual audiences whom they wish to persuade or influence. In so doing the speakers constitute, or reconstitute, through their performance, a social universe in which they and their audience are the principal actors; they define and make real a set of values or motives to which they appeal; and they create a sense of the facts of the world and what counts as reason within it. The judicial opinion is in this sense a socially constitutive literature. But so, of course, is the poem or the novel, which of necessity defines both its author (as well as its various "narrators") and its reader (as well as its various "readers") and establishes a relation between them. This is an actual relation, made through language but not wholly expressed or expressible in it. Most obviously where the text is ironic, but in a sense always, the relation is not expressible in the language in which the text is made. Just as we have read law as a kind of literature, so we can read literature as a kind of law, or at least as a kind of rhetoric, and thus devote explicit attention to its politics: to the character the writer gives himself (or herself), to the way the writer talks about others, to the relation he establishes with his reader, to the language of value or motive that he uses, and to its adequacy for the purposes of general social life.

To look at textual relations from this point of view is to suggest a set of questions about human relations more generally: to what degree does this speaker recognize and speak to the situation of his or her audience? To what degree does he or she recognize, validate, and seek to promote the autonomy of the reader, in this relation or in relation to others about whom the text speaks? For example, to establish relations between a slaveholder writer and a slaveholder reader—say in an antebellum Southern novel—that validated the principles of freedom and equality, as these are united in the act of reading, would create a reality that would work to destroy the slavery itself. This is in a sense the point of Fanny's question. It is what Sartre means when he says it is impossible to imagine a good anti-Semitic or racist novel: the premises of the art are directly opposed to the ideological position claimed.

Our questions can focus on the reader's integration as well as his (or her) autonomy: to what extent does this text ask the reader to reduce himself to a certain aspect of his mind or spirit only, to what extent does it urge him on the contrary to respond with all that he is and knows? Does it offer a ground that increases the integration of self and experience by bringing tensions and contraries into simultaneous view? Or does it tend to disintegration, by omitting relevant facts, appealing simply to logic, or simply to feelings? Is it what I earlier called sentimental?

When these questions are asked of a text, they have the kind of meaning, and permit the kind of learning, that comes from immediacy of context. We are asking questions not about the general nature of autonomy or integration, as abstract matters, but about the way a particular text advances or impedes them. This rootedness in experience can give to what are otherwise rather bland and empty terms a richness and specificity of meaning that can carry over to our more general, more explicitly political talk. We shall know that it is not enough to use "autonomy" or "equality" as self-defining words, or as words stipulatively defined at the level of concepts, but that responsible political thought requires that we accept responsibility for the meaning we give such words both within our own compositions and by performance in our relations with our readers.

Many-voicedness; the integration of thought and feeling; the acknowledgment of the limits of one's own mind and language (and an openness to change them); the insistence upon the reality of the experience of other people, and upon the importance of their stories, told in their words—these values, implicit in the kind of reading I have described above, are all in fact essential to our own best ideas of justice. They are political as well as intellectual and aesthetic virtues. And they are political virtues not only in the reading and writing of law, but in the reading and writing of anything, including poetry and political speeches and novels and billboards and newspapers. When we teach law properly, we teach a kind of literature as well; when we teach literature properly, we teach politics as well; and both activities can be seen as serving the same values, under the same standards. In this way we can hope to find a point at which rhetoric and poetry are themselves seen to fuse, or at least to be comprehended in a single field of vision; at which the concerns of law and art, and of justice and beauty, that they represent can be seen not as competing or divergent or unconnected but as one; and at which we are engaged in an activity that can serve as the center of life.

This means that in my view the purely aesthetic is not an adequate test for literature (or other art)—indeed that there is no such thing as the purely aesthetic. All literature, all art, all expression, is ethical and political in nature and part of its meaning—its excellence or viciousness—lies in those dimensions. As I have tried to show in detail in *When Words Lose Their Meaning*, the "literary" greatness of certain texts is inseparable from their political and ethical greatness; and it follows, for me as for Sartre, that the morally vicious cannot be aesthetically great. To say this may throw into jeopardy the professional neutrality or objectivity that seems to some literary critics, and to some law professors, essential to the standing of their craft. But that is of no concern to me. I am talking not about the profession of criticism but about what texts actually mean and the kind of response to them that we, as individual and independent minds, should feel entitled and obliged to make.

As one example of the kind of criticism I mean, let me point briefly to the achievement of William Faulkner. In his novels, especially *Absalom! Absalom!* and *The Sound and the Fury*, he managed to bring to the surface where it could not be denied, the contradictions deep in the white attitude towards blacks, who were to whites at once inferior beings and members of their own families. Yet he did this in a way that was at once accepting of the history, loving towards people of both groups, and—of necessity—determined to effectuate change. He created a mythic past and present for his white community that implied a continuous and reformed future. In this way he moved his culture in the direction both of comprehending its contraries—all of them—in a whole view with a shape of its own, and of recognizing the essential humanity of its human members. To say this is necessarily to praise the work. One could praise quite different works, in different cultures, for the same essential reasons: Dickens and Austen, for example, or Aeschylus and Euripides; or even, I think, such apparently "conservative" writers as Burke and Gibbon.

Let me now put the point in a legal context, using custody and sentencing judgments as my examples. What are to be the standards by which custody is determined when two adults are quarreling over a child, or where the state seeks to intervene to protect a child? The "child's best interests," we are told (and this is indeed an advance over regarding the child as someone's property): but how on earth are those "best interests" to be determined? Or consider sentencing judgments: how is the punishment proper to an offense and an offender to be determined? To think in categories is to produce evident injustice: a fixed punishment for burglary will fail to distinguish among burglars; a variable punishment will produce different consequences for the "same" crime. Rules that further specify what is meant by the "best interests" or "proper sentence" have the defect that they too are categorical and will be both over-inclusive and under-inclusive. (Not all alcoholic mothers are bad mothers; not all third offenses are the same.) So what are we to do? To what ideal conception of law should we aspire?

The answer implicit in what I have said is that we conceive of the law less as a bureaucratic system than as a language and a set of relations. What we should demand in each case is that the judge give to the case attention of a certain sort and make it plain in writing that he or she has done so, for there, in the attention itself, is where justice resides. We are entitled not to "like results" but to "like process" (or "due process"), and this means attention to the full merits of a case, including to what can fairly be said on both sides: to the fair-minded comprehension of contraries, to the recognition of the value of each person, to a sense of the limits of mind and language. On this view it is not a bad but a good thing that sentences vary from any categorically determined precision and that custody decisions do too.

An example from domestic life may help clarify what I mean when I say that justice is at its heart a matter of relations and attitudes rather than results. Suppose the parents of a teenaged child ask, as they often and understandably do, what rules they should adopt governing such things as curfews, dating, housework, allowances, school work, conduct towards siblings, music lessons, and so on. What answer could you—or Dear Abby or anyone else—possibly give them? Obviously there is no one set of correct or just or wise rules. Many fine parents have resolved these matters with their children very differently; many bad parents have no doubt used rules that looked very much like those used by parents of whom one would approve. Within very wide bounds what is critical is not the content of the rules but the relationship out of which the rules grow and which they in turn help to reconstitute. *What* the parent decides matters less than *how*: with what attention to the child's needs and circumstances, with what respect for his or her feelings and claims, with what voice, with what kind of listening (or "hearing"), and so forth. If this analogy is thought to be inappropriately paternalistic, the same point could be made in connection with relations more explicitly equal—in a marriage, a professional partnership, certain business relations, and so on. The point is that the heart of what we mean by justice resides in questions of character and relationship and community—in who we are to each other—for this is what determines the meaning of what is done. If these things are got right, the material manifestations—the rules, the results—will take care of themselves; if they are not got right, the rules and results will be wrong, and this is true in the family, in the custody hearing, in the sentencing proceeding, in the ordinary trial, in national political arrangement, and in international relations. Talk about justice is at its heart talk about character and relations.

How, then, are the judicial opinions of which I speak to be judged: by whom, and under what standards? In the first instance by appellate courts, but ultimately by the community as a whole, by the legal community and the community beyond it. The standards are implicit in what I have said: putting aside pathological extremes that can be disposed of summarily, we shall ask for attention to the case, to the parties, to what can be said on all sides; for openness to new characterizations; for a sense of the limit of one's own language and mind and for respect for the experience of others. The responsibility is ours, to make ourselves better judges and better critics. It is hard to discharge, hard even to contemplate. But it cannot be evaded, for example, by making the law bureaucratic, conceptual, and systematic. For if we do that we are still responsible, and by the same standards, for who we become in our conversations with each other.

My point here may be misunderstood. I am not saying that "results" in the usual sense do not matter; indeed in all the legal conversations I envisage the speakers are in some sense continually addressing the question which result or outcome—which material disposition—is best. But I think these conversations will be most responsive to the conditions of the world, and most likely to lead to the "best" results, if primary attention is continually given to the questions I identify above: How completely is each relevant voice given the opportunity to speak? How fully is it heard? How adequate is our recognition of the equal humanity and equal worth of all people? How adequate is our recognition of the contingency of our own language, the limits of our own minds? To what extent does our ultimate legal composition comprise the relevant contraries and acknowledge the existence of what it does not comprise? As Sophocles shows, and Neoptolemus learns, attention to these questions and others like them makes real, in experience and in character, certain fundamental ethical and political values, in which each of us needs perpetual education; and I think that in an uncertain world, where nothing stays the same, those values, so realized in our actual intellectual and social life, in our characters, are a more reliable guide to conduct and decision than any programatic or systematic scheme could possibly be—in part because such a scheme assumes as stable what is in flux, as knowable what is unknown. Attention to who we are in relation to each other and to our language is, by contrast, within our competence and is far more certain, stable, and practical than any reaching after cause-and-consequence could ever be. If we address the ethical and literary questions well, good answers will emerge to the other questions too. If we can get our voice right—our sense of self, language, and audience—all else that matters will follow more surely than we can ever seek to compel it.

All this, I think, is built into the practices of reading and expression in which we have been schooled. What this means for the practice of criticism and judgment is that we can best begin, not by razing what we have been left and starting over, not by defining abstract principles and applying them to the world, but with what we know how to do already, with our social and linguistic competence, with our reading of law and literature: with the kind of knowledge of our capacities and conditions that Plato perhaps means when he talks about knowledge as a species of remembrance.

9

This returns us to a point raised above, our discomfort with the claims of authority traditionally made for the literary and legal canon, indeed with our own claims to authority as teachers. If everything has a political dimension, and the essence of our political belief is the equal right of individuals to choose their own values, risks, and attitudes, how can we justify the sort of ideology-confirming education in which we engage? Should we perhaps rather strike an unremittingly rejecting stance towards all claims of authority? My view is that we need not fear such claims to authority, in ourselves or others, any more than we need fear the conditions of uncertainty that so distress the rationalistic mind. And the reason is much the same: the claims we make for the authority of the canon, of the past, of what we admire, are themselves tentative and presumptive, ready to be qualified and conditioned by other texts, other voices, and by our own conversations with other people. To become a universal skeptic is no answer at all, for that is also to choose to establish one kind of community and culture rather than another. It implies a basis of preference for which authority is claimed, and authority of a kind that is inconsistent with the skepticism itself. In our world we must choose, and must do so under conditions of uncertainty; we are thus as a matter of necessity always acting on faith and making claims of authority. For my part it seems far better to start by choosing what others have learned to value, by trying to remake our world on the basis of what it is and what is presumptively best within it, rather than to assume that we can start completely fresh, in a place we alone have made, to realize our own ideal. For one thing, that cannot be done, for there is no such place, and our ideals are never purely our own. But even if it could, who are we to claim to know so much better than our predecessors and contemporaries? The truth is a simple but hard one, that neither our acceptance nor our rejection of our inheritance should be unquestioned; it is in the life of our questioning of it and of ourselves, in our remaking the language that defines us, that our true work goes on, and our true community is defined.

We need not fear the claims of authority we make for what we admire but should always be prepared to qualify them; and should in addition always recognize that what is truly authoritative, not authoritarian, is so only by the free and informed acquiescence of others. Whatever presumptive authority we claim for ourselves and others is thus radically conditioned by our recognition that we always speak to those who are entitled to be persuaded, not commanded; that the most we can ask is a fair hearing; and that (whatever we may claim) whenever we speak we can never ask less. What our claims of presumptive authority call for, in law and literature aiike, is not presumptive submission, not obedience, but trusting and responsible engagement.

10

But there is a problem with all this. For who is to say that the attitudes and methods of reading that I associate with the humanities, and with a certain kind of justice, are the right ones? Why should you believe me rather than a real or imagined adversary who takes an opposite position: locating justice in the maximization of net social utility, for example, or in equal distribution of material goods, rather than in the way in which the members of a community regard and speak to one another? Or locating literary excellence in the degree to which the text supports certain *a priori* truths, to such a speaker the most important truths of all, rather than in the way it exposes the resources and limits of the common language in a new way? There is no authority to which I can appeal higher than your own experience: to be persuaded you must agree that this way of talking, as I outline or practice it, or as you can imagine yourself doing it in an improved version, makes more sense of your experience than those posed as alternatives. But what kind of "sense" do we seek to make of our experience, and what can "more" mean? Here I can do no better than to call upon the standards at work in what I have already said, and ask which serves better the cause of truth by including relevant contraries; of beauty by placing them in organized relations with one another; and of justice by recognizing—by constituting—oneself and others as whole and autonomous persons.

The Judicial Opinion and the Poem

BIBLIOGRAPHIC NOTE

Here is an alphabetical list of texts referred to in this chapter:

Mikhail Bakhtin, *The Dialogic Imagination: Four Essays,* ed. Michael Holquist, trans. Caryl Emerson and Michael Holquist (Austin: University of Texas Press, 1981), esp. chap. 4.

Owen Barfield, *Poetic Diction: A Study in Meaning* (London: Faber & Gwyer, 1928), esp. chaps. 7 and 8.

Cleanth Brooks, *The Well-Wrought Urn: Studies in the Structure of Poetry* (New York: Reynal & Hitchcock, 1947), chap. 2.

S. T. Coleridge, *Biographia Literaria* (Modern Library ed., New York: Random House, 1951), chap. 14, pp. 263, 269.

T. S. Eliot, "Tradition and the Individual Talent," in *Selected Essays* (New York: Harcourt, Brace, 1932), p. 4.

William Empson, *Seven Types of Ambiguity* (London: Chatto and Windus, 1930), chaps. 1 and 8.

Robert Frost, "The Constant Symbol," Prefatory Essay to *Collected Poems* (Modern Library ed., New York: Random House, 1946), and "The Figure a Poem Makes," in *Selected Prose,* ed. Hyde Cox and Edward Lathem (New York: Holt, Rinehart & Winston, 1966), pp. 17–18.

Samuel Johnson, "Life of Cowley," in *Rasselas, Poems, Selected Prose,* ed. Bertrand H. Bronson (San Francisco: Rinehart Press, 1971), pp. 353, 358.

Katz v. United States, 389 U.S. 347 (1967).

F. R. Leavis, "The Irony of Swift," *Scrutiny* 2 (1934): 364.

McCulloch v. Maryland, 17 U.S. (4 Wheat.) 316, 407, (1819).

J.-P. Sartre, *What Is Literature?,* trans. Bernard Frechtman (New York: Harper and Row, 1965), pp. 63–65.

Sir Philip Sidney, *The Defense of Poesie,* in *The Complete Works of Sir Philip Sidney,* ed. Albert Feuillert (Cambridge: The University Press, 1922–26), 3: 4–5, 13–14.

7 FACT, FICTION, AND VALUE

IN HISTORICAL NARRATIVE

GIBBON'S ROADS OF ROME

This essay and the next are both about narrative. In the first I focus attention on the ways in which ostensibly "factual" narratives are also necessarily "fictional" and—perhaps even more surprising—the ways in which, however empirically scrupulous they may be, they necessarily express "values" as well. I do this by examining a great historical text, Gibbon's *History of the Decline and Fall of the Roman Empire*, one purpose of which is to bring these structural characteristics of historical narrative repeatedly to the attention of the reader, where they cannot be evaded.

In our reading of Gibbon's *History* we shall pursue several of the themes raised in "The Judicial Opinion and the Poem," for Gibbon's view of history, and of civilization itself, is that each is a kind of composition; for him excellence lies in integration, especially in the integration of aesthetics and utility, and the meaning of the component parts is derived largely from the order in which they are arranged; he practices his own kind of cultural or "civilizational" criticism of the general sort I say we need to develop; and, finally, his text has both great excellence and great flaws, and thus requires us to engage in a complex process of criticism of our own.

The next essay will deal with the relation between legal and social narrative. In it I ask both what special hopes we can have for legal stories, with their authoritatively determined conclusions, and what vulnerabilities those narratives may have, especially when they are placed against the ordinary-language narratives from which they always arise. The context in which I do these things is a reading of Aeschylus' *Oresteia* and Katherine Anne Porter's story "Noon Wine."

If a modern reader tries to read Gibbon's *History* seriously as history—rather than as literature, or for its style or bibliographical ref-

139

erences—he or she will immediately be presented with two serious difficulties. First, in nearly every phrase, in nearly every move it makes, this text expresses value judgments of just the conclusory and attitudinal sort that we expect the historian or serious student of culture to avoid. Second, much of what it represents as factual is so highly caricatured as to make it impossible for us to regard what we are told as being in any usual sense of the word true. These two difficulties are deeply (though perhaps not obviously) related, for each involves a violation of the historian's supposed task of stating the "facts" alone, rather than propounding his "values" on the one hand or making "fictions" on the other. What is more, in Gibbon's case the usual explanations fail—that the historian, scrupulously distinguishing between the objective and the subjective, has reasoned himself to a balanced judgment on the facts he presents, or that his created version of events is the one that makes the most responsible use of the evidence available. Gibbon's judgments seem not to be reasoned, but to operate as unexplained premises, and his fictions are often caricatures that could not survive the pressures of a novel, let alone those created by fragmentary and conflicting historical evidence about real people and events.

But in my view these qualities of Gibbon's text are not defects to be patronized away—say by reference to his earlier (and hence presumptively lower) standards of historical scholarship, or by reducing his text to the status of *belles-lettres,* or by admiring it for the solid work that underlies its unfortunately rhetorical surface—but merits to be celebrated, and merits of an extraordinary kind: for they continually bring to the reader's attention fundamental questions about the very nature of historical writing itself. These questions, about the nature of facts, values, and fictions, are unavoidably present in historical writing of every kind, including "histories" not usually conceived as such: stories about one's own life, statements of fact (or law) in a legal brief, politicians' descriptions of circumstance and character—in short, in every attempt to talk about, and in talking about to constitute, our shared experience. But in most texts, including those of our own composition, these questions are either unaddressed or actually hidden from view. Gibbon's text not only defines these questions for us with a special clarity but forces them upon our consciousness, and into our field of responsibility, where they belong. This text thus provides an education in an intellectual activity that is as universal and deeply rooted in human nature as any could be, the activity of telling stories about the world and claiming meanings for them.

1

To start with the judgments of value: while in his *History* Gibbon organizes factual material, tells stories, and does the other things we expect historians to do, he also tells his reader over and over what he should think and feel about these matters, and does so in no uncertain terms. This aspect of his text may be a real irritant to the modern reader, who is likely to resent Gibbon's constantly judging presence. Yet the judgmental side of this text is not secondary or superficial, but essential to its life and structure. The very title commits it to a view of civilization by which the "decline and fall" of which it promises to speak can be described and measured. And the judgments we find here are of a breathtakingly bold and global kind, for Gibbon sets himself up as nothing less than a judge of civilization itself, and he asks his reader to become one too—one just like him, that is. This is not value-free social science, to say the least, nor the kind of nonjudgmental anthropology that is careful to respect the forms of life other people have made or chosen, but an explicit literature of value and judgment.

My questions are these: What are the central terms of value in Gibbon's discourse, and how are they given meaning for the reader? Taken as whole, what do his judgments add up to: what language of value does he make, what idea of excellence in civilization does he express? And how should we respond to—how judge—the invitations this text makes us, to speak its language, to share the position from which these judgments are made, and thus to become members of the "civilization" it defines, by which the other civilizations—of Rome, of Christianity, of the Arabs—are judged?

Gibbon's language of value is made a subject of the reader's attention right from the opening paragraph, which is full of apparently undefined terms of praise and blame. How are we to read this, and what do we expect to follow from it by way of clarification or elaboration?

> In the second century of the Christian Era, the empire of Rome comprehended the fairest part of the earth, and the most civilized portion of mankind. The frontiers of that extensive monarchy were guarded by ancient renown and disciplined valour. The gentle, but powerful, influence of laws and manners had gradually cemented the union of the provinces. Their peaceful inhabitants enjoyed and abused the advantages of wealth and luxury. The image of a free constitution was preserved with de-

cent reverence. The Roman senate appeared to possess the sovereign authority, and devolved on the emperors all the execu-
tive powers of government. During a happy period of more
than fourscore years, the public administration was conducted
by the virtue and abilities of Nerva, Trajan, Hadrian, and the
two Antonines. It is the design of this and of the two succeed-
ing chapters, to describe the prosperous condition of their empire; and afterwards, from the death of Marcus Antoninus, to
deduce the most important circumstances of its decline and fall:
a revolution which will ever be remembered, and is still felt by
the nations of the earth.

This paragraph defines a central subject, the "prosperous condition"
from which the empire fell, and proposes a set of terms by which that
condition can be defined: "ancient renown and disciplined valour,"
"laws and manners," "union," "enjoy[ment] of wealth and luxury,"
the "virtue and abilities" of the benign emperors, the "free constitution" of which this stage of Imperial Rome has only the "image,"
and the "abuse of wealth and luxury," which is apparently its signal
vice.

As the text proceeds, we naturally (and properly) expect it to make
fuller and sharper definitions of these central terms. But the experience Gibbon actually offers us is puzzling, for he seems to have little
interest in working out more refined and complex definitions of the
words he uses. Rather, he seems to use his words of value throughout as terms of undefined conclusion, empty labels of praise or
blame, without apparent consciousness that they need further definition. In this paragraph, for example, he seems to assume that we
all know what "abuse of luxury" and "disciplined valour" are, as if
they were bright checkers of determinate meaning to be moved about
on the page, a view of language that one would expect any good
teacher to correct as a failure of thought.

This use of undefined terms of value fits with a larger impression
the text makes upon the reader—that he or she is constantly being
told what to think, and what (rather reduced) terms to think it in.
Gibbon's prose is full of wholly unsubstantiated judgments. To take
one brief example: of the war in Britain Gibbon tells us that it was
"undertaken by the most stupid, maintained by the most dissolute,
and terminated by the most timid of all the emperors." We are in no
way told what is meant by these adjectives nor how their application
is justified. We certainly have no opportunity to engage with the text
either by challenging or by confirming these judgments.

What is the effect of this kind of writing? It is not to tell us very much about the war, or about the emperors, nor even to assert, in however unsatisfactory a form, the values of intelligence, temperance, and bravery. The assertion effectively achieved by this sentence is not about these things but about the text and the reader's relationship with it: we are told that this is a text in which conclusory judgments of this sort will be made, and that we are expected to accept them, indeed to enjoy or to admire them. The primary value actually at work here is thus not stated but performed, and it bears no special relation to the meaning of any of the words of value: it is that of firm and categorical judgment itself. One learns here not so much that Gibbon thinks it good to be brave, intelligent, and temperate—what else could he think?—but that he thinks it good to talk in this judgmental and elegant way.

To modern ears this kind of literature may sound like advertising or propaganda, a stripping of complexity from life and language, and it is easy to imagine someone turning away from this prose, not wanting to be talked to in such a way, perhaps believing that nothing true can be said in such a style. Similar effects are produced by Gibbon's irony, much of which seems heavy-handed; and by the way he represents people, many of whom are mere caricatures. One cannot complain of Gibbon, as one might of Swift or of Melville, that he offers us nothing firm or stable. He offers us an impossibly reduced place to stand and insists that we stand there with him; he admits, indeed, no other possibility. This literature seems to be written not to acknowledge and to assist the freedom and autonomy of the reader, but to control him—to force the reader to accept a smug and limited view of the world, in a language of caricature that cannot be true. Not only can it not be true "historically"; it seems that it cannot be true imaginatively either, and it may be hard to see how it can even be interesting.

But while Gibbon does not give meaning to his initially rather empty terms in the way we most naturally expect (that is, by elaborating increasingly rich and complicated definitions of them), he does give his language meaning in other ways—by performance—and thus expresses directly what he values in mankind and in civilization.

Consider again for example the sentence about the "stupid, dissolute, and timid" emperors. Since Gibbon does not name or otherwise identify them, the sentence assumes that his reader will know who they are and take pleasure in the invocation of that knowledge; or, if he (or she) does not know, that he wishes he did, so that this pleasure could be his. A value thus actually performed here is that of belonging to a community based upon common knowledge, a community indeed of the kind that it is the purpose of the *History* as a whole to create with its readers. What does it mean to belong to such a community? Partly the pleasure and meaning of activating what one knows, of confirming the value of the knowledge itself, and of sharing it; partly, here at least, the pleasure of elegance and wit, of the reduced characterization that is to be admired for its force and boldness, as well as for what may be, from one point of view, its truth.

Or consider the way Gibbon tells us what he means by the "free constitution" of which the first paragraph said that the empire had only the "image." He gives meaning to this phrase, not by explicit definition, but by the very structure of his next sentence:

> The principal conquests of the Romans were achieved under the republic; and the emperors, for the most part, were satisfied with preserving those dominions which had been acquired by the policy of the senate, the active emulation of the consuls, and the martial enthusiasm of the people.

The republic of which this sentence speaks is enacted in its structure. This is achieved not merely by the balance, complexity, and directness of the sentence, though these are important qualities of the republican form of government as Gibbon conceives it, but by the nature of the items thus placed in relation to each other. The senate, the consuls, and the people represent the divisions of the republican constitution, while policy, emulation, and enthusiasm are the contributions of each: wisdom from the experienced, performance from the excellent, and simplicity and strength of sentiment from the multitude. In establishing these pairs Gibbon defines each term by reference to its correlative, telling us at once what to hope for from each kind of actor and where to look for each sort of contribution to the healthy republic. And, most important, in writing this sentence Gibbon tells us that we can look for the same kind of meaningful organization—of composition—at once in our utterances and in our governments.

The sentence about the true constitution, like that about the "three emperors," employs a method of defining value—I call it definition by performance—that will prove central to the character and achievement of the *History* as a whole, and to it we shall frequently return.

The paragraph goes on to speak of the "spirit of moderation" that led first Augustus, then the other emperors, to confine the empire within those limits which Nature seemed to have placed as its natural bulwarks—the Atlantic, the Rhine, the Danube, the Euphrates, and the deserts of Africa. Augustus was led to this policy, Gibbon says, by his "temper and situation," which made it "easy for him to discover that Rome . . . had much less to hope than to fear from the chance of arms." Experience confirmed this disposition: his generals "marched near a thousand miles to the south of the tropic but the heat of the climate soon repelled the invaders and protected the unwarlike natives of those sequestered regions." As for the land to the north, it "scarcely deserved the expense and labour of conquest. The forests and morasses of Germany were filled with a hardy race of barbarians, who despised life when it was separated from freedom."

In a highly stylized form Gibbon has here sketched two relationships—between Rome and the barbarian, and between Rome and nature—that will quickly be developed into major themes, and ultimately become central to the structure of the *History* as a whole. What begin here as mere "barbarians" or "natives" will become Germans, or Persians, or Goths, or Mongols, or Arabs, or Franks, members of distinct cultures that are given separate and extensive treatment, until at the end it is the "barbarians" themselves who supplant Rome and raise a new civilization out of its ruins. ("The most civilized nations of modern Europe issued from the woods of Germany, and in the rude institutions of those barbarians we may still distinguish the original principles of our present laws and manners." [chap. 9]) The relationship between Rome and nature is developed in a different way, but it is no less important; it becomes, as we shall shortly see, the center of Gibbon's idea of civilization.

These movements from schematic relations lightly sketched to structures central to the work as a whole are instances of an important quality of Gibbon's text: the marking out within small structures, such as the sentence or paragraph, of a set of relations that will reappear on a different scale in other parts of the work. The entire first paragraph is itself a model of this technique, for in a sense it contains within it the structure of the *History* as a whole: it establishes the scale of the empire, contrasts it with the politically happier countries that enjoy a "free constitution," identifies the abuse of luxury that will destroy it, and promises to carry the story to the present moment, when the fall of Rome is "still felt" by the nations of the earth and to affect the way it is "remembered" for ever. In retrospect, at least, we can see the entire work compressed into its first paragraph. The replication of such relationships on different scales contributes to one's sense, which increases as one proceeds, that, despite its enormous range and variation, the text is at heart one thing. And this principle of organization is one of movement and development, as well as one of structure: what is lightly touched in one place, barely hinted at, will later expand into an important subject of work and attention. One is reminded of the way in which a musical theme might at first be heard very lightly, in a second or third voice, and only later be developed and complicated on a larger scale.

In going on to say that Britain was inhabited by a people who "possessed valour without conduct, and the love of freedom without the spirit of union," Gibbon defines what is *not* civilized by employing positive terms of value drawn from his first paragraph: what civilization unites—valor and discipline (or conduct); freedom and union—its opposite divides. This is a way of giving meaning to words not by defining their content, but by establishing a relationship between them. Since the relationship is good for any ordinary meaning of the terms, Gibbon need not, indeed he should not, define "valour," say, or its complement "conduct," with any greater specificity: it is part of his point that however the terms are defined, the achievement of civilization requires both. Another example of this method of definition can be found in the pairings of negative terms in the "three emperors" sentence: the war was "undertaken" by the "stupid" emperor, "maintained" by the "dissolute" one, and "terminated" by the "timid." In these pairings Gibbon defines the dangers especially associated with each bad characteristic: he tells us to look for bad initiatives from the stupid, bad execution from the dissolute, and bad terminations from the timid. And a similar point is made, as we have already seen, in his sentence about the republic (the "policy of the senate," etc.). In each of these cases what I have called the reduced content of Gibbon's terms is in fact a way of clarifying the relationships among them and thus of establishing their meaning.

After defining the "spirit of moderation" that led Hadrian and the Antonines to retract the frontiers of the empire to their "natural" limits Gibbon shifts to an account of the military force that supported it; only then does he describe its physical extent. This order (which a modern writer might well reverse) establishes an important pattern that is reduplicated elsewhere in the *History*. Gibbon's account of the army, for example, begins with the motives that animated the soldiers—their spirit and character—and only then moves to the structure of the institution itself and its methods of training and of operation. In his lengthy description of the Roman military force, we see Gibbon once again enact in his prose what he admires in the world: in this instance, the organization into a single living order of an enormous universe of details, which have no function until they are placed in disciplined relation with one another. As the Roman legion makes rational, orderly, and powerful the conflicting impulses of men in battle, Gibbon's *History* organizes a vast array of facts and events into a comprehensible and living whole. In both cases no small part of the excellence to be admired is the remarkable combination of greatness and multiplicity on the one hand, with swift and coordinated movement on the other.

The opening chapter concludes with a splendid survey of the Roman world, in which Gibbon describes at once the magnificent reach and variety of the empire and the scope of his own work. His attention is double: both upon the natural forces and features of the world—the sea, mountains, rivers, deserts, and so forth—and upon their human or social significance. For Gibbon, civilization takes place in nature, and, at best, the forces of nature will be at once employed and respected:

> When Augustus gave laws to the conquests of his father, he introduced a division of Gaul equally adapted to the progress of the legions, to the course of the rivers, and to the principal national distinctions, which had comprehended above an hundred independent states.

But the historian of the Roman Empire insists that the mind of man has its own independent force, answering to that of the rivers and deserts, a capacity to impose order and meaning of its own invention. Compare:

> Phoenicia and Palestine were sometimes annexed to, and sometimes separated from, the jurisdiction of Syria. The former of these was a narrow and rocky coast; the latter was a territory scarcely superior to Wales, either in fertility or extent. Yet Phoenicia and Palestine will forever live in the memory of mankind; since America, as well as Europe, has received letters from the one, and religion from the other.

2

Gibbon begins the second chapter by reminding us that "it is not alone by the rapidity or extent of conquest that we should estimate the greatness of Rome. . . . The obedient provinces of Trajan and the Antonines were united by laws and adorned by arts." This sentence anticipates the structure of the chapter as a whole, half of which will be devoted to the laws that united the empire, half to the arts that adorned it: together, defining its civilization. We already know enough to expect that this chapter itself will exemplify unity and order on the one hand and elegance and beauty on the other, and we are not disappointed.

Under the first heading, Gibbon deals with laws of three kinds: those tolerating a wide diversity of religions; those by which the rights of citizenship were extended first to the Italians, then to soldiers and other deserving provincials, and at last to practically every free man within the empire; and those that meliorated the status of slavery.

Among the religions of the ancient world, similarities of image, method, and sentiment encouraged universal toleration: "the deities of a thousand groves and a thousand streams possessed in peace their local and respective influence; nor could the Roman who deprecated the wrath of the Tiber deride the Eygptian who presented his offering to the beneficent genius of the Nile." Rome, which was "incessantly filled with subjects and strangers from every part of the world," gradually became "the common temple of her subjects"; and "the freedom of the city was bestowed on all the gods of mankind."

The policy of extending citizenship beyond the city itself obliterated the "partial distinctions" among the Italians, and the people of the peninsula "insensibly coalesced into one great nation, united by language, manners, and civil institutions, and equal to the weight of a powerful empire." As for the provinces, "a nation of Romans was gradually formed" among them by the "double expedient of introducing colonies, and of admitting the most faithful and deserving of the provincials to the freedom of Rome." The use of Latin was extended by the Romans with their arms, so that the "western countries were civilized by the same hands which subdued them"; and as time went on, "education and study insensibly inspired the natives of those countries with the sentiments of Romans." The Greek-speaking eastern countries were not Latinized, but a linguistic and intellectual union was established the other way, by the spread of Greek throughout the empire. As Latin was the language of government, Greek was the language of letters: it became "almost impossible, in any province, to find a Roman subject, of a liberal education, who was at once a stranger to the Greek and to the Latin language." Such were the "institutions" by which the "nations of the empire insensibly melted away into the Roman name and people."

The institution of slavery, which seems to establish an irremediable division among the people, was softened by the laws and manners of the Romans. When the fear of insurrection had died away, "the sentiments of nature, the habits of education, and the possession of a dependent species of property, contributed to alleviate the hardships of servitude." The master's humanity was encouraged by his self-interest; and in time the protection of the laws as well extended to the slave. "Hope, the best comfort of our imperfect condition, was not denied to the Roman slave," for manumission by gradual degrees was possible and often achieved. "Without destroying the distinction of ranks, a distant prospect of freedom and honours was presented, even to those whom pride and prejudice almost disdained to number among the human species."

In each of these sections, the Roman Empire is conceived of by Gibbon as a composition: a putting together of material, an arrangement, that balances unity with variety, and makes a new object: the "laws," in fact, are "arts."

In his promised account of the "arts that adorned" the empire Gibbon begins as usual with spirit and motive: the "innumerable monuments of architecture" left by the Romans might deserve our attention by "their greatness alone, or their beauty . . . but they are rendered more interesting by two important circumstances, which connect the agreeable history of the arts with the more useful history of human manners. Many of those works were erected at private expense, and almost all were intended for public benefit."

The practice of public building had its roots in the "commonwealths of Athens and Rome," where "the modest simplicity of private houses announced the equal condition of freedom; whilst the sovereignty of the people was represented in the majestic edifices destined to the public use: nor was this republican spirit totally extinguished by the introduction of wealth and monarchy." The result was that Rome and the provinces were embellished by a "liberal spirit of public magnificence, and were filled with amphitheatres, theaters, temples, porticos, triumphal arches, baths and aqueducts, all variously conducive to the health, the devotion, and the pleasures of the meanest citizen." The aqueducts in particular deserve attention: "The boldness of the enterprise, the solidity of the execution, and the uses to which they were subservient, rank the aqueducts among the noblest monuments of Roman genius and power."

From the monuments Gibbon turns to the number and magnitude of the cities, and then to the roads, which in an important passage he describes thus:

All these cities were connected with each other, and with the capital, by the public highways, which, issuing from the Forum of Rome, traversed Italy, pervaded the provinces, and were terminated only by the frontiers of the empire. If we carefully trace the distance from the wall of Antoninus to Rome, and from thence to Jerusalem, it will be found that the great chain of communication, from the north-west to the south-east point of the empire, was drawn out to the length of four thousand and eighty Roman miles. The public roads were accurately divided by milestones, and ran in a direct line from one city to another, with very little respect for the obstacles either of nature or private property. Mountains were perforated, and bold arches thrown over the broadest and most rapid streams. The middle part of the road was raised into a terrace which commanded the adjacent country, consisted of several strata of sand, gravel, cement and was paved with large stones, or, in some places near the capital, with granite. Such was the solid construction of the Roman highways, whose firmness has not entirely yielded to the effort of fifteen centuries. They united the subjects of the most distant provinces by an easy and familiar intercourse; but their primary object had been to facilitate the marches of the legions; nor was any country considered as completely subdued, till it had been rendered, in all its parts, pervious to the arms and authority of the conqueror. The advantage of receiving the earliest intelligence, and of conveying their orders with celerity, induced the emperors to establish, throughout their extensive dominions, the regular institution of posts. Houses were everywhere erected at the distance only of five or six miles; each of them was constantly provided with forty horses, and, by the help of these relays, it was easy to travel an hundred miles in a day along the Roman roads. The use of the posts was allowed to those who claimed it by an Imperial mandate; but, though originally intended for the public service, it was sometimes indulged to the business or conveniency of private citizens. Nor was the communication of the Roman empire less free and open by sea than it was by land. The provinces surrounded and enclosed the Mediterranean; and Italy, in the shape of an immense promontory, advanced into the midst of that great lake. The coasts of Italy are, in general, destitute of safe harbours; but human industry had corrected the deficiencies of nature; and the artificial port of Ostia, in particular, situate at the mouth of the Tiber, and formed by the Emperor Claudius, was

an useful monument of Roman greatness. From this port,
which was only sixteen miles from the capital, a favourable
breeze frequently carried vessels in seven days to the columns
of Hercules, and in nine or ten to Alexandria in Egypt.

In this passage the roads of Rome are held out for our admiration as
great works of man. What is it about them that Gibbon remarks
upon? It is their enormous scale; the incredible solidity of their construction; the rationality and boldness of their design; the unity and
order they impose on the world; and their utility for commerce and
for arms. They constitute a system of great simplicity that makes one
thing out of many, by the imposition of the mind of man upon the
world of nature. In making the world one, the roads make intelligible
and manageable what was theretofore incomprehensibly various and
disjunctive. Two things are at once admired here: the spaciousness
and variety of the geographic world, and the force of mind and industry that can organize it and make it usable by man. For Gibbon
the "arts that adorn" are not fine arts for private consumption, but
public works for public benefit, and they are characterized by greatness, boldness, rationality, and simplicity.

When this passage is considered in connection with what has gone
before (especially with the survey of the empire, the appeals to the
lost republic, and the images of the barbarians) and with what comes
after it (especially with the next section, where we are told of the new
fruits, flowers, and grasses that the system of transportation enabled
the Romans to introduce throughout their empire, converting it into
an "immense garden"), what I have called Gibbon's idea of civilization emerges with considerable clarity: at its best, civilization for him
is the active and equal engagement of the mind of man with the
forces of nature, including the forces of human nature. Gibbon sees
civilization, that is, as a special kind of art, by which the materials,
both of nature and of culture, that exist around man and within him
are given order by the mind: the order should employ the strengths
and respect the limits of its materials, but the order itself must come
from the mind.

Gibbon has no romantic sense that nature is best when undis-
turbed, nor does he express the value of harmony with nature in the
usual sense ("nature to advantage dress't"). The roads impose a new
order upon the face of the earth, and the lines they draw are straight;
the aqueducts move water from where nature placed it to where man
wants it; and when the harbor at Ostia was built, we are told, "human industry . . . corrected the deficiencies of nature." It would be

proper to say that Gibbon's conception of culture is aesthetic, but only if one adds that his standards are not formal but substantive: the ideal is not beauty so much as integrity and force, the goal not appreciation but use. (His word for consumption, including aesthetic consumption, is "luxury," and we shall soon learn what he thinks of it.) The mind does not merely arrange or dispose the materials of nature in harmonizing patterns or in designs that bring out strengths or beauties latent within them, but imposes itself upon them, making something of its own.

Gibbon's idea of civilization as composition extends to human as well as to material nature. The barbarians have all their natural vigor and strength and courage, but lack the "discipline" or "union" to convert themselves into a real force: they have "valour without conduct." The imperial legion, by contrast, has the organization that the barbarians lack, but since it cannot draw upon the deepest of human motives, it must make do with a set of more or less artificial inducements—honor and religion, pay and fear. For Gibbon the ideal is the republic, where self-interest and public interest merge into one, and the community has available to its service the most powerful feelings and motives of its citizens. ("In the purer ages of the commonwealth, the use of arms was reserved for those ranks of citizens who had a country to love, a property to defend, and some share in enacting those laws which it was their interest, as well as duty, to maintain" [chap. 1].) It is the genius of the republic to employ the natural forces of human desire in balanced and constructive ways: not to banish, but to civilize them. Thus the "emulation of the consuls" (by which he means their competitive striving for success and excellence), which is in the republic so productive of public good, is a channeling of forces that in another set of circumstances could easily be destructive. Likewise, as we have seen, it is one merit of Roman slavery to give place and function to the force of human hope.

Gibbon's idea of civilization, then, is an idea about the relationship between man and nature, including human nature, a conception not of organic harmony—"man at home in nature"—but a kind of struggle or tension, almost a competition, in which the mind of man both imposes itself upon the world and respects its qualities and limits: a kind of productive art, of which the roads and aqueducts can perhaps serve as the best example. In the course of his text this idea, lightly sketched in the early paragraphs, is developed over and over in different contexts until it becomes what might be called an informing or structural idea: it offers a method for approaching any aspect of civilization, a way of thinking about culture both as a whole and in its parts. Gibbon's idea becomes the central location defined by his text, the place from which he proceeds, and to which he withdraws: the place he offers his reader to stand, and the measure by which a civilization is to be judged.

It should by now be apparent that Gibbon's idea of civilization is also an idea of history, and that it is in the life of his prose that it receives its fullest definition. Think once again, for example, of the roads. The qualities for which they are held out as admirable are self-evidently qualities of Gibbon's own text: the sheer magnitude of the work, the greatness of the ambition, and the unification of an enormous body of disparate material under a single bold design, which makes one thing out of many. As the civilization of the Roman Empire organizes the materials of nature into productive patterns determined by man, so the "civilization" of Gibbon's *History* organizes the facts and evidence of history, the raw materials of the past, into a set of patterns that are the products of Gibbon's own mind. And as it is not Gibbon's idea that nature should be interfered with as little as possible in the physical world (that roads should be lovingly adapted to the contours of the terrain, for example), so it is not his idea that the "facts" of history should be allowed "to speak for themselves," nor his conception of his task that he is merely to clear away cobwebs and place things in their own natural order. For him history—like civilization— is made by the force of a mind acting upon its materials, at once respecting their essential character and imposing an order of its own upon them.

As the account of Roman religion shows—and his account of the Christians, who denied the claims of culture with a vehemence matched only by their denial of nature, shows even more clearly[1]—

1. The Christians denied their own sexual nature, their ambition to govern, and their ties to their culture. For example, their "abhorrence of every enjoyment which might gratify the sensual, and degrade the spiritual, nature of man" led them to adopt extraordinary doctrines of chastity, including demonstrations of purity such as those by which nuns and priests would sleep together without violating their vows of chastity. "But insulted Nature sometimes vindicated her rights," Gibbon says, and "this new species of martyrdom served only to introduce a new scandal into the Church." (Some, judging it "most prudent to disarm the tempter," indulged in self-mutilation.) The Christian belief in miracles involved a similar turning away from the facts of nature to fantasy, as Gibbon presents it in the paragraph reproduced above, on p. 85 n. 2. As for culture, it was "the first but arduous duty of a Christian to preserve himself pure and undefiled by the practice of idolatry." But the "innumerable deities and rites of polytheism were closely interwoven with every circumstance of business or pleasure, of public or of private life," and it seemed "impossible to escape the observance of them,

Gibbon's ideas of civilization and history are founded upon respect for the facts of culture, as well as those of nature. His ideas of civilization and of history thus literally merge: for as the citizen respects the facts of his culture, and starts from those, making what he can from them, the historian does likewise; beginning with the facts, the evidence from which a life can be inferred, and making from them a history of his own; and both history and civilization—like the laws themselves—are species of art.

3

But this is to get ahead of ourselves, for there remains one important feature of Gibbon's art to describe. So far in his second chapter, Gibbon has defined, both by description and by enactment, what he means by "united" and "adorned," and has established the central elements of his informing idea of civilization. Gibbon concludes this section by describing the views of the inhabitants, who "celebrate[d] the increasing splendour of the cities, the beautiful face of the country, cultivated and adorned like an immense garden; and the long festival of peace, which was enjoyed by so many nations, forgetful of their ancient animosities, and delivered from the apprehension of future danger."

Here it seems, with the conversion of the empire into a united and prosperous garden, the chapter may end. Gibbon's idea of civilization has been fully expressed; the structure promised us in the first paragraph—"united by laws and adorned by arts"—has reached its conclusion; and the chapter itself is a splendid enactment of what it means to unite diversity into a single organization, to adorn it with the useful arts. But instead the text takes a surprising turn:

> It was scarcely possible that the eyes of contemporaries should discover in the public felicity the latent causes of decay and corruption. This long peace, and the uniform government of the Romans, introduced a slow and secret poison into the vitals of

without, at the same time, renouncing the commerce of mankind and all the offices and amusements of society." The result is both comic and pathetic: "when the bride, struggling with well-affected reluctance, was forced in hymeneal pomp over the threshold of her new habitation, or when the sad procession of the dead slowly moved towards the funeral pile; the Christian, on these interesting occasions, was compelled to desert the persons who were the dearest to him, rather than contract the guilt inherent to those impious ceremonies" (chap. 15).

the empire. The minds of men were gradually reduced to the same level, the fire of genius was extinguished, and even the military spirit evaporated. The natives of Europe were brave and robust. Spain, Gaul, Britain, and Illyricum supplied the legions with excellent soldiers, and constituted the real strength of the monarchy. Their personal valour remained, but they no longer possessed that public courage which is nourished by the love of independence, the sense of national honour, the presence of danger, and the habit of command. They received laws and governors from the will of their sovereign, and trusted for their defence to a mercenary army. The posterity of their boldest leaders was contented with the rank of citizens and subjects. The most aspiring spirits resorted to the court or standard of the emperors; and the deserted provinces, deprived of political strength or union, insensibly sunk into the languid indifference of private life.

The text is here once again performative, but in a new way: it achieves what might be called a negative enactment of Gibbon's idea of civilization, offering the reader an experience that directly parallels that of the empire in decay. We have been lulled by the luxuriousness of Gibbon's prose (and by his defense of luxuries themselves, which he justifies by saying that their production promotes the redistribution of wealth) into a kind of relaxation, an oblivion of what he has already told us; like the empire, we are "insensibly" led into a kind of false happiness. Gibbon corrects us with an appeal, by now familiar, to the age of the Republic, where citizens had the "public courage" that derives from the "love of independence, the sense of national honour, the presence of danger, and the habit of command."

With a decline of republican virtue, Gibbon tells us, came a decline in letters (an "art" of which we should have felt the absence in his earlier catalogue): "if we except the inimitable Lucian, this age of indolence passed away without having produced a single writer of original genius or who excelled in the arts of elegant composition." In the midst of this paragraph another major shift of perspective and attitude occurs:

On the revival of letters, the youthful vigour of the imagination after a long repose, national emulation, a new religion, new languages, and a new world, called forth the genius of Europe. . . . [The Romans had degenerated into] a race of pigmies, when the fierce giants of the north broke in and mended the puny breed. They restored a manly spirit of freedom; and, after the revolution of ten centuries, freedom became the happy parent of taste and science.

By the end of this chapter we realize that the golden age that it describes is a golden age of empire only. The historical embodiments of Gibbon's central values are offstage: the age of the Republic and now, for the first time, modern Europe, that world created by the barbarians when they at last united their natural vigor with the learning of the ancient world. This is a redefinition both of the familiar figure of the "barbarian" and of the "decline and fall" itself; we now learn that the true subject of the work as a whole will include not only the fall of Rome but the rise of Europe.

Such dramatic shifts in perspective mark a characteristic of the life of this text as a whole, both in its largest and in its smallest structures, in its general design and in its sentences and turns of phrase. The reader's experience of this work has what can be called an architectural character, for it is like one's experience of a great building: the text works by shifting one's sense of space and object across time. Think, for example, of the experience offered by one of the great Gothic cathedrals. One knows with great immediacy where one is: at the doors, say, examining the details of the sculpture in the arch overhead, or at the entrance to the nave, where the space sweeps upwards, or in the lady-chapel, complete in itself, yet a part of something else. But these experiences are not discrete, for one does not jump but moves from one full and immediate engagement to another, and much of the experience of the architecture is the experience of such movement. Each new perspective redefines what has gone before, until a sense of the whole is achieved. Great landscape gardening has something of this same character, and so do the best cities: one suddenly emerges onto an extensive view one had not imagined. So too with this text: what is at one moment seen in one way, with clarity and assurance, is later seen very differently as perspectives shift and relations change.[2] In an important sense, indeed, what this text is ultimately about is the set of positions it establishes for its reader and the movement from one to another.

---

2. Think of the sentence in the first paragraph of the whole work, for example, that points to the "arts and luxuries" section in these words: "Their peaceful inhabitants enjoyed and abused the advantages of wealth and luxury." Notice how the word "peaceful," as was the case with "adorn," obtains in retrospect a complication of meaning that one would not have noted the first time through. In such ways the shifts of perspective work on the language itself.

Shifts of this kind occur at the largest level. At the end of the history Rome herself has undergone a remarkable transformation: no longer an empire, by many hundreds of years, she is now merely a city, and a modern one at that, among whose decayed and ancient ruins the reader himself, like Gibbon, may walk. Gibbon makes it one of his last tasks to explain how even the physical remains of the lost empire were gradually degraded into ruins, until, in the words he quotes from Poggio: "The forum of the Roman people, where they assembled to enact their laws and elect their magistrates, is now enclosed for the cultivation of pot-herbs or thrown open for the reception of swine and buffaloes" (chap. 71). Perhaps nowhere is the distance of the old Rome from the new more dramatically displayed than in Gibbon's account of the attempt of Nicola di Rienzi, the self-styled Tribune, to recreate the Roman Republic, of which he did not understand the structure and which of course the world could not accept, a story marked by the comic and tragic exaggerations of Italian opera.

As architecture is about space, history—like music—is in part about time, for both the events of which it tells and the reading of the text itself take place in time: time is the dimension in which they move. The structured length of Gibbon's text makes this fact extraordinarily vivid, for the reader who finishes this text will of necessity be different from the reader who began it, and not only by virtue of reading it. Months of life will have altered the conditions of his (or her) existence: when he looks back from the end of the book to the lost Antonine past, he looks back upon a past of his own, which is also lost. This is the result not merely of the length of the book but of its shape—its movement from one condition to another—and of its interest in what is past and lost.

At the end of the text, the barbarians have become Europeans; Rome has become merely Rome; and Gibbon himself descends from the special position he has maintained in his prose, as the historian of the Roman Empire, to become one of us. "It was among the ruins of the Capitol that I first conceived the idea of a work which has amused and exercised nearly twenty years of my life, and which, however inadequate to my own wishes, I finally deliver to the curiosity and candour of the public" (chap. 71).

The true standard of civilization for Gibbon is not the prosperous condition of the empire in the second century, but the less luxurious and more energetic worlds of republican Rome and modern Europe (which, in his "General Observations on the Fall of the Roman Empire in the West," he says can be called "one great republic" [appendix to chap. 38]). But the story he tells is not that of the republic, nor that of modern Europe, and for an expression of his central values we must look to the life of the text itself, to the experience it offers its reader, for it is here, and here only, that his idea of civilization—by which he judges Rome, the barbarians, and Europe—is given content and meaning. His idea of civilization can be directly enacted in his text, rather than merely talked about, because it is also his idea of history: as it is the nature of civilization at once to employ and to respect the forces of nature in making objects of man's design—in the construction of the aqueducts, in the development of agriculture, and in the constitution of a republic—so it is the proper nature of history to respect the facts that are the ultimate constituents of its composition, but to put them to work in the service of purposes determined by the mind.

4

But how can Gibbon's idea of civilization possibly function as an idea of *history*? It is founded upon a split, between mind and material, that entails incompatible imperatives: to respect the material and to impose the mind. Perhaps it is possible for the architect or city planner or engineer or sculptor to reconcile these opposed demands, but how can the historian even attempt to do so and remain true to the craft? The sole concern of the historian should be with his (or her) materials—with the facts—for his sole job is to tell us what is true about the past. He has no business "imposing his mind," we may be inclined to say, or "creating a design" or "making new structures of significance." That would be literature, not history; we expect the historian to confine himself to the evidence, and to the story it tells.

Gibbon's text is from this point of view a puzzle: it is plainly not what we would call mere literature, for his use of evidence is enormously thorough and careful, and it is obviously his purpose to root his text in fact and detail; but it is equally plainly not the sort of history we would expect to be written today, for it is full of characterizations, indeed of stories, that one simply cannot regard as true, nor even as false, and that must, therefore, have some other kind of meaning. To consider a small example, how are we to take it when Gibbon tells us (in chapter 3) that Augustus, at the age of nineteen, "assume[d] the mask of hypocrisy, which he never afterwards laid aside"? When he further tells us that he was led to this action by a "cool head, an unfeeling heart, and a cowardly disposition"? Here is the whole passage: in what sense can we regard it as either "true" or "false"?

> The tender respect of Augustus for a free constitution which he had destroyed can only be explained by an attentive considera- tion of the character of that subtle tyrant. A cool head, an un- feeling heart, and a cowardly disposition, prompted him at the age of nineteen to assume the mask of hypocrisy, which he never afterwards laid aside. With the same hand, and probably with the same temper, he signed the proscription of Cicero and the pardon of Cinna. His virtues, and even his vices, were arti- ficial; and according to the various dictates of his interest, he was at first the enemy, and at last the father, of the Roman world. When he framed the artful system of the Imperial au- thority, his moderation was inspired by his fears. He wished to deceive the people by an image of civil liberty, and the armies by an image of civil government.

Or consider the following sentence (in chapter 1), in which Gibbon speaks of the Roman decision not to extend the conquest of Britain beyond the Firths of Scotland:

> The masters of the fairest and most wealthy climates of the globe turned with contempt from gloomy hills assailed by the winter tempest, from lakes concealed in a blue mist, and from cold and lonely heaths, over which the deer of the forest were chased by a troop of naked barbarians.

Of what "masters" can Gibbon be speaking here? The soldier or com- mander in Britain, the emperor or senator in Rome? (Or is he rather telling us what we should feel about the decision to draw the line of empire there?)

And think of the caricatured ways in which he represents the Christians, the Roman republicans, the Germans and Persians, and the other peoples of his history, as well as its great individual figures: Julian, Constantine, Athanasius, Justinian, indeed the Antonines themselves. Or of such impossible statements as this one: "the obe- dience of the Roman world was uniform, voluntary, and permanent" (chap. 2).

Gibbon's text is in fact alive with a tension between fact and imag- ination, arising from the split at the center of his idea: his history must be true to the facts of nature and culture with which it deals, yet it is to be an artifact with a shape and significance of its own. It is rather like a tapestry, filled with many scenes and panels, that is meant both to be a picture of events that have occurred in the world and to have a kind of coherence and beauty that will make it valuable aside from the truth of any of its pictures. Like such a tapestry, Gibbon's text looks two ways at once, and forces the reader to do likewise: towards the world of the past, which it is intended to represent, and towards the world of the present, to which it is intended to speak.

Such a text frustrates the modern reader because it refuses to be merely art or merely science, and the combination seems just impossible. Whenever one makes an objection that is drawn from one kind of discourse, it is likely to be met by a move based upon the other.[3] One can refute this fact or that, for example, or show that this panel or that scene is wrong in this or that detail, yet one will not succeed in answering the whole work, even as a representation, unless one can establish that it is so riddled with inaccuracy as to lose its essential shape. To make still another analogy, we can say that both the history and the tapestry are in this respect like a law case: the lawyer knows that to prove his (or her) case he must not only demonstrate the truth or probability of certain propositions of fact; he must present to the judge or juror a way of looking at the case as a whole that will make sense; and it must "make sense" not merely as a matter of factual likelihood, but as a predicate to judgment, as a basis for action. While a case can in a technical sense be refuted by disproving one element or another, in practice the lawyer knows that he must do more than that: he must offer the judge or juror an alternative place to stand, another way of making sense of the case as a whole. To do his job, that is, the lawyer must both engage in an accurate retelling of the facts and make his own claim for what they mean.

The same is of course true of the historian as well, although contemporary critical rhetoric often hides the fact. Even the reader of history who says that he or she is interested only in the accuracy of representation cannot test that accuracy merely by looking from the text to the real world and back again, checking for correspondences; the text "represents" what can be "seen" only by one who engages in an act of creation of his or her own, who becomes for the moment an historian interested in meaning, as well as fact. Otherwise what

3. Gibbon's own work provides an example. In 1779 he published "A Vindication of some Passages in the Fifteenth and Sixteenth Chapters," in which he defends himself in masterly fashion against charges of factual inaccuracy in his account of the Christians; but of the larger questions of tone and value and attitude, which were presumably more provocative to his critics than his purely factual assertions, he says nothing.

one "sees" is an unintelligible jumble. The evidence alone tells no story at all.

There is, of course, a sense in which history can be reduced to matters of pure fact, or nearly so, by the expedient of asking questions that omit or assume away almost all questions of characterization or significance. How far did the Roman conquest extend into Britain? When did it happen? What did the emperor, or a general, say his motives for extension and limitation were? These are important questions, and Gibbon will answer them if he can; but the answers, standing alone, will do nothing to tell us what it meant that the Roman Empire came to a halt at this point. To speak to that question requires a language of generalization, of purpose and motive, a way of "making sense" of what one "knows," of giving meaning to the facts. (Think again of the way that Gibbon speaks of the boundaries that "nature itself" seems to have placed upon the empire, or of his sentence about the "masters of the globe" turning with contempt from Scotland.) What Gibbon understands is that facts are not facts—they have no meaning—until they have been made into history; that they will make no sense until the historian makes sense of them. That is what Gibbon does himself, and what he requires of anyone who would answer or surpass him. As a historian Gibbon is not merely reporting on evidence: he is creating, or recreating, a world, telling us what to think and what to feel about the events he speaks of, for he tells us not merely what happened, but what it means. He knows that for history to be true, it must be a fiction.

Gibbon's performance of his idea of history brings to the center of his text the tension that marks the activity of history itself, the tension between fact and meaning, between material and mind; between the text as a "true" historical record of a past world, forever dead, and the text as a design or narrative constructed in and for the present, a contemporary cultural artifact. The discomfort caused by his caricatures, his confidence, his constantly judging mind—the strong lines and bold colors of his design—is an exaggerated version of the discomfort inherent in the very process of making history, and it is a great merit of his text, not its defect, that it keeps this tension or paradox, this uncertainty, constantly before the reader, where it must be faced and responded to, rather than hidden in his premises or assumptions. Gibbon's text is a construction of culture, but so is every history, including those contemporary personal histories by which we locate ourselves and give meaning to what we do. The "Rome" that Augustus actually knew, for example, was certainly not the "Rome" that Gibbon offers us; but, though "real," it must also in its own way have been incomplete and artificial, constructed by the individual mind of the boy, the man, the emperor. And much the same is true of the world that each of us lives in as well. The disturbing tension or split that Gibbon keeps constantly before us is thus at the heart not only of history, but of all cultural life. In this sense his insistence upon the artificial character of the world he makes is an insistence upon what is most real about it.

5

Gibbon's idea of history is literary or imaginative, rather than theoretical, in character. He does not seek to explain what he means by excellence in civilization, or in history, by setting forth premises, justifying them by reference to assumptions still more basic, then carrying the reader by a chain of reasoning to assent to certain rules or standards of judgment, which he or she may take away, in distilled form, to be applied elsewhere. (One can indeed imagine how Gibbon would mock such exercises.) His idea has its meaning not in its summary statement, nor in arguments that support it, but in its performances, in the life it makes possible for the reader.

Think back again to the passage in which Gibbon describes the "slow and secret poison" that worked its way into the vitals of the empire, and then expresses his admiration for the Renaissance, when "freedom became the happy parent of taste and science." The value defined in this section is that of coherence and force of mind. What the empire lacks is a constitution, an organization of the communal self, that will enable it to act as a firm and consistent center of energy and achievement, of nerve and will, of exploit and creation. At the individual level, such a constitution is what its citizens lack too, those "cold and servile imitators" of ancient genius. In the structure and life of Gibbon's text the same value is given affirmative definition, for the center that is missing in Rome, and among the Romans, is aggressively present here. The fabric of this history is made by a mind that constantly asserts its own coherence and capacity, claiming to control and order the enormous body of material by which the story of the fall of empire, and the rise of Europe, can be told.

The force and quality of this mind is present in its single paragraphs, indeed in its sentences and clauses:

> In the various states of society, armies are recruited from very different motives. Barbarians are urged by the love of war; the citizens of a free republic may be prompted by a principle of

duty; the subjects, or at least the nobles, of a monarchy are animated by a sentiment of honor; but the timid and luxurious inhabitants of a declining empire must be allured into the service
by the hopes of profit, or compelled by the dread of punishment (chap. 17).

In the second sentence of this passage Gibbon creates a world that is
in some sense a microcosm of his entire text: each clause defines, in
a schematic or caricatured way, a different kind of society, with its
characteristic motive; we know clearly which Gibbon admires, and
asks us to admire; and the sentence itself has a movement and a
shape that turns upon the relationship between citizen and state defined in the verb "allured." The center from which this sentence
arises is the center from which the entire history is composed; and
the sentence and the work accordingly share a structure, a movement, and a life.[4]

The ideal reader contemplated by this text, who learns what it has
to teach, will move from the *History* to the rest of life with a recogni-

---

4. Other historians have ideas of this informing kind: Parkman, for example, sees
himself as telling the story of the attempt to extend French civilization by cross and
sword and trade, as opposed to the English method of settlement and farming; Clarendon is interested in the process by which the virtues and vices, capacities and weaknesses, of individual men produce direct consequences in the public world, and the
center of his history is his repeated attempt to trace such lines of responsibility. (For
further discussion see *The Legal Imagination*, pp. 903–25.)

It would be superfluous to give instances of what I mean by the play of Gibbon's
mind: nearly every sentence is a new and remarkable creation, and the continuous
variety of the text effectively resists any attempts to reduce it to a set of rhetorical
devices or techniques. The reader's sense is of a mind perpetually examining and complicating its own utterances, producing a series of surprises that are, after all, not surprises, for they express and confirm the central attitudes with which we are familiar.
And it is important to see that Gibbon's sentences are not mere comments on the
world, but creations: "A candid but rational inquiry into the progress and establishment of Christianity may be considered as a very essential part of the history of the
Roman empire. While that great body was invaded by open violence, or undermined
by slow decay, a pure and humble religion gently insinuated itself into the minds of
men, grew up in silence and obscurity, derived new vigour from opposition, and finally
erected the triumphant banner of the cross on the ruins of the Capitol" (chap. 15).

And compare the following, from chapter 22 (Gibbon is speaking of Julian): "The
Barbarians of Germany had felt, and still dreaded, the arms of the young Caesar; his
soldiers were the companions of his victory; the grateful provincials enjoyed the bless-
ings of his reign; but the favourites who had opposed his elevation were offended by
his virtues; and they justly considered the friend of the people as the enemy of the
court." In this sentence, as in the structure of the *History* as a whole, Gibbon creates a
set of actors, establishes relations between them, and suggests the conflict that will
give movement to the world he has defined.

tion that all of his or her own "histories" and the judgments based upon them—whether in law, in politics, or in art—must face the tensions between fact and value, fact and fiction, that Gibbon has made so inevitably a part of the experience of this text, tensions that are indeed central to the intellectual history of Gibbon's era and our own. And while the reader will wish to see those tensions resolved, Gibbon has given us a double lesson: both teaching us that complete resolution is in the nature of things impossible, and showing us, in his performance, something of the art by which they can be addressed.

Gibbon invites the reader to conceive of this art in such general terms that it becomes in fact a neutral ground for judgment, committing the reader in advance to neither one side nor another of a particular dispute—a ground indeed for the modern pluralist who is committed to no one set of knowable and unchanging truths, yet who is committed also to the process of judgment itself, and refuses to cast his or her capacities for having and defending values into a sea of universal relativism.

But it is worth saying at the end what Gibbon does not do as well as what he does. He creates one of the great artifacts of our culture, reconstituting a civilization and subjecting it to coherent and constant judgment by a standard enacted in his own work; but he does not establish what I would call a reciprocal community with the reader. For what is there for the reader of this text to do, but to applaud its achievement? Thucydides, by contrast, sets his reader a puzzle he himself cannot solve, and one could spend a lifetime trying to make sense of the world he gives us, and one's own world, in the ways he suggests we try. The reader is recognized by Thucydides' text, for the problems that the text faces are defined as shared ones; the text offers to the reader the education that Thucydides has been giving himself. Gibbon, by contrast, seems to offer one little to do but to admire what he has done. The reader comes from this experience with a greatly enhanced capacity for admiration and contempt, for judging and perhaps for making, artifacts of civilization, but not for establishing and managing relations with others, for acting in the world. The text creates a civilization, but not a community. There is a sense, that is, in which Gibbon's text fails to meet his own test of civilization: "In a civilized state every faculty of man is expanded and exercised; and the great chain of mutual dependence connects and embraces the several members of society." This is perhaps not a fault in Gibbon's work; but it leaves us still wondering what a history would be like that established the terms in which one might function in one's own world—that defined a language of value and fact and fiction, a language of character and community, and taught it to its reader.

BIBLIOGRAPHIC NOTE

The general ideas of this essay can be rather simply stated: that "factual" history necessarily involves making "fictions," yet it cannot be purely fiction; that "facts" cannot be separated from "values," at least in history. My intention here is to give meaning to these ideas not so much through conceptual elaboration as through experience and example.

Many current theorists are of course conscious that history, like science, has a creative and cultural component (see, e.g., Hayden White, *Metahistory: The Historical Imagination in Nineteenth Century Europe* [Baltimore: Johns Hopkins University Press, 1973], and *Tropics of Discourse: Essays in Cultural Criticism* [Baltimore: Johns Hopkins University Press, 1978], and more generally Thomas S. Kuhn, *The Structure of Scientific Revolutions* [Chicago: University of Chicago Press, 1962], but such work is often marred by a tendency to see history as merely creative, no longer as "factual" in any meaningful way. As yet we have no generally accepted way of talking about history as an activity that is at once creative and faithful to the evidence (both "fictional" and "factual"), at once concerned with what is true and what is good (both "factual" and "judgmental"). For a fine general account of the current state of our discourse about facts, values, and reason, see Alasdair MacIntyre, *After Virtue: A Study in Moral Theory* (Notre Dame, Ind.: University of Notre Dame Press, 1981).

On the stock diction with which Gibbon delineates his characters—"they blush or sigh or tremble"—see Harold L. Bond, *The Literary Art of Edward Gibbon* (Oxford: Clarendon Press, 1960), pp. 92, 156. Similarly, on his "stiffly brocaded style" and its inconsistency with the "unadorned truth," see J. B. Black, *The Art of History: A Study of Four Great Historians of the Eighteenth Century* (New York: F. S. Crofts, 1926), pp. 178–79, who gives the nice example of the chieftains of Scandinavia "who sighed in the laziness of peace, and smiled in the agonies of death." He also gives examples of Gibbon's highly repetitive "standard diction."

On Gibbon's value of "republican virtue," and its enactment in the sentence quoted at p. 144, see J. G. A. Pocock, "Between Machiavelli and Hume: Gibbon as Civic Humanist and Philosophical Historian," *Daedalus* 105 (1976): 153–70, especially p. 157; and H. R. Trevor-Roper, "Gibbon and *The Decline and Fall of the Roman Empire*," *Journal of Law and Economics* 19 (1976): 489–506, especially p. 496.

For a fuller statement of the view that the structure of the *History* includes the rise of modern Europe, see H. L. Bond, *The Literary Art of Edward Gibbon*, pp. 40–45.

Fact, Fiction, and Value

On Gibbon's "factuality" see Arnaldo Momigliano, "Gibbon's Contribution to Historical Method," in *Studies in Historiography* (London: Weidenfeld and Nicolson, 1966), pp. 40–55. For more on Gibbon's European center of value, see H. R. Trevor-Roper, "Gibbon and *The Decline and Fall*."

For an elaboration of a somewhat different version from my own of the view that the *History* is united by the force of Gibbon's organizing mind, and the character of his voice, see Leo Braudy, *Narrative Form in History and Fiction: Hume, Fielding, and Gibbon* (Princeton: Princeton University Press, 1970), pp. 213–68.

My general view of Gibbon's history fits with what might be called its presentational or theatrical character, its interest in association rather than causation. Consider, for example, the relationship between spirit and structure: we have seen that in his account of the scope of the empire in the first chapter Gibbon carefully gives the "spirit of moderation" first place; likewise, his description of the army begins with the question of motive. So far it may seem that he regards spirit as primary, structure as secondary. But in his account of military motives he invokes the republic, where he says the structure or constitution of the state naturally engaged the interest as well as the duty of the citizen, and led to his voluntary and committed participation, almost as though the form of the republic would automatically harness the natural forces of human feeling in the most appropriate way. But this implication is immediately undercut by the next chapter, where Gibbon tells us of the process by which Augustus seemed to support, but actually subverted, the republic, producing "an absolute monarchy disguised by the forms of a commonwealth"; for the success of Augustus seems to be due to a general supine lassitude that is itself not really explained at all—that is, to want of proper spirit. In Gibbon's world it is thus not true either that spirit determines structure, or that structure determines spirit. What is required is both: "A martial nobility and stubborn commons, possessed of arms, tenacious of property, and collected into constitutional assemblies, form the only balance capable of preserving a free constitution against the enterprise of an aspiring prince" (chap. 3).

In this connection, compare Gibbon on the emperor Decius, who investigated the decline of Roman greatness. "He soon discovered that it was impossible to replace that greatness on a permanent basis without restoring public virtue, ancient principles and manners, and the oppressed majesty of the laws." In aid of which, he reestablished the office of censor, only to find that a "censor may maintain, he can never restore, the morals of a state" (chap. 10).

Gibbon's history proceeds then neither in the mode of political science, as a way of tracing consequence from structure, nor in the mode of romantic history, tracing the manifestations of national spirit or heroic individuality, but as a narrative of the single cultural reality of which spirit and structure are aspects.

In fact, as has been observed, Gibbon's statements about the causes of the fall of Rome are not infrequently inconsistent with one another. See, e.g., J. B. Black, *The Art of History*, pp. 166–67; David P. Jordan, *Gibbon and His Roman Empire* (Urbana: University of Illinois Press, 1971), p. 213. To chapter 38 Gibbon appended a section entitled "General Observations on the Fall of the Roman Empire in the West," in which he concluded rather lamely that "the decline of Rome was the natural and inevitable effect of immoderate greatness. Prosperity ripened the principle of decay; the causes of destruction multiplied with the extent of conquest; and, as soon as time or accident had removed the artificial supports, the stupendous fabric yielded to the pressure of its own weight. The story of its ruin is simple and obvious; and, instead of inquiring *why* the Roman empire was destroyed, we should rather be surprised that it had subsisted so long." As Braudy points out, Gibbon's interest shifts during the course of the *History* from causation to the process and passage of time: Braudy, *Narrative Form in History and Fiction*, p. 251.

Consistent with this view of Gibbon's text is Oliver's interesting argument, based in part upon a psychological reading of his biography, that for Gibbon the activity of history was an escape from present experience, a way of dealing with an essential fear of life. The chief examples from Gibbon's life are his indecisiveness about his own religious conversions and his incapacity to act coherently in his romance with Suzanne Curchod. The idea is that the experience that is so unmanageable and frightening as it occurs, so incomprehensible, can afterward be reduced to order, and made safe, by being converted into history. See Dennis M. Oliver, "The Character of an Historian: Edward Gibbon," *E.L.H.* 38 (1971): 254–73.

For more on what I mean by the community established with the reader, see *When Words Lose Their Meaning*, especially chapter 3, on Thucydides.

The best analyses of Gibbon's prose style I know are Bond, *The Literary Art of Edward Gibbon*, pp. 136–58, and Braudy, *Narrative Form in History and Fiction*, pp. 213–68.

8 TELLING STORIES IN THE LAW

AND IN ORDINARY LIFE

THE *ORESTEIA* AND "NOON WINE"

One way in which the law is poetic is that it works by narrative. From the outside it can of course be described as a structure of rules or a set of institutions, as a tool for policy implementation, and so on, but if it is looked at from the inside, as an activity in which individual minds engage, I think, as the reader well knows, that it is better talked about in other terms—as an art of language, as a way of creating versions of experience in cooperation or competition with others. From this point of view the law always begins in story: usually in the story the client tells, whether he or she comes in off the street for the first time or adds in a phone call another piece of information to a narrative with which the lawyer has been long, perhaps too long, familiar. It ends in story too, with a decision by a court or jury, or an agreement between the parties, about what happened and what it means. This final legal version of the story almost always includes a decision or an agreement about what is to remain unsaid. Beyond the story is a silence it acknowledges.

Much can be said about what happens when a person starts off to tell a story, or brings one to a close. Of particular interest to me are the pressures towards fiction relentlessly at work in the process, and I have spoken to these matters a bit both in the preceding essay on Gibbon and in *The Legal Imagination* (Chapter 6). Here I wish to focus on two kinds of questions that constantly arise in connection with legal narratives: (1) What kind of relation can exist between an authoritative legal story and the narratives of ordinary life that lie behind or beside it? Does one kind of narrative typically depend upon the other, and if so in what way? Where does the authority of a story, legal or nonlegal, come from? (2) Sometimes we regard a story as adequately told in an adequate language; sometimes we think the language, or the telling, is in an important sense defective. How do,

and how should, we make these judgments of adequacy and inadequacy?

As a way of exploring these questions I shall discuss two works,
each of which is both about the relation between legal and nonlegal
narratives and about the adequacy of certain languages—Aeschylus'
Oresteia and Katherine Anne Porter's story "Noon Wine."

One fundamental characteristic of human life is that we all tell stories, all the time, about ourselves and others, both in the law and out
of it. The need to tell one's story so that it will make sense to oneself
and to others may be in fact the deepest need of that part of our
nature that marks us as human beings, as the kind of animal that
seeks for meaning. In this essay I want to explore certain aspects
specifically of legal narrative, but I shall begin with some reflections
on the process of narrative in ordinary life.

1

The story is the most basic way we have of organizing
our experience and claiming meaning for it. We start telling the stories of our lives as soon as we have language and we keep it up until
we die. We make narratives literally all the time, for at some level we
are constantly engaged in the process of telling and retelling the stories of our lives, trying to make sense of what is past and to allow for
the force of what might happen next. We perpetually process new
material, checking it against old claims, revising our story where necessary, repressing parts of it when that is the only alternative. This is
among other things a central way in which our sense of our own
individual character is made. "I am one who . . ." (Think how Philoctetes, Neoptolemus, and Odysseus each might finish that sentence.) Our need and capacity for narrative is collective as well as
individual, and we constantly tell the stories of our communities:
think of family legends retold at the dinner table, of village or city
traditions, of national histories ("from the Declaration of Independence to World War II"), or ethnic histories, all beginning with the
word "we."

The stories we tell about our own lives, individual or collective,
have the fixed characteristic that they are always incomplete, always

unfolding, and we accordingly find ourselves constantly trying to work into our narrative new events that may or may not fit comfortably with what has gone before. From our earliest years, each of us is constantly telling his or her story over and over again and claiming a meaning for it in the light of new events; or, more precisely, claiming slightly shifting meanings as new experiences add new material. The old story won't quite work with this new chapter; the design breaks down; so we rewrite the earlier chapter with new highlights and emphases, putting back in what we had earlier left out as irrelevant, dropping into the background what had been central, and so on. We now see that what had seemed at the time so minor—the peculiar tension that Thanksgiving dinner, covered by that tone of strained sentimentality; our insistence in seventh grade upon playing soccer instead of football, against our parents' wishes—is actually of great importance. Likewise, what had seemed to be of cosmic significance—this victory, that defeat, winning the scholarship or failing the exam—lapses into triviality. Or a part of the story perhaps retains its level of significance but alters its substantive meaning: what was a defeat is now a triumph, or the other way round.

What if your story so far has been one of virtue rewarded and suddenly vice becomes a part of the picture? Or of virtue unrecognized, and suddenly unimaginable success comes your way? Great adjustments must be made. The process of adjustment is necessary at the collective level too. Think, for example, of the way people have to take into account the ugly development (or beneficial progress) that mars (or saves) their New England village; of the shift from American autonomy to American imperialism; and so on. Or think of Gibbon, who started out to tell the story of the decline of civilization in the West, but to his reader's surprise, and perhaps to his own, ended up telling the story of the making of modern Europe, a triumph of "barbarian" (not Roman) civilization.

The kind of constant adjustment and revision I mean can be illustrated by thinking of the way a person follows a baseball game, or perhaps a baseball team through a whole season. Every game and every season starts with the teams at exactly the same point; but every game and season ends with winners and losers. When things begin to go against your team at the beginning, you have lots of explanations and excuses, various imagined futures that will lead to victory at last. But in every game, and every season, there is a moment, often recognized only in retrospect, when the fan must finally give up. No probable imagined future will lead to victory. This is the turning point; our recognition of it, in baseball or elsewhere in life, is a recognition that life falls into art forms, and part of the activity of life is learning what those forms are.

Related to the process of revision is the fact that we do not know, or cannot remember or cannot say, everything that belongs to the story, at either the individual or the collective level. We normally deal with this problem by making skeletal outlines or formulas, which we *can* remember and which we use to organize the rest of what has happened and what will happen. We can see such formulas at work in both Neoptolemus and Philoctetes, for example: the one is the young man who "never stooped to deceit," the other is one who "suffers terribly and unjustly at the hands of others." The *Oresteia,* as we shall see below, derives its structure from a set of competing formulas, each urged on us as authoritative. Orestes suffers from having two such formulas, starkly opposed: he is one who "must avenge his father's death" but also one who "must not kill his mother." In "Noon Wine" we see that Mr. Thompson, the failing farmer, also has a formula, seen in his repeated reference to "his dear wife, Ellie, who was not strong." This formula sums up his career by justifying his failure and in fact making a kind of success of it, for when it is understood that he is burdened with a wife so frail, it actually is success to do as well as he has managed to do.

Our stories, big and little, share another feature: they all end up in some essential way all right. If not in triumph, in acceptance. To tell a story that ends in total failure is simply not endurable. Thus a tragic series of losses can be seen to have a kind of saving grace, by becoming the object of superhuman endurance—this is what Philoctetes feels about his wound and why in a sense he loves it—or by leading to a new level of understanding of the nature of human life. Or they may be saved by being seen as part of a larger history, of ethnic repression or revenge, for example, that has its own tolerable meaning, resting either on future events or on the moral significance of the suffering of the just. What is in experience intolerable can sometimes be made tolerable, if only barely so, by conversion into a story, a narrative with a meaning of its own.

Something like this happens to our own worst or stupidest actions too: I am no longer defined by my terrible mistake, by my crime or folly, for I have become someone who has learned something from it that I would not otherwise have known. This is indeed the promise and appeal of psychoanalysis: by retelling your story in ways that include what you at first leave out, your weaknesses, your losses, shall be turned into strengths and gains. The crippling blight will become something else, the object of understanding; the person, no longer merely blighted, will become one who rises above his limits by understanding them, in this sense achieving something more than he could have achieved without his illness. The story of Philoctetes shows both kinds of redemption: the injury as an occasion for the display of courage and endurance; and the re-told narrative as ordering all aspects of life, including his exceptional suffering, into a new story, leading to new knowledge and new action.

Our stories are always written against two possible evils: that they will make no sense at all, or that they will make sense, but of an unendurable kind. The power of narrative is a power by which the self maintains its integrity in the face of threats of total destruction.

I say that the process of storytelling is both collective and individual. One could go further and say that the idea of community itself depends upon both language and story: a community is a group of people who tell a shared story in a shared language. Of course the "same language" at one extreme may be a family of languages, like the languages of Europe, or at another may consist of the kind of private language that a family often makes for itself, a language of almost private symbols and gestures. Within the community defined by a story there may also be different versions of the same narrative, which may conflict or compete, but it is always the same story of which they will be different versions. (The nation that has contributed the most to European civilization is—take your pick—England, France, Germany, Greece, or Italy; but all would lay claim to the special identity and merit of European civilization itself.) We can disagree about the meaning of certain key terms in our discourse or about key events—say about the meaning of "liberty" or of the Emancipation Proclamation—but in speaking and arguing about these meanings we affirm both the common language by which our disagreement is made intelligible and the common history against which the disputed event takes its place and from which it derives its meaning.

Another way to put this is to say that telling a story can never be a purely private art. To tell a story at all you need a language: a set of terms for describing the natural world, for defining the roles and relations and activities that constitute the social world, for establishing motives and values. And language itself is always social; it implies a community of those who speak and understand it. A language can never be wholly private. Not even Thoreau at Walden can make a private language; the meaning he claims for his life at the pond is expressed by the ironic use of the language of his culture that he purports to reject: "I have travelled much in Concord." As speakers we depend absolutely upon our languages and the communities they define. Narrative, like rhetoric, is in this sense culture-specific. As artists we can of course redefine the terms of our discourse, and in so doing try to redefine the community it constitutes. (What is commerce? What is prostitution? It is a new connection between those terms that lies at the heart of Shaw's play, *Mrs. Warren's Profession*.) But we must always start where we are.

The storyteller thus fears not only that his (or her) story will make no sense (or an intolerable sense), but that no one will listen to him at all. We are all like the Ancient Mariner, seeking to fix our stories in another's mind, and afraid we are failing; or, like Mr. Thompson in "Noon Wine," we go about the community trying to find an audience who will listen to our story, to our account of what has happened and what it means.

When we tell our stories, at either the individual or the collective level, we must always face the question whether our language is adequate to the story we have to tell. In a sense, of course, it never is. Who can find words to express just what a particular sunset looks like, or a moment of a certain kind of sadness or pleasure, or our sense of another person? All too often when we try to do these things, as we talk and talk our impoverished cliches string themselves along in a line so that this sunset comes to seem just like any other, anywhere. Our prose sounds like a Hallmark card. (Think how utterly inadequate our language is for writing a letter of sympathy to a bereaved friend.) Sometimes our language is not merely inadequate; it is really wrong and commits us to morally impossible statements. This is what happens to Huck Finn, on the raft, when he suffers remorse at the great "wrong" he has done in helping Jim escape, as a result of which Jim will steal "his" children from their "owner"! There is a conflict between "his" and "owner" in that sentence that is simply unresolvable; it reflects the contradiction of a culture, of a nation.

But we do not always feel that our language is inadequate. Usually it seems good enough for our purposes. What characterizes these moments of adequacy? When do we feel that we have said the right thing and that it is enough? I will say more about this below, but in general I think the answer is to be found not at the intellectual or conceptual level, not in a correspondence between "idea" and "word," but in the social and cultural context in which we act. We feel our language is adequate when we are confident in the social and ethical meaning of what we do. We know that what we are saying will be taken by this person as a gesture of mild affection, or as establishing a distance; we know that this other person will not subject this utterance to the misconstructions that a stranger might; and so on. Upon what kind of knowledge does this sense of adequacy rest? Not conceptual or merely verbal, but knowledge of the best and most reliable kind: social, ethical, experiential.

2

How about storytelling in the law? To start with, it is plain that narrative is central to the intellectual activity of the lawyer, for whenever the lawyer acts, he or she is telling a story about the world and claiming a meaning for it. This fact has great linguistic and intellectual consequences, for to tell a story is to choose a language in which it is to be told, and to choose a language is, at some level, to recognize that there are other possible languages, other possible meanings. This is part of what distinguishes legal from bureaucratic talk, where the language is a given, about which there is no choice and can be no argument. (We have the form—the blue one, Number 1165-B—and you must respond to its questions in its terms.)

The process of storytelling in the law takes its form in part from another fact: that legal stories are told by lawyers and judges not about themselves, but about other people, and told in competition with each other, on the necessary understanding that each is incomplete. This means that there is in the law an openness to multiple stories, multiple languages. This openness is not accidental but structural, and it has significant political and ethical consequences as well as intellectual ones. It is in fact built into the idea of the hearing, the central form of legal life and discourse, for at the hearing two stories are told in competition with one another, and a choice between them—or of a third—is forced upon the decider. This array of competing stories drives the listener to the edge of language and of consciousness, to the moment of silence where transformation and invention can take place, and a new story, perhaps in a new language, can be told.

Once one realizes that stories can be told in different ways, with different meanings, as the law requires us to do, one's sense of the world, and of the relation of one's speech to it, changes profoundly. In addition to the choice of terms, there is the choice of beginning: in telling Philoctetes' story, for example, do we start with isolated suffering, with the step on sacred ground, with the wrongs done by the

Achaeans before that, or with Helen's capture by Paris—and was that a rape or a seduction anyway? As the beginning shifts, so does the sequence, and the meaning of it all is transformed.

The meaning of the story, uncertain as it is, extends into the future, in the law and elsewhere, for stories about the real world are told as grounds of action. The injury requires revenge; innocent suffering requires compassion; and so on. The idea of Hume and others that the domains of fact and value are by definition distinct—"one can't get an 'ought' from an 'is'"—is certainly not supported by our experience of narrative and moral action. It *is* from the "is," from the story told a certain way, that we get our most important "oughts": our sense that a particular story is incomplete without a certain ending, which we can supply.

As lawyers we are engaged in a discipline that teaches us again and again what Gibbon also teaches us: that no story can include everything, that every story is a reduction, a fiction, made from a certain point of view. In looking at competing stories, and trying to decide between them, or upon a third, we thus naturally think in terms of inclusion and exclusion: what—or who—belongs in this story that is now left out? What—or who—is present that can be dropped? Where should it begin, how should it end? The lawyer who reads and remakes a story, like the poet and the reader of poetry described in "The Judicial Opinion and the Poem" (Chapter 6), is constantly at work seeking to integrate tension and inconsistency into a coherent whole, to "comprehend contraries": different languages, different inclusions and exclusions, different senses of ending and beginning. In all of this we are schooling ourselves in the recognition of radical difference in point of view and central experience, in the contingency of language and expectation, in the uncertainty of life, and in the inevitability of individual responsibility. And in both telling and reading the stories of our clients and others we make active, in a way that renders them available for scrutiny, the suppositions of our culture—the sense of what is "natural" that inheres in one's mind and marks it as sharing a common world with others. The narrative is the archetypal legal and rhetorical form, as it is the archetypal form of human thought in ordinary life as well.

What are the similarities and differences between legal and ordinary narratives? What relation can exist between them? In particular, what dissatisfactions with ordinary narratives give rise to the need for legal ones, and vice versa? These are our questions, and in examining them we turn first to Aeschylus' great trilogy, the *Oresteia*.

3

The outline of the plot will be familiar: on his return from Troy, Agamemnon is murdered by his wife, Clytemnestra, and her lover, Aegisthus. Aegisthus had his own motives for the murder, for he was the son of Thyestes, to whom Agamemnon's father, Atreus—who was also Thyestes' brother—had served a dish made from the bodies of two of Thyestes' murdered children. This was itself done to retaliate for Thyestes' earlier attempt to seduce Atreus' wife and to take over the throne of Argos. What justifications Thyestes may have had—an agreement to share power?—we do not know, but some can be readily imagined. In any event it is essential to an understanding of the *Oresteia* that we see that it begins in the middle of a long chain of reciprocal acts of retaliation the exact origins of which are lost in the mists of time.

After the murder of Agamemnon, his son Orestes is under an excruciating double injunction: to avenge his father's death and to refrain from matricide. He chooses the former, and kills his mother (and Aegisthus). He is then driven mad by the Eumenides—the Furies who punish the shedding of kindred blood—and pursued to Athens, where he seeks asylum. Athena establishes a homicide court, the Areopagus, by which the community—the *polis*—will respond to cases of homicide, convicting or acquitting but in either case breaking the cycle of infinite revenge. Orestes is acquitted. The Furies will hereafter have a transformed role in the world: they will enforce the sacredness of law and legal judgments, rather than the prohibition against kindred murder. This story represents a movement from a primitive world of feud, in which one homicide creates a duty to avenge it with another, to a world of law. The court will now determine the true story and inflict a proper punishment, all without incurring blood guilt. The drama is obviously meant to celebrate the institution and the progress it represents.

The trilogy directs our attention first to the world with which it begins, the impossible moral universe to which law is represented as being a solution. As Aeschylus presents it, this is a world in which the actors struggle, always without success, to find proper ways to tell their stories. How they struggle, and why they fail, are of special significance, for this failure does much to define the defect in life to which the law is a response.

The first play of the trilogy, the *Agamemnon*, begins in the dark just before dawn with a Watchman awaiting a beacon signal that will announce the fall of Troy—a fire on a mountain top, the last of a chain of such fires that will carry the news from Troy in a single night. While he is speaking, the signal suddenly appears. We naturally ask, what will that beacon, and the Fall of Troy that it announces, prove to mean? The Watchman claims that for him the answer is a simple one: it means that his master will return and offer his hand to his servant, who loves him. For "the rest"—the whole prior history of crime and revenge, from Atreus' murder of Thyestes' children to the usurpation of Agamemnon's place by Aegisthus, to which the Watchman has darkly alluded—he will be silent. "A great ox stands upon my tongue" (line 36). His is the kind of mind that senses the intolerable and turns away from it to an act or a relation that it can comprehend and bear, from his knowledge of past crimes and fear of future ones to his pleasure at his master's return. Yet the turning away, here and always, is imperfect. The monstrous and the fearful remain on the margin of consciousness, never erased. It requires a great force— an ox—to maintain one's silence, and this can be done at best imperfectly: the Watchman cannot help hinting at what he does not say about what has been going on in Agamemnon's house.

The chorus of elders, who enter now, also ask what the beacon will mean, and see that question, naturally enough, as a version of what the Trojan War itself will mean. They start with a clear view, clearly stated: this was a just war of revenge, ordered and supported by Zeus and by the moral order of the universe. But this view cannot hold. No sooner is it stated than it is undercut, first by reference to the terrible cost of the war—and all for "one promiscuous woman"—and more seriously by their telling the terrible story of the sacrifice of Iphigenia by Agamemnon on the way to Troy. (She was Agamemnon's daughter, whom he killed in a sacrificial ritual to appease the gods, who were sending adverse winds that kept the fleet from sailing.) Of course the Chorus need not have told that story, but it is part of the meaning of the war for them, a part they wish to deny and cannot face but cannot help revealing. It emerges, as in a dream, by a process of association: the idea of Paris' original sexual wrong being punished by the war and by the destruction of Troy suggests a contrasting (but related) form of sexual wrong and implies that its punishment lies ahead. The emergence of this scene is dreamlike in another way too: it drifts from a place in the darkness, in the background, where it is felt by them and by others without their knowing it, to the foreground, where it is seen with unbearable vividness. "But the girl's cries of 'Father!' were nothing to the men" (lines 228–30). Once this story is out, the Chorus, like the Watchman, retreats to silence.

The war, and the victory, are given a new meaning by this story of the murder of Iphigenia, for we now see that they are rooted in what we feel to be a horrible crime. The Chorus's earlier invocation of the sense of universal justice that punishes wrong, originally stated as a proud justification of the war, has now a threatening significance that we could not have seen before. This story actually provides a kind of narrative justification for Clytemnestra's murder of Agamemnon, which we can now see as an understandable response to it. But the mind of the Chorus, and of the audience, cannot comprehend these contraries. They represent an intolerable incoherence to which the only response is silence.

These speeches of the Watchman and the Chorus establish the shape of the kind of narrative, and of the kind of life, that is characteristic of this world, and we soon see it repeated in the speeches of others. Clytemnestra, for example, begins by triumphantly describing her achievement of setting up the beacon fires—which carry the news from Troy in a single night, defying the very laws of nature—but ends by imagining the looting of Troy that must just then be going on, including perhaps even the sacrilegious destruction of the altars, an event pregnant with danger. From triumph to fear, fear of others' lawless destructiveness and perhaps fear of her own desire for revenge. Similarly, when the Herald enters to announce the victory, he describes, with an irony he cannot feel, the utter devastation of Troy—"the sons of Priam have paid twice over for their crimes"— inducing a shudder in the audience that has heard Clytemnestra's speech.[1] (She feared just the sort of excess that he describes; and in this world we know that that kind of wrong leads to punishment.) He briefly alludes to the cost of war, to the death of his friends, but, like the Watchman, tries to put all that behind him, saying, in essence, "It is for us, the living, to forget and live on." Yet he cannot do so: his own narrative concludes with a tale of shipwreck in which his friends were lost. His attempt to think hopefully, to start afresh, is

---

1. In one place (line 527) he even refers to the destruction of the altars, but this line has been deleted as spurious in the most authoritative edition (Eduard Fraenkel, *Agamemnon*, 3 vols. [Oxford: Clarendon Press, 1959]). Others have criticized the deletion: e.g., J. D. Denniston and Denys Page, *Agamemnon* (Oxford: Clarendon Press, 1957), and Hugh Lloyd-Jones, *Agamemnon* (translated with commentary) (Englewood Cliffs, N.J.: Prentice-Hall, 1970).

On the tone of the Herald's speech compare both Fraenkel and Denniston and Page, who think it is wholly optimistic, with D. M. Leahy, "The Representation of the Trojan War in Aeschylus' *Agamemnon*," *American Journal of Philosophy* 95 (1974): 1–23, whose view is closer to my own. "His attempt to speak personally about the war leads him, whatever his original intention, into a description of its unhappy side" (pp. 7–8).

undercut by his need to think about disaster. In the world represented here no speaker can maintain any version of the story he has to tell, any claim of its significance, against the pressure of other versions. For each speaker, the story as it is first told is broken apart by an upheaval from beneath and the emergence of an intolerable "other story." What is excluded as unbearable ultimately intrudes upon and incapacitates the speaker, rendering him or her silent and incoherent.

This is what happens when Agamemnon returns and is invited by Clytemnestra to step on the magnificent carpet, an act of triumph that he knows is inappropriate to the full meaning of the events in which he has participated, complicated as they are by crime and by success alike. Yet he cannot maintain his knowledge against his desires, including his desire to be entangled and punished for what he has wrongfully "trod down," and he submits.

Cassandra, his captive, speaks to the Chorus while Agamemnon is inside the house being prepared for murder and being murdered, and she describes in the plainest terms what is happening and will happen. But her audience cannot believe her. The effect of this disbelief is to make vivid and explicit—to enact before our eyes—the process of repression by which the other stories were given their initial shape, the shape they could not hold.

In the final scene of this play Clytemnestra repeats the original pattern of the stories: she begins by telling the story of the murder of Agamemnon with triumphant pride—"as for me, I glory" (line 1394). But as she talks her assertions grow increasingly weak: "let us do no more evil" (line 1654). She ends with a claim of future power, whatever the wrongs upon which it rests: "we have the power and let us set the house in order" (line 1673). Of course the kind of power she has is no power at all, but a kind of disintegration of mind and self.

As for us, we learn that we too have left out what we in some sense knew, when we see, triumphant over Agamemnon, not only Clytemnestra but the hideous Aegisthus—*this* is what the murder means! Then, in an additional surprise that is no surprise, at the very end our attention is directed to the existence of Orestes, offstage, whom in the rush of events we had naturally forgotten. But we now see that he can be expected to act upon this story as it appears to him, as a ground for revenge. The play in this way puts us in a position like that of its characters, affirming stories only to have them undone before our eyes and undone on grounds that are in some sense already known to us. Perhaps never in literature did a work have an ending that concluded less, promised more, than this play.

As the *Agamemnon* teaches us that the worst kind of murder can have a kind of justice to it, the next play in the trilogy, *The Libation Bearers*, shows us that a murder that is in one sense most highly moral—Orestes' killing of Clytemnestra, which is ordered by Apollo and enforced by his threats—of necessity has also a hideous dimension. Orestes can screw himself up to the killing of his mother by focusing on a part of its meaning, as revenge for his father, and by insisting upon that formula as if it were the whole story. But once the killing is done, its other meanings—as a matricide, as fulfilling desires of his own to kill his mother, and perhaps to penetrate her in other ways, hostile and not so hostile—take over, and he is driven mad by the Furies (invisible to us) who visit those whose crimes include the unspeakable shedding of kindred blood.

One especially revealing moment is Orestes' initial interpretation of Clytemnestra's dream. She dreamed she gave birth to a snake, which bit her breast as she suckled it, and drank the blood with the milk. Orestes sees this, accurately, as a kind of schematic confirmation of his role as avenger, but is completely blind to the hideous way it characterizes his conduct—blind, that is, until the act is done and the Furies take their revenge, when he is driven to the edge of madness by recognition of what he has denied.

In the final play, the *Eumenides*, the intolerable becomes visible in an extreme way, for here the hideous Furies themselves appear on stage, hounding Orestes to destruction. But they are placed in confrontation with other forces beyond the zone of conscious human life, represented by Apollo (who defends Orestes) and Athena (who resolves the conflict by establishing the new homicide court). In the clear light of day Athena achieves a new organization or composition of these forces in the establishment of the court of the Areopagus. These forces are here integrated into a new form of life and activity, an institution that will tell stories with authority, so that they will remain the same and not slide into other intolerable and mysterious meanings. The law will thus rescue us all from the unbearable incoherence of the world that has been presented to us—an incoherence of story, of intellect, of action, of the very self.

Notice that here, as in the *Philoctetes*, the drama celebrates its own form, for it is the drama that actually brings the intolerable before us and teaches us to accept and address it. The play in fact marks a central connection between law and drama, for it is as a kind of drama—a way of telling a story, fixing a meaning, and going on with the rest of life—that the law is celebrated here. The poet sees that the law is at its heart a species of narrative and dramatic poetry.

4

This is one version of the relation between the narratives of ordinary life and those of law. "Noon Wine"—which is a fine story but by no means a work of the stature of the *Oresteia*—is of particular interest to us because it presents with great clarity quite another version of that relation. I shall begin with a summary of the story; one of its topics is the adequacy of a language to a story, and the reader who is familiar with the original, or who rereads it now, may want to ask how adequate my language is to the story I retell.

Mr. Thompson, a failing south Texas farmer, takes on as a hired hand Mr. Helton, a drifter from North Dakota. Mr. Helton transforms the Thompson farm and the Thompson family: with a silent skill he puts everything right that had gone wrong. By his industry and knowledge the failing farm is made to succeed in every way. He himself is something of a mystery. He keeps to himself, seeking no companionship but that of his harmonicas, which he plays in the evening. His favorite song, about noon wine, gives the story its title. Only one untoward event occurs over the several years he is with the Thompsons (before the final catastrophe): he catches the Thompson boys playing with his harmonicas and shakes them with a mute ferocity that should perhaps have scared Mrs. Thompson, who saw it, more than it did.

The harmonious and productive existence of this extended family is destroyed by the visit of Mr. Hatch, a bounty hunter from North Dakota. He tells Mr. Thompson that Mr. Helton is an escapee from a lunatic asylum, to which he had been sent for killing his brother (who had damaged his harmonicas). Mr. Hatch wants to return Mr. Helton to the authorities and get a reward. Mr. Thompson takes a powerful dislike to Mr. Hatch and refuses to cooperate, even when Mr. Hatch threatens to tell the neighbors he is harboring "a loony." Mr. Thompson is shouting at Mr. Hatch to get off the property when Mr. Helton turns the corner of the house and comes upon the two men. Mr. Thompson then sees, or thinks he sees, Mr. Hatch stab, or stab at, Mr. Helton with his bowie knife, and he fells Hatch with an axe. Mr. Helton is later killed in the course of his capture by a posse, but no sign of the knife wound Mr. Thompson thought he saw is found on his body.

For this homicide Mr. Thompson is tried and acquitted by a jury. Yet the acquittal does not work: he is known by his neighbors as the one who "killed Mr. Hatch." He spends his time and energy obses-

sively going about the neighborhood, telling his story without success to unbelieving or uncaring listeners. At last he cannot stand it
and kills himself, leaving a note that tells his story one last time:

> "Before Almighty God, the great judge of all before who I am
> about to appear, I do hereby solemnly swear that I did not take
> the life of Mr. Homer T. Hatch on purpose. It was done in de-
> fense of Mr. Helton. I did not aim to hit him with the ax but
> only to keep him off Mr. Helton. He aimed a blow at Mr. Helton
> who was not looking for it. It was my belief at the time that Mr.
> Hatch would of taken the life of Mr. Helton if I did not inter-
> fere. I have told all this to the judge and the jury and they let
> me off but nobody believes it. This is the only way I can prove I
> am not a cold blooded murderer like everybody seems to think.
> If I had been in Mr. Helton's place he would of done the same
> for me. I still think I done the only thing there was to do. My
> wife—"
>
> Mr. Thompson stopped here to think a while. He wet the
> pencil point with the tip of his tongue and marked out the last
> two words. He sat a while blacking out the words until he had
> made a neat oblong patch where they had been, and started
> again:
>
> "It was Mr. Homer T. Hatch who came to do wrong to a
> harmless man. He caused all this trouble and he deserved to
> die but I am sorry it was me who had to kill him."

One question this story leaves with us is why the legal verdict did
not work. Why did it not give Mr. Thompson what he needed? Why
was this gesture in legal and authoritative language—the acquittal—
inadequate to its ostensible purpose? And behind this question there
is another one: whatever the law did, why was Mr. Thompson unable
to make a version of his story that would work for his neighbors?
Why could he not find a way to tell his story as he saw it (perhaps
including and resting on the legal acquittal, perhaps not), so that
others would accept it? And, most seriously of all, why could he not
make a version of his story that he could himself accept, that ended—
as I earlier said all our stories must end, on pain of suicide—in some
fundamental way "all right"?

Another way to put this set of questions is to ask why neither the
language of the law nor his ordinary language was adequate to the
story he had to tell. Katherine Anne Porter implicitly invites us to ask
that question by comparing the verdict, and Mr. Thompson's own
narratives, with examples of languages that *are* adequate to the needs

of their users. What she shows us about adequacy teaches us something about inadequacy as well.

Consider for example the opening paragraph of the story:

> The two grubby small boys with tow-colored hair who were digging among the ragweed in the front yard sat back on their heels and said, "Hello," when the tall bony man with straw-colored hair turned in at their gate. He did not pause at the gate; it had swung back, conveniently half open, long ago, and was now sunk so firmly on its broken hinges no one thought of trying to close it. He did not even glance at the small boys, much less give them good-day. He just clumped down his big square dusty shoes one after the other steadily, like a man following a plow, as if he knew the place well and knew where he was going and what he would find there. Rounding the right-hand corner of the house under the row of chinaberry trees, he walked up to the side porch where Mr. Thompson was pushing a big swing churn back and forth.

This is the language of fiction—especially, I think, of the short story—and it is wonderfully adequate to its purposes. It is a language for the quick delineation of scene and character and for the creation of narrative expectation. In the first sentence the author creates a whole world: it has people, a sense of place, and a sense of relationship among the people. She even gives it a past. The combined complexity and simplicity of this sentence has an aesthetic appeal all its own. The paragraph ends with a confrontation between Mr. Thompson and Mr. Helton, and we necessarily wonder what will happen during their conversation. This means that we are caught up in this narrative and we function on its terms. This language seems so natural, and it does its job so well, that we may find it hard to perceive its limits, or see that it is chosen in the first place.

But take the "two tow-haired boys digging among the ragweed." This characterization is adequate for these purposes, but it would be inadequate for others. Suppose you were one of those boys, how would you like to be talked about this way? This phrase doesn't even distinguish you from your sibling—your greatest rival and only friend. People sometimes actually do talk about children that way, sometimes even about their own children: they look out the window and what do they see? "Two tow-haired children." That is a form of sentimentality, a verbal equivalent of a Norman Rockwell painting. (Mrs. Thompson in fact falls victim to this temptation when she calls her children her "little tads.") That kind of cute language, if habitual in the real world, would create a serious problem both for the child and for his parents. But in the story it all works fine. The "ragweed" renders the scene less sentimental, the long introductory sentence gives us the pleasure of a world created at a single stroke, and the account of the man walking as if he were following a plow makes the scene real for us in a moment.

Mr. Thompson is described in ways equally adequate to the world of the short story fiction—"a tough weather-beaten man with stiff black hair and a week's growth of black whiskers." And the description of the two men creates a moment of tension: who will these characters be to each other and to us? There is a sense of threat at the intrusion. But it turns out all right: the stranger is looking for work, and knows exactly how to say so: "I need work." The farmer knows he needs help—though not all the ways in which that is true—and knows how to say so too: he has been "lookin' round for somebody" ever since his "two niggers got in a cuttin' scrape." He knows exactly where he is and has a language adequate to his needs.

Here is another example, one that sums up Mr. Thompson pretty well.

> Slopping hogs was hired man's work, in Mr. Thompson's opinion. Killing hogs was a job for the boss, but scraping them and cutting them up was for the hired man again; and again woman's proper work was dressing meat, smoking, pickling, and making lard and sausage. All his carefully limited fields of activity were related somehow to Mr. Thompson's feeling for the appearance of things, his own appearance in the sight of God and man. "It don't *look* right," was his final reason for not doing anything he did not wish to do.
>
> It was his dignity and his reputation that he cared about, and there were only a few kinds of work manly enough for Mr. Thompson to undertake with his own hands.

What makes this language adequate is not its conceptual clarity or intellectual richness, or even its correspondence with social, natural, or ethical facts. What makes it adequate is that it works socially. Mr. Thompson has a sense that he knows what to do, and how to do it, with his language. But by the end of the story all this has changed: neither his acquittal nor his own story is adequate for Mr. Thompson's needs. Why is that so? What has happened?

We can start with the legal story: why is the verdict of acquittal inadequate to Mr. Thompson's needs? It seems on the face of it to be perfect: a public and authorized statement by the representatives of the community that he is innocent of any crime. Why is that not enough?

There seem to me two lines of explanation. The first has to do with the nature of the legal process itself, as it is represented in this story and as it actually works in the world. The acquittal does not work as the undisputed end to the narrative of the killing of Mr. Hatch because at trial no attempt is made to tell that narrative truly and fully. The acquittal is not a judgment about what really happened in the world, but about what happened in court. Mr. Burleigh, the lawyer for Mr. Thompson, completely misunderstands or discredits everything that Mr. Thompson tells him. He even compares what Mr. Thompson did with his own father's killing of a trespasser he hated: "He had waited a long time to catch the other fellow in the wrong, and when he did he certainly made the most of his opportunity." This imputes to Mr. Thompson just the sort of motives that he is at pains to disown. At the trial itself, on Mr. Burleigh's advice, Mr. Thompson pretends that he knew nothing about Hatch's own motives, which are of course central to his own view of the meaning of the act of killing him. Mr. Thompson's stream of consciousness concludes: "they never did get to the core of the matter"; they "hadn't let him talk."

The second reason the verdict does not work for Mr. Thompson is that this legal judgment, like all legal judgments, is not self-validating but requires community acceptance. The text of a judicial judgment, like the text of a contract or a statute, is in its own terms purely authoritative, but it is always a question what role any such text will have in the community that it seeks to govern. Think for example of a divorce decree, or an antitrust decree, incorporating an agreement between the parties. It is an open question what weight and authority the parties will in subsequent years treat that document as having and by what standards or means it will be interpreted. The same thing is true of real estate sales contracts, statutes, and so forth. The text does not conclude the difficulties of the real world, but begins a process, a process of its own interpretation. This is the process by which the law is connected to the rest of life.

Whatever it may purport to say, what a judgment shall come to mean is thus a matter for the parties and their audiences to address and decide. And here it is important that the process, always imperfect, always leaves open the possibility of attack or disregard. After all, as we just saw, the evidence upon which the judgment rests is itself always constructed, second hand: What can the jury, sitting there in a high-ceilinged room on a summer afternoon, ever know about what it was like, for either side, that day on the highway when disaster struck without warning, or when in the chicken yard the farmer hit the stranger with an axe? At best, the juror can only decide whom to believe. The paunchy lawyer, his sensibilities dulled by routine, speaks in cliches and platitudes, invokes technicalities—pleading questions, or jurisdictional or conflicts issues—and what can all this have to do with what really occurred and what it means? It is always fictional, and this helps, really: the victor never wholly wins, the loser never wholly loses. What the judgment will mean after all, the judgment that pretends to end the story, is still open, as the trial and judgment themselves become the elements of a story: perhaps in a court of appeals, perhaps just in the neighborhood.

But at most this explains why the legal verdict failed to speak with authority, why the legal story did not work. There remains the question why Mr. Thompson's story was in its own terms inadequate. Why could he not tell his story in such a way that his neighbors could accept it, that he himself could accept it?

One reason is the sheer difficulty of the moral questions presented by any version of this narrative, which Mr. Thompson's mind and language, at least at the outset, are simply too crude to define and elaborate. Suppose for the moment that this story were to be presented as a law case, not as Mr. Burleigh did it, but properly: should Mr. Thompson be found guilty of homicide, and if so to what degree? His own first line of defense, as he explains it himself to others, and in his suicide note, is to say that he didn't do it "on purpose." But in a sense he obviously did: he brought the axe down on Mr. Hatch's head knowing what he was doing and with the object of injuring him. What does he mean by the phrase "on purpose" then? We all know the answer, for this is the universal defense of children in our culture whenever they are blamed for something they did. "I didn't do it on purpose" means "I shouldn't be punished for it." But the word "purpose," in this case at least, does very little to express any reason why one should not be punished. This was not in the usual sense an accident, after all.

Mr. Thompson's second line of defense is that it was done in defense of Mr. Helton, who was apparently threatened with a bowie knife. This raises a difficult legal question: when may one use deadly force in defense of another? Must one have a special relation with the person in whose interest one acts? Must he or she be threatened with death, or great bodily harm, or will something less suffice? Does a capture of the kind threatened here qualify, especially if it was in some sense authorized by law? (It might predictably lead to Mr. Helton's death, but not right away; and other steps could be taken to challenge his seizure; and so on.)

Of course, as Mr. Thompson thinks he remembers the events, the issue is clearer: he saw a knife flash towards Mr. Helton and he acted to save him. But there was no wound on Mr. Helton's body, no knife on Mr. Hatch, so apparently Mr. Thompson was in error. What is the effect of such an error on a claim that the defendant was acting in defense of another? Does he lose the defense automatically if he was wrong? That is, do we say that he can act to save another from death or great bodily harm, but he does so at his peril if he is in error about the circumstances? Or, does he lose the defense if, but only if, his mistake was under all the circumstances unreasonable? Or does an honest (even if unreasonable) belief in the necessity of his action justify him? (Here a lawyer would think of an *imperfect* defense: in the last case at least, he might properly be convicted not of murder, but of manslaughter; in a sense it was his unreasonableness that caused the death.)

But what can reasonableness and unreasonableness of belief actually mean in a case like this, where the defendant apparently suffered from a hallucination, to which he responded, on its own terms, appropriately? (Does this really entitle him to a defense of insanity?) And what if the hallucination—as is no doubt frequently the case— is an expression of a wish or creates the conditions for the achievement of a wish—here the very killing of Mr. Hatch for which the defendant is being tried? For the truth is that Mr. Thompson hated Mr. Hatch and hated him on his own account: for his disturbance of Mr. Thompson's view of himself, for threatening to take away Mr. Helton, and so on.

Throughout the conversation, Mr. Hatch makes a continual assault on all Mr. Thompson's social expectations and values. In the following passage, for example, he rejects both Mr. Thompson's language of praise for Mr. Helton and, even more important, his central formula about his "poor wife, Ellie, who's not very strong." (We take up the story when Mr. Hatch has just revealed, over his offensive leer, that Mr. Helton had been a violent mental patient.)

> "He never acted crazy to me," said Mr. Thompson. "He always acted like a sensible man, to me. He never got married, for one thing, and he works like a horse, and I bet he's got the first cent I paid him when he landed here, and he don't drink, and he

never says a word, much less swear, and he don't waste time runnin' around Saturday nights, and if he's crazy," said Mr. Thompson, "why, I think I'll go crazy myself for a change."

"Haw, he," said Mr. Hatch, "heh, he, that's good! Ha, ha, ha, I hadn't thought it jes like that. Yeah, that's right! Let's all go crazy and get rid of our wives and save our money, hey?" He smiled unpleasantly, showing his little rabbit teeth.

Mr. Thompson felt he was being misunderstood. He turned around and motioned toward the open window back of the honeysuckle trellis. "Let's move off down here a little," he said, "I oughta thought of that before." His visitor bothered Mr. Thompson. He had a way of taking the words out of Mr. Thompson's mouth, turning them around and mixing them up until Mr. Thompson didn't know himself what he had said. "My wife's not very strong," said Mr. Thompson. "She's been kind of invalid now goin' on fourteen years. It's mighty tough on a poor man, havin' sickness in the family. She had four operations," he said proudly, "one right after the other, but they didn't do any good. For five years handrunnin', I just turned every nickel I made over to the doctors. Upshot is, she's a mighty delicate woman."

"My old woman," said Mr. Homer T. Hatch, "had a back like a mule, yes, sir. That woman could have moved the barn with her bare hands if she'd ever took the notion. I used to say, it was a good thing she didn't know her own stren'th. She's dead now, though. That kind wear out quicker than the puny ones. I never had much use for a woman always complainin'. I'd get rid of her mighty quick, yes, sir, mighty quick. It's just as you say: a dead loss, keepin' one of 'em up."

This was not at all what Mr. Thompson had heard himself say; he had been trying to explain that a wife as expensive as his was a credit to a man.

What this means in the end is that the issue comes back to the one towards which Mr. Thompson was originally groping: whether he did it "on purpose" or not, and we can see that in a profound sense that he did.

Mr. Thompson's suicide note expresses a movement of understanding very much like the one outlined in the preceding paragraphs, from one simple view of the matter through a great deal of complication to another rather simple view: "He caused all this trouble and he deserved to die but I am sorry it was me who had to kill him." This letter, far from being a pathetic and inadequate version of the story, is in fact a sophisticated, complex, and intelligent piece of moral analysis. It achieves a version of the story that is almost sufficient for Mr. Thompson's purposes of life and for ours as readers.

Why is it not totally adequate? Because, as I implied above, it leaves out something essential: the fact that Mr. Thompson was protecting not Mr. Helton but himself. What actually precipitated the blow was Mr. Hatch's threat to tell the neighbors that Mr. Thompson was harboring a lunatic fugitive, and Mr. Thompson could not bear the loss of esteem that this would entail. Nor could he bear to give up Mr. Helton, the ministering angel who had saved his family and himself. To say that the killing was rooted in fear and hatred is not to say that it was not justified: we too hate Mr. Hatch as we read about him, and cannot regret what happens to him. But it does say something about a story of justification: that it will always be felt to be inadequate, it will be told and heard with queasiness, so long as it fails to face all the facts upon which the charge of guilt can be said to rest, and this one does not. This message is familiar to us from the *Oresteia:* Orestes' act of vengeance cannot mean what he claims because it means something else as well, to which his narrative gives no place. When that fact intrudes upon him, he is driven mad.

Why can Mr. Thompson not tell the story of his hatred of Mr. Hatch? I think the reason is that to talk about what the loss of Mr. Helton would mean he had to have a language in which to talk about what Mr. Helton's presence in his life did mean to him, a language in which to express his gratitude, his acknowledgment of dependence, his sense of love. The closest he can come is to say, "If I had been in Mr. Helton's place, he would of done the same for me." If he had been able to say some of those things more fully, he would have a ground upon which his own sense of the rightness of the killing could rest, and perhaps a strength of character that would have enabled him to endure either verdict.

There is another, deeper reason why the story told to the neighbors fails at the end and would have failed even if Mr. Thompson included what has been left out. The reason is that he has no audience that is willing to pay the kind of attention that such a story requires. The neighbors simply do not care very much about Mr. Thompson or what he did. They are far more disturbed about his behavior in insisting on talking to them than they are about the killing itself, for that behavior intrudes upon them as the killing of a stranger from North Dakota certainly did not.

At the core of this story is the truth that intense moral experience is by its nature isolating. No one will, no one can, listen to your central story as you tell it to yourself. At some point the person with the story finds no one nearby to listen, so he (or she) writes to the world. In doing so he hopes to establish a community somewhere, somehow, with someone who does read and understand his story. Even the law, which is meant to provide a special kind of audience and of attention—the kind established in the *Oresteia*, both in the trial scene and in the play itself—ultimately fails to pay the kind of attention that this sort of story, the central story of a person's life, really requires. At the end, writing from what seems a permanent isolation, Mr. Thompson thus writes a message to the world, trying to establish a relation with an unknown reader; and that is what Katherine Anne Porter also does, in writing this story to us.

Who is Mr. Helton for us? He is a mystery, a kind of angel capable of satanic rage. It is impossible in reading this story not to try to find a formula for Mr. Helton, to try to sum him up, to claim we have a meaning for him, but I think this cannot be done. This is in fact a great merit of the text: it forces the reader in his or her own experience to face the radical fact upon which the story itself is based, by providing an experience for which a language is necessary, but none is available.

5

These two works of literature establish a tension between two kinds of stories and between the two domains in which they are told, legal and nonlegal. In the *Oresteia* the movement is from an utterly impossible world without law, in which no one can maintain a story of his or her life that both includes all that the teller knows and makes a tolerable kind of sense of it. Every version is partial; to focus upon it obscures the rest; action upon it is instantly eroded when the story is told differently. The law and, in a different way, the drama are celebrated as public places where the different versions can be placed in open comparison and competition, where the contraries can be comprehended within a larger whole. This new version can have a kind of authority that none of the others, standing alone, could possibly have; and action taken on the ground it affords can have a new kind of authority too. It is now public action taken on a publicly determined story.

"Noon Wine" moves in the other direction, from the authoritative story back into the social world in which its authority must receive a new validation and beyond that into the private zone of individual life where each actor must make a story to meet his or her own standards of acceptance. Neither work disproves the other. It is true that the collective judgment of guilt or innocence, which insists to the defendant and victim alike that the full story must reflect the presence and equality of both actors, is a great step in the making of civilization. It is also true that this judgment is always incomplete, for it always depends upon what happens in the other world of ordinary narrative and private life in which it must work and which it cannot control. This is not a defect, as it might seem, but is, in my view at least, a great merit. The effect of this dependence upon the processes of ordinary life, like the dependence upon the jury at trial, is a validation of the ultimate authority of the community over its institutions and its instruments, an insistence upon the integration of legal speech with ordinary speech as a condition of its effectiveness. It is not that the legal judgment has no authority, but that its authority is not absolute and should always be defensible in other terms, in the language of the community itself.

For lawyers this means that they are not to expect too much from the law, or too little, for themselves or for their clients. The final isolation of Mr. Thompson and of all moral actors teaches us that the center of life cannot be found in institutions or formulas, or even in communities, but in the self. Even Philoctetes and Neoptolemus are imperfect audiences for each other.

9 MAKING SENSE OF

WHAT WE DO

THE CRIMINAL LAW AS A

SYSTEM OF MEANING

In this essay I turn to a particular field of the law with the idea of bringing to bear some of the concerns expressed above. The question I address is whether the criminal law can be said to make sense and, if so, on what terms. The position I work out is that on the usual view of it—which is bureaucratic in nature, thinks in terms of ends-means rationality, and treats people as "means," not "ends"—the criminal law in a deep sense does not make sense, for it suffers from impossible internal contradictions, most seriously in the relations it establishes with those it addresses. The result is that the criminal law, so regarded, is "senseless" in three overlapping ways: it is unintelligible, irrational, and unjust. But on another view of it, resting on the ordinary-language practice of blaming, I think the criminal law can be seen to make sense of all three kinds. What is needed is a language that is adequate to the activity of punishment, and I think the practice of blaming provides such a language. Its function, at bottom, is to insist that one person recognize the reality and value of another.

When a person comes to law school, he (or she) leaves behind a world he knows and understands and turns to another world, that of the law, which at the beginning he cannot comprehend. The body of literature in which he is immersed is at once assertive and confusing, and it is not at all clear what he should do with it. He attends a series of classes in which his teacher seems to make the unsettling assumption that he already knows what he came to learn. One question he will naturally ask himself about all this—his experience of the law—

is whether it makes any sense. And for a long time, if he is honest with himself, he will find that it does not. Of course others will assure him that if he buckles down and does his work, things will come into a sort of order, and this is indeed what normally happens. For learning the law is a kind of learning the ropes; we learn it, as we learn to engage in other activities, by doing it. One comes to know how to do what one could not do before, and in this sense at least things can be said to become clear.

It may seem an odd sort of clarity, for one cannot wholly reproduce in words what one knows—the law must be taught as it is learned—but it is a true clarity nevertheless, based upon a true knowledge. You come to know what you are up to and how to go about it. The experience of making sense by learning to do is one that every person has, over and over, as one works one's way through life, and an experience that every lawyer has as he or she learns to make the arguments—the countering characterizations, explanations, appeals, and justifications—that make up the stuff of the law. It is an experience known to all of us.

The question I wish to address here is this: can one have this experience of making sense, of watching things come clear, as one learns to engage in the activity of criminal law? Or is this set of social and intellectual practices in some fundamental way incoherent—a sort of social and intellectual monstrosity of which no sense can be made, and by which, of necessity, no justice can be done? This is a question I have heard asked over and over in the classroom by those who are trying to learn this branch of the law. I have never heard an adequate response, and this essay is my own attempt to make one.

There are at least two respects in which the law can make sense or fail to do so, two kinds of coherence to look for: internal and external. We can ask, that is, whether the law is internally consistent—whether it makes sense in its own terms; and we can ask whether it fits in a coherent way with the other things we do, with the other conceptions we have of ourselves. "Making sense" thus includes the topic of justice as well as that of intelligibility, and the student who says that the criminal law "does not make sense" can mean it both ways.

When I say that the criminal law does not "make sense" when talked about in a certain way, I do not mean that it is impossible for a lawyer to learn to make appropriate arguments for and against a particular defendant, for that can be done and done well. The question is not whether one can learn the arguments but what, if anything, they all add up to, and how they fit together. This is a puzzle to every thoughtful lawyer with a criminal practice, for it goes directly to one's sense of the meaning of what one does. And the judge and juror must face this question every time they have to decide what they should do in a particular case. "Shall I convict or acquit? If I convict, of which of the crimes with which the defendant is charged? What should the sentence be? How can I explain to myself or to another why I did what I did?"

It is those who ask such questions as these to whom the criminal law may, I believe, make no sense. The problem is not that there are no possible answers to the questions; in a sense there are far too many, cast in different terms and heading in opposite directions.

1

The standard way to analyze the criminal law is by reference to its "purposes." The assumption is that this institution can best be explained, regulated, and justified by a proper understanding of the purposes it is meant to serve. As usually asked, this is not a question about what substantive interests the criminal law should serve, such as security of property or personal liberty, for those ends can be served in many ways. Instead it is a question about the methods by which the criminal law serves those ends: that is, about punishment.

The standard view among lawyers, as reflected in most discussions of the matter and in most recent proposed or enacted codifications of the criminal law, is that the infliction of criminal punishment serves four purposes: (1) the deterrence of future misconduct by threat of punishment; (2) the incapacitation of offenders by restraint; (3) their rehabilitation by treatment (perhaps including the imposition of sanctions as well as therapy of one sort or another); and, though some argue about this, (4) the satisfaction of a need to exact pain by way of retribution or revenge from someone who has done a wrong.[1]

---

1. "Deterrence" is a somewhat ambiguous term. I use it to mean the punishment of one person to affect the conduct of others—I punish you for stealing, for example, so that others will decide not to steal. The term can also refer to the punishment of a person to affect his or her own conduct in the future, but I prefer to follow the general practice of treating that as a species of rehabilitation.

"Retribution" can be used to mean the need or desire to retaliate for an injury and so defined can serve as a justification of punishment that entails its own limits, for the injury imposed must be proportional to the harm inflicted. It can also be used in a more theoretical or conceptual way, not as a ground for punishment—which is motivated by the other purposes—but as imposing an outer limit on that punishment: you

Most contemporary writing about the nature of criminal law asks whether, and how far, each of these purposes serves as a justification either of the practice of punishment in general or of its infliction in a particular case or class of cases. The idea is that once the purposes have been agreed upon, they can form a basis upon which the institution of the criminal law can be shaped and action within it guided and controlled. This is a version of a way of talking about social institutions, as bureaucratic mechanisms, that is very widespread indeed. It serves as the basis of most contemporary talk about social policy, indeed of our very conception of the state. This is the mechanical and instrumental language of systems design and cost-benefit analysis. Of this way of talking it is sometimes said that it, and it alone, is "rational."

I want to put aside for the moment the question whether this kind of talk about institutional and collective life can ever be rational. For present purposes let us accept its premises and accept the further claim that each of the purposes stated is, standing alone, a valid one. My question then is this: What can it mean to say that the law serves all of these purposes at once?

It would be possible to imagine a system of criminal law directed to one of these "purposes" that would be, at least at the level of theory, coherent and intelligible. Suppose for example that our only object was to exact retribution for certain kinds of wrongs. The law would have to decide what acts should qualify as wrongs, what punishment each act should deserve, and so forth. Argument about those things would necessarily proceed not in terms provided by the criminal law system itself, but in a language of fact and value found elsewhere in the culture.[2] There would of necessity be imperfections

---

may not be punished beyond your "deserts."

In this paper I ultimately propose a version of the first kind of retribution—what I call "blaming"—as the proper ground for punishment, but see it as motivated not simply by a desire for revenge but more importantly by a desire to insist upon the equal reality and value of all human beings. So understood, blaming both provides a justifying motive for punishment and imposes a limit upon it.

2. To punish arson, for example, one needs a set of terms in which to talk about fire and buildings, a language in which to differentiate burning from other wrongs and one burning from another. Then, and only then, can the retributive judgment be made. One might distinguish, for example, among temples, houses, and barns; deliberate, careless, and accidental fires; personal, economic, and political motives; and so on. Such distinctions as these are not in the first instance created by the criminal law but exist prior to it. They are rooted directly in the language and culture of the community and constitute, as it were, part of the material out of which the criminal law is made and upon which it acts.

both in the conception and in the execution of such a purpose. But one would have, at least on the surface, an internally consistent language in which to make arguments as a lawyer, in which to make and to explain decisions as a judge or juror. One's sole concern would be with fitting "punishment" to "wrong," and we can imagine ourselves doing that. The process might not "make sense" in another way—it might be intolerably discontinuous with our other ways of talking about our experience and conduct—but it would be intelligible in its own terms. In this sense at least one would know what one was up to, and one could shape one's efforts accordingly.

Internally consistent systems could similarly be based upon the goals of restraint, rehabilitation, and deterrence. In each case, there would be argument about what conditions or conduct should expose the individual to corrective sanctions and about what the sanctions should be. As before, the argument would have to proceed in a language external to the criminal law itself. But in each case one can imagine an internally coherent and intelligible system of punishment.

When we try to imagine a system that serves all of these purposes at once, we seem to turn from what makes at least one sort of sense to what makes none. How can one possibly mold an institution, or a set of practices, to serve such deeply conflicting goals as these four? Consider this case, for example. Imagine yourself as the judge charged with sentencing a woman—a wife and mother—who has killed her husband in a rage; in a rage occasioned perhaps by jealousy, perhaps by prior brutality toward herself or her children, or perhaps just in a rage. Assume, as is often the case, that there is general agreement that she is unlikely to do such a thing again, and is thus in need neither of restraint nor of rehabilitation. Is she to be put on probation, as her own situation may seem to require, or is she to be punished severely, to her own injury and that of her children, as a lesson for the deterrence of others? How would you decide such a case? How would you explain your decision to yourself or to someone else?

Or, to take a less dramatic case, consider what should be done with a first-offender tax evader. Once the offender has been identified, future violations are unlikely. Exposure is its own sort of practical rehabilitation and retribution, and it makes restraint easy, for the IRS will keep tabs on him (or her). The offender does not need a prison sentence. But to put him on probation will impair the credibility of the threat to others who may be tempted to commit tax fraud, and our whole revenue system depends on truthful and voluntary compliance. What is to be done with such a person? How is what is done to be explained? These are questions that the conception of the criminal law as a mechanism designed to serve the four stated purposes simply does not answer in a coherent or sensible way, or, more precisely, to which it gives contradictory answers.

Both of these examples involve a conflict between deterrence and the other stated purposes of punishment, but other divisions are possible as well. For example, if the original conduct in either of the examples were perceived as deliberate, retribution might be thought to line up with deterrence on the side of punishment, rather than on the side of lenity.[3]

Some seek to reconcile the inconsistencies of purpose by conceiving of the different aims as operating in different fashions or at different times. For example, one could say that unless the defendant has committed a wrong for which retribution could properly be exacted, he or she is not to be punished at all—retribution is used, that is, as a limit on, rather than as a reason for, punishment. Once that threshold is past, punishment should be shaped not by retributive considerations, but by a kind of compromise among the goals of deterrence, restraint, and rehabilitation. This is what I call the modern orthodoxy, and I will discuss it below in section 3.

These questions are not hypothetical or academic, interesting only as a puzzle or because of their theoretical implications. The question "What is the right thing to do?" is a real one, for judges and jurors, and those who must answer it have an enormous, sometimes a terrible, responsibility. How can the law speak intelligibly and decently to people who must make judgments of this kind?

---

3. Conflicts between rehabilitation and restraint are very common. Frequently a judge will feel torn between sending an individual to prison and placing him or her on probation. The prison sentence makes it unlikely that the defendant will commit crimes in the short run, but it is also likely to result in a worse ultimate social and personal adjustment. Probation entails a higher likelihood of real reform, but also a greater likelihood of repeated crime in the short run.

There are also cases, such as those involving an insane or infant defendant, where one would judge that some coercive action is required for the protection of society, and perhaps also for the rehabilitation of the individual, but where neither retribution nor deterrence would call for sanctions. In our system, such cases are typically treated as civil, not criminal, matters. Both the remedy and the procedure reflect that difference in character.

2

When it is conceived of in the traditional way, the criminal law forces a choice among its competing purposes but affords no method by which that choice can be made and explained. Is it possible to find or devise such a method—a language in which to think and talk about these choices, a body of law to govern them? In particular, does it help to regard the law, as I have been arguing from the beginning that it should be regarded, not as a bureaucratic but as a rhetorical system? On this view we might try to conceive of the contradiction among its purposes not as an anomaly but as a rhetorical topic, as the problem that this branch of the law is meant to be a way of addressing.

To test this possibility, let me turn once more to the examples of the first-time tax evader and the wife who killed her husband. Imagine that you are the sentencing judge and that you have decided that if you considered only the need for rehabilitation and for restraint and the reprehensibility of the conduct when judged in light of all matters of circumstance and motive, you would put the defendant on probation. But you are also told by the law that it may be your duty to sentence the defendant to a substantial term in order to deter others from committing other crimes in the future. Can you conceive of a respectable process by which such a choice as this can be made?

I think not. The conflict between deterrence and rehabilitation cannot be converted into a topic of an intelligible discourse, in the way that say "crime control versus due process" or "restraint versus liberty" can be. The reason is that one choice by its nature excludes the other, and that the difference between them is not a matter of degree. In terms familiar to us, the choice is between treating the offender as a person and treating him or her as an object. How could such a polarity be the subject of an intelligible discourse, whether of choice or of harmonization or compromise? Another way to put the point is to say that the opposition is really a conflict between two fundamental conceptions of character—of the character of the court, of the defendant, and of the relation between them—and that consistency is essential to any coherent or workable conception of character. Think of this in the terms established for us by the *Philoctetes:* you cannot choose at one time, or in one relation, to be an Odysseus, at another to be a Neoptolemus. If you tried, you would either be an Odysseus all the time or no one at all.

Let me explain what I mean. Essential to the creation of a working rhetorical and social universe is the creation of a set of intelligible voices and comprehensible positions—authorized ways of talking—with respect to which the individual, whether official or private citizen, can locate himself or herself in an intelligible way. For example, it is one function of the law of the Fourth and Fifth Amendments to define an important part of what it means in our world to be a police officer and what it means to be the citizen with whom he (or she) interferes. This body of law is meant to constitute a coherent set of ways of defining each party, telling each, in some respects, what he must, and in others what he may, do and say: giving each, in the context of their relationship, a way of conceiving of himself or herself, of the other, and of the world in which they both act. Similarly, one function of the substantive criminal law is to create and make real a coherent conception of the judge, of the lawyer, of the juror, and of the criminal defendant, by giving each role a character of its own. The law is a constitutive rhetoric, which works through the creation of characters in relation to each other, and it can work only if the rules, the relations, and what is said are coherent with each other.

The conflict between rehabilitation and deterrence is irresolvable because it is a conflict between different conceptions of character and relation. On matters of this sort we cannot get away with vacillation—treating someone now as a person, now as a thing, now as a friend, now as an enemy. If we claim to perform two contradictory characters in alternation, what we have is neither of those, but the character either of a chameleon—an alternating contradiction—or of a hypocrite. If I hear a judge say, with deep sincerity, "My concern is with the welfare of those who come before me," I will believe him (or her) only if that voice, and conduct consistent with it, are regularly maintained; if in every third or fourth case he makes plain that the person before him is to be considered as an enemy or as a resource, I know how to read what he earlier said. I know what character he has given himself, and it is not that of a friend or of an honest person. When the meaning of what we do lies in the relation we establish with others, that relation must be consistently maintained.

3

But is it conceivable that the judge might explain such a shift from one role to another, thus giving himself or herself a new character with a new relation to the defendant, which might somehow incorporate both possibilities and for which a claim of consistency could be made?

Consider for example this possibililty, put by a judge speaking to a group of convicted defendants whom he or she is about to sentence: "What we shall do," says the judge, "is to treat you all as cases for restraint and rehabilitation, unless we are persuaded that the public interest would be served in your case by a punishment designed to deter, in which case we shall inflict it. While it is not an easy task to identify the cases in which the public interest requires a deterrent sanction, it is a familiar one; the usual methods we have of identifying and measuring costs and benefits, of estimating risks and determining preferences, will serve us here as they have elsewhere.

"It may at first seem that this power of discretionary 'punishment to deter in the public interest' is inconsistent with the rule of law, but in fact it is not. In a narrow sense our power rests firmly upon the rule of law, for no punishment can exceed the maximum established by the legislature for your offense. It is consistent with the rule of law in a larger sense as well, for it is perfectly fair: it is only those who, like you, have violated the law and have thus forfeited the right to consideration of their interests (except as they coincide with those of the public) who will be subject to this treatment. You can even be said to have inflicted this exposure on yourselves, for no one in our system is convicted of crime unless he or she (1) has adequate notice of a sufficiently clear prohibition to be able to avoid violating it and (2) is personally at fault with respect to the prohibited conduct.

"By fault we mean both that the offender has whatever guilty mind the particular criminal statute requires for liability—intent to kill, recklessness with respect to life, intent to defraud, and so on—and that the offender is a competent person, able to conform his or her conduct to the requirements of the law. It is upon a voluntary and wrongful act that the forfeiture of which I speak is conditioned and its fairness rests."

This is not an imaginary explanation or justification, but the best statement I can make of what I would call the contemporary orthodox view. What are we to think of it?

At heart this position claims that it is fair to use the class of persons convicted of crime for deterrent purposes because we told them that we would do it this way if they violated the law and they went ahead and voluntarily violated the law anyway. This justification of punishment thus depends completely upon the judgment that conduct is "voluntary"—otherwise no "forfeiture" can fairly be imposed.

There are many difficulties with this position. For one thing, what can "voluntary" mean? As we all know, the rudimentary image of human freedom to choose is far too simple to be an adequate account of deviant and criminal behavior. None of us is wholly free, and in some sense those among us who commit crimes, at least crimes of certain kinds, are likely to be less free than the rest of us.

It is also not clear what the function of the word "forfeiture" is. In these cases we do not have a conscious waiver or willing relinquishment of a right. We have a class of offenders, situated equally with respect to fault and circumstance, who are treated in radically different ways, the difference being based upon the relative usefulness to society of one kind of sanction or the other in the particular case. The forfeiture argument assumes what is at issue, namely that upon conviction (and within certain limits) one is exposed to whatever sanction seems to be most useful to the public. It is true that conduct justifies punishment, to be sure, but that is not to say that any kind of punishment—torture?—is justified, nor that inconsistencies of treatment should be permissible.

The true function of the forfeiture argument is perhaps not to justify a punishment but to reassure an audience. It tells us, the socially competent, that we need not fear that the power of discretionary punishment will be used against us. The practice of punishment as justified by the forfeiture theory may in fact be seen as a sort of cruel joke. Under it many people are punished who have indeed done harmful actions, but whom it is hard to call free in the sense required by the theory itself; and the audience for and beneficiaries of the practice are those who—like us—are for the most part much more nearly free to choose, as is demonstrated in part by our managing not to commit the forbidden acts. We punish those who are not free in order to control the conduct of those who are.

Even more important, this view of the criminal law does nothing to solve the problem of character and relation with which we began. Each of the four purposes of the criminal law implies its own conception of the character both of the individual and of the judge. If you act with a genuine solicitude for the offender's welfare, and seek—however misguidedly in practice—to rehabilitate him (or her), you can properly be said to respect his humanity. You treat him as a person in a different sense when you act to restrain him—for you do no more than he should be required to recognize it is necessary to do, to him and to others who threaten the security of the community. In still a different sense, to be elaborated in section 5, you treat him as a person when you punish him as an act of that special form of retribution I call blaming. But when you impose a punishment not required by any of the particular characteristics of the defendant's personality or the circumstances of his life or the nature of his conduct, merely to make him serve as an example to others, what you have done is to convert him from a person into a resource or object to be employed in the public interest. You have, as it were, drafted him into a population control program.

It does not harmonize these inconsistent relations to say that the court has the character of none of these but that of the agency that chooses which character it should have at any one time. That simply reduces all the characters to one, that of the agency with despotic, if limited, control over the offender, which will use him or her as it seems to suit the agency's view of the public interest.[4] This makes wholly false the ethical claims upon which the powers to rehabilitate and to restrain rest, namely that the law respects the offender's humanity. Under this justification, then, there is either an impossible alternation of roles or the single role of the judge who disposes of the offender in the public interest but sometimes speaks in other voices. Either is inconsistent with our conception of what it means to be a citizen or a judge in our world, indeed with our conceptions of law, of justice, and of honesty.

It may make my point clearer if you think of punishment in the family. In the family punishment usually rests on one of two grounds: the need of a child to be corrected for his (or her) own sake; or the need of the community, and the child, that he be incapacitated from certain kinds of destructive acts. It would be wholly different for the parent to punish one child, not for the sake of that child, but for the benefit of his or her brothers and sisters. (This would happen, for example, if the parent judged that the child had already learned his lesson but punished him anyway.) What would be the nature and effect of an alternation between the two modes of punishment? If one punished a child sometimes for his or her own good or on account of his or her own propensities, sometimes as an example to others, the result would not be that one sometimes had the character of the parent who respected the humanity of each child, sometimes not, for that is simply impossible. One would be either a chameleon or a hypocrite. It is just such an impossible shift in role and character that the criminal law, as we have conceived it, requires the judge to try to make.

---

4. One way the defendant might want to respond to a judge who speaks to him or her in the way that the orthodox view would suggest is to ask, "Who on earth do you think you are, to talk to me in such a way?" I think that any respectable conception of the criminal law should include or suggest an answer to that question. To say, "I am one who uses you as I believe (or as the legislature believes) the public interest requires" fails in my view to meet any standard of acceptability.

What all this means is that the incoherence of purpose in the criminal law does not, after all, disappear when the criminal law is analyzed as a rhetorical system, the central topic of which is the conflict among its stated purposes. For the contradictions in the criminal law are not merely competing statements of value that can serve as a rhetorical topic, but give a contradictory character both to the institution itself and to those who must act within it. They thus define impossibly incompatible ways of proceeding. They order the judge, as it were, to be, to do, and to feel inconsistent things at the same time. The contradiction destroys the very world the language seeks to constitute, the coherence of which is a necessary precondition to all else it seeks to achieve.

Is there another way to conceive of the practice of punishment that would render it intelligible and coherent? Is there some way, that is, in which we can make sense of this activity after all?

4

I think that the first step is to abandon the "purpose-structure" or "ends-means" language of bureaucratic analysis. The assumption of such a way of talking is that we can produce in schematic language, like a blueprint, both a description of the mechanism of a social institution and a statement of the goals by which it is to be directed. Argument is permitted on the questions whether the goals are proper (and properly stated) and how to design the machine to achieve them. Once these matters are settled, the only question is an empirical one, whether the design "works" in practice. In my view, to talk this way about the criminal law misrepresents the nature of human action and experience and misconceives the nature of language.

Of course, there is a sense in which the practice of punishment, like the practices say of lawyering or teaching, is intentional or purposive. We naturally want to be able to say that we know both what we are up to and how to go about it. The question, then, is not whether our practices are in some sense intentional but how we should talk about our intentions, in what language we should define our motives and claim meaning for our actions. The reduced language of the purposive machine is not adequate to our needs, for it does not permit us to say what we actually know about what we do. This way of talking, which may seem at first to be so "rational," in fact prevents us from making sense of our experience.

Consider the nature of the practice we call punishment, for example. It has been with us much longer than any self-conscious talk about institution-building or the design of social systems. It is a practice in which every government, perhaps every community, engages. Indeed, in some form it may be necessary to the very idea of a community, for its subject is approval and disapproval, acceptance and rejection, inclusion and exclusion. It is something we do; and something we seem, for the most part, to know how to do. Punishment is an activity that like many others—family life, warfare, education, making beautiful objects and sounds, arguing, and believing—is not wholly subject to theoretical comprehension or restatement. It is only partly guided and controlled by the logical faculty in rational pursuit of statable objectives. It is guided by feelings as well: of anger, of revulsion, of sympathy, of appropriateness, just as other such activities—teaching, raising children, tending gardens, and the like—are guided by feelings. Punishment is guided, in fact, just as forgiveness is guided.

Activities of this sort engage much more of the mind than its quantitative or mechanical capacities, and they cannot be adequately represented in a language of mechanism or regulated by it either. They are based not upon processes of calculation but, at best, upon a sort of educated self-evidence, a sense of what is natural or appropriate, which is at once the simplest ground of action and the most complex, for it is the point at which intellect and instinct, mind and nature, meet.

I do not mean that such activities cannot be learned, shaped, and modified, or that they cannot be the object of critical contemplation and understanding, for of course they can; I mean only that the language of purposive mechanism is too simple and too mechanical to describe and judge what we do. It does not respect the limits we should acknowledge upon our capacities to explain and justify ourselves. Only a wholly mad judge, for example, would think that any of his or her decisions could be wholly explained, wholly rationalized, or wholly justified. One does the best one can to decide the right way, and to say what is possible by way of explanation, but one knows that one cannot say everything. One cannot justify, or even reproduce for criticism, "every stage of the process." Explanation, in the real world, is always incomplete. Suppose, for example, that someone asked you why you chose your college or your career. Both your questioner and you would know that something could be said by way of response, perhaps something illuminating, but neither would expect you to produce some equivalent of a computer tape, showing with precision and completeness every operation of your mind, nor to state with accuracy a list of the relevant "purposes" you were pursuing. Meaningful talk about such matters partakes of the uncertainty of the experience that is its subject.

5

But if the language of mechanism and purpose is inappropriate to these matters, how are we to talk about them?

I want to begin by thinking of communal punishment as a practice of a special kind, the function of which is to claim a certain kind of meaning for events. In this it is like law more generally, which, as you know, is in my view best regarded not as a machine for social control, but as what I call a system of constitutive rhetoric: a set of resources for claiming, resisting, and declaring significance. It is a way of asking and responding to questions; of defining roles and positions from which, and voices with which, to speak; of creating and maintaining relations; of justifying and explaining action and inaction. It is one of the forms in which a culture lives and changes, drawing connections in special ways between past and present, near and far. The law, of which legal punishment is a part, is a system of meaning; it is a language and should be evaluated as such.

What kind of meaning does punishment make? Here I wish to turn to the aspect of the criminal law tradition that speaks in terms of "blaming."

The old common law formulation, that there can be no criminal guilt without a "mens rea" (guilty mind) reflects a conception of the criminal law as a species of blaming. The Model Penal Code, which codifies enlightened modern opinion, states as its central principle the allocation of criminal responsibility according to blameworthiness. Within the criminal law as well as outside it, punishment has traditionally been regarded as a special form of the social and intellectual practice we call "blaming." If we can make sense of that practice, we may be able to make sense of the criminal law as well, and indeed discover a ground, very different from a statement of purposes, upon which that activity may be shaped and guided.

The idea that the criminal law is a species of blaming is an uncomfortable one. Blaming seems to entail retaliation or retribution, and we like to think that we have outgrown that as an element of punishment. And blaming itself, even in ordinary life, is problematic: we all engage in it but feel uneasy about what we do—more uneasy perhaps than we should.

I think that the heart of the difficulty for most people, both in ordinary life and in the law, is that there is an apparent conflict between blaming on the one hand and sympathizing and understanding on the other. It is sometimes said, indeed, that when enough is sympathetically understood about a person, blaming becomes impossible, even in the case of the person who commits atrocities or is utterly selfish. *Tout comprendre, c'est tout pardonner.* And in some logically extreme sense that is true: if one were to step wholly into the shoes of another—to see what he (or she) sees, to feel what he feels—one would not blame him for what he did, at least not any more than he blamed himself. Our own experience seems to prove the conflict, for as we learn more about a person we are blaming, we notice that the impulse to blame weakens, and often disappears—perhaps to our momentary chagrin. Blaming, in short, seems incompatible with one of our deepest wishes, to regard ourselves as sympathetic and understanding.

But to rid ourselves of blaming seems simply impossible. As a matter of ordinary experience, blaming is something we do in fact and will continue to do. It is part of our constitution. Suppose, for example, that you found your tires slashed when you next went out to your car, or the pages you wanted cut from a library book. What would you do? The refusal to blame is equally impossible, I believe, at the level of community action. We blame collectively as we do individually, not by choice or will, but by nature.

One might take the view that the impulse to blame, however ingrained in us, is an unfortunate carryover from an earlier stage of evolution, a mere instinct that it is the work of time and conscience, indeed of civilization, to overcome. At least in our official world, one might say, we ought to be able to act rationally, free from such impulses. This view is in the first place unrealistic—our official life is not free from instinct and impulse!—and I think it misconceives the nature both of blaming and of civilization. Indeed I think that what I call "blaming" is in fact essential to whatever dignity and decency the criminal law has, and that one cannot even imagine a tolerable system of criminal law that did not operate by blaming.

To test this point, ask yourself how you might try to remove the practice of blaming from the criminal law. One possibility—present in our own system to at least some degree—would be to hold people criminally responsible for their conduct, and the consequences thereof, without regard to fault. But this would seem to us both unfair and, in its extreme form, willfully senseless, a kind of crazy obliteration of distinctions that are essential resources for our collective life. The difference between accidental and deliberate injury is important to any judgment about conduct. (As Justice Holmes said, even a dog knows the difference between being stumbled over and being kicked.) Such a system would exclude from consideration just those elements of motive and feeling that contribute most to the meaning of events, from whatever point of view; like Odysseus, the law would see only the bow and not the social relations that give it significance and power. This would be blaming without blameworthiness, both unfair and foolish.

Another alternative would be to dispense with both the act and state of mind requirements of the criminal law—indeed with all aspects of what we now call the trial stage of the process—and instead have a compulsory treatment system operated on the model of our present involuntary commitment practices. The basis for detention would be a judgment not about the blameworthiness of one's conduct but about the propensities of one's personality. No one would ever be blamed or punished for what he or she did; but we would all be subject to compulsory detention when the interests of the public were judged to require it. This is unthinkable. It would expose every citizen to the incompetence, caprice, and corruption of coercive official action. In the terms suggested earlier, it would define every citizen not as a free person with defined liberties, but as simply belonging to the bureaucratic state for its use. It would also abolish distinctions that are natural and important to us: the distinction, for example, between responsible and irresponsible conduct, and that between dangerous people who never act on their propensities and those who do. It would be an abdication by the community, or by its official part, of its function as the maker of a language of approval and disapproval, of praise and blame. The practice of punishment is by nature a practice of blaming conduct, and we cannot live without it.

I would like now to reconsider the claim that blaming is inconsistent with understanding and sympathy, for I think I have put that incompletely. It is true that the more fully one steps into the shoes of another, adopting his (or her) experience, his feelings, his view of the world, the less one is inclined to blame him (or to blame him more than he himself does). From his point of view, then, blaming is indeed inconsistent with sympathy and understanding. But the more one steps into his shoes, the less one can inhabit those of the victim, the less one can sympathize with and understand *him;* and the less, likewise, one remains aware of one's own position, whatever that may be. Blaming can thus be seen as a way of limiting one's imaginative or sympathetic identification with the actor, but this is done in the interest of maintaining one's capacities to remember what one knows and feels about others as well. It is a way of saying to the offender and to his victim that in the eyes of the community both have claims to recognition and sympathy. For one's identification with the victim is also qualified by the practice of blaming. The victim is not entitled, that is, to demand public condemnation on a showing of some injury alone; he or she must speak a language of fault and blame. Similarly, the defendant will not be excused on the grounds that perfect sympathy would lead to forgiveness, if it would, for he is not entitled to that. He and the victim are alike entitled to a sympathy that runs at least two ways, that recognizes both parties. The defendant will indeed be held to standards of conduct; but only those that he can meet.[5]

For both people the function of the practice of blaming, like that of Neoptolemus' speech and *Philoctetes* itself—like poetry and law more generally—is to insist upon recognition and integration, a putting together into one composition of what we know about the world: a truly constitutive process. The community insists to each of the characters that it will recognize the existence of the other, and it forces each to speak a language that does this too. In doing this, the com-

---

5. In holding people responsible for their conduct, the practice of blaming affirms, as a general matter, the power of a person to choose what he or she does. Of course the question of freedom of will is problematic: sometimes, or in some respects, we perceive ourselves and others to be truly free agents; in others, we are so confined by past and present circumstances that the word "free" cannot intelligibly or fairly be used. And the sense of freedom that we do have may be illusory or exaggerated. But any ethical system, which is by definition about choice, must posit the power to choose. And a criminal law that is "ethical" in this sense is surely far more respectful of the offender than one that, denying his or her freedom to choose, simply treats the conduct as a product of circumstance. In this sense both the modern criminal law and the practice of blaming are ethical systems. But the practice of blaming seems to recognize more fully than the modern orthodoxy the uncertainties and doubts that surround our sense of freedom; it admits more openly that the "voluntary" act may be "involuntary," that the defendant would, if all were known, be forgiven by a remote and omnipotent judge. For it does not proclaim a forfeiture. It insists only that the imperatives of social life be recognized, an insistence compatible with the recognition of the defendant's humanity but not with a collective use of him or her. This is no more than parents lovingly insist upon.

munity claims and performs a meaning for its action or inaction; it defines and maintains a character of its own. This last, indeed, is the critical achievement of the practice of blaming, for there is no guarantee that the communal insistence I describe will much affect the subjective view either of a particular defendant or of his or her victim. The one may simply want to get off; the other may simply want revenge. It is in its own interest above all that the community acts when it insists upon recognizing the claims of both, for this insistence gives the community an important part of its character. This achievement is not dependent upon the understanding or acquiescence of others.

The community so created is not an abstraction but is a living world defined by the actions of individual people responsible for particular judgments. For the judgment of blame is made by one jury or one judge about one person; the sentence a person must suffer is passed upon him or her by another who is responsible for the judgment. The law happens, as it should be studied, one case at a time. It is one of the merits of the law, especially of the criminal law, that the judge not only may but must turn from the impossible institutional ideal of deciding every case perfectly in accordance with some set of rules, to deciding, within limits, each case on his or her view of its merits. The defendant speaks to the person who is responsible for his case, the proper disposition of which requires an individualized judgment about him. This is an important way in which the criminal law defines the citizen and his relation to the community.

Even when he (or she) is sent to a special place of punishment, the defendant remains a member of his community, entitled to all protections and recognitions not taken away as punishment. The idea is not the theory of the modern orthodoxy, that he has forfeited to a bureaucracy his sovereignty over himself by his wrong, for he has not, but that he has exposed himself to a sanction whose very premise assumes his continued responsibility for himself. This is in practical terms a wise assumption because nearly all of the people we punish eventually come back from prison or jail to join the larger society.

To say, as I do, that the criminal law can be made sense of if—and only if—it is regarded as a system of blaming is not, of course, to answer every question about it. Decisions still must be made regarding what conduct should be blamed and how much; about admissibility of evidence, instructions to the jury, and the like; and about questions of guilt and disposition. What the conception of the process as "blaming" affords is a method of organizing the activity, a premise upon which intelligible questions can be asked and responded to at each stage. In making these judgments people will still address tensions that can be seen as conflicts between the individual and society and may even use language that bears some resemblance to the terms in which the "purposes" are stated. A judgment about blaming, for example, often includes a statement of fear, or of a need to repress or restrain. My suggestion is not that the participants in the process, conceived of this way, will have nothing to do, or that their decisions will be easy; but that, however difficult any particular judgment is, they will be able to say to themselves and others that they know both what they are up to and how to go about it.

It follows that the language in which offenses are defined should reflect a conception of the criminal process as blaming. This can be done through the use of terms expressly inviting judgments of moral fault, such as "mens rea" or "guilty mind" or "scienter" or "wicked," as the common law originally did; or it can be done in the apparently more refined and objective way recommended by the Model Penal Code, with its careful definitions of purpose, knowledge, recklessness, and negligence. (In his interesting book, *An Inquiry into Criminal Guilt* (1963), the late Professor Peter Brett argued for the use of the older terminology.)

The defenses should likewise reflect this conception of the criminal law, as to some extent indeed they already do. It may be thought that the set of excuses and justifications that evolved at common law—especially self-defense, duress, insanity, infancy, and necessity—constitute an adequately exhaustive catalogue of the sorts of circumstances in which an actor, otherwise guilty of an offense, should be excused. Or one might prefer a catch-all defense, as Professor Brett does. He would have the court in borderline cases "tell the jury that they must endeavor to put themselves in the defendant's place, and ask whether they can truly say, 'I understand why he did this, but he ought not to have done it; if I had been in his place, I would not—or I hope I would not—have done it myself.' If they cannot say this, they should absolve him from guilt" (p. 77).

Blaming is a practice that, like other important cultural practices, cannot be reproduced in the language of systems design, but it is intelligible to all of us. No tolerable system of criminal law can be imagined without it. It is not, as it may at first seem, inconsistent with the ideal of sympathy and understanding, but is a way in which the community extends its sympathy two ways at once, insisting upon the equal worth and humanity of each member against those who arrogate to themselves what they should not. It imposes no forfeiture and makes no use of the defendant, but punishes him or her as a parent punishes a child, to teach us what that act makes true, that we all live here together.

6

You may want to know what flows in practical terms from the view I express in this essay. I think quite a lot does.

1. Criminal punishment ought to be based upon blameworthiness only, and not imposed upon those who cannot be blamed. The determination of what is blamable is the task in the first instance for the legislature and ultimately, within the boundaries so established and subject to constitutional limitations, for the judge and jury.

2. The criminal law should use a language of blame, so far as possible a language continuous with that of ordinary English. Only then will it make sense to the defendant, the victim, and the public; only then can the jury and the judge understand what they are up to and how to go about it.

3. The jury should be retained, for the properly instructed community of lay men and women is in fact peculiarly competent at the practice of blaming that lies at the center of the criminal process. It is more competent at this practice than any one person could be, for collective judgment reduces idiosyncrasy; and it is more expert than any professional, for whom each case necessarily tends to be just one of many, the material upon which his or her profession or the bureaucratic institution of the criminal law acts.

4. The insanity defense should be retained. Its object is to permit the jury to separate out for different treatment those people whom they believe cannot fairly be blamed for what they did. Its formulation should express this function.

5. We should stop talking of deterrence as a "goal" of punishment that should in any way affect individual judgments of guilt, grading, or disposition. Of course it is true that deterrence will continue to be one of the effects of the practice of punishment, and we can be pleased that that is so. But the criminal law proper concerns itself only with instances of violation, and these should be punished only as blame requires, never for exemplary or deterrent reasons.

The rationale for deterrent punishment sometimes takes this form: "We agree that the circumstances of the particular offender and his offense call for lenity, but if we treat him that way we are afraid that the force of our threat to others, upon which compliance with our rule depends, will be reduced." What this fear rests upon is the view that if one attempts to explain why this defendant was being treated leniently, others, failing to understand our distinctions, would more readily engage in much more blameworthy conduct. I think this is wrong, even in the clearest kind of case for exemplary punishment— say that of a person involved (but in a manner we regard as only marginally blameworthy) in an airplane hijacking. For trust in our capacity to make clear the distinctions upon which judgments of blame rest and to enforce them in future cases is an essential part of the character of the law in our culture. To draw the distinctions as we honestly perceive them and to rest confidently upon them are necessary to the making of a genuine language of fact and value.

BIBLIOGRAPHIC NOTE

For accounts of the four purposes of the criminal law, see, for example, the proposed Federal Criminal Code, S. 1437, 95th Cong., 2d Sess. § 101(b) (1977); the Model Penal Code, § 1.02 (Proposed Official Draft, 1962); Herbert L. Packer, *The Limits of the Criminal Sanction* (Stanford, Calif.: Stanford University Press, 1968), chapter 3; *United States v. Bergman*, 416 F.Supp. 496 (S.D.N.Y. 1976). A useful treatment of the literature appears in Sanford H. Kadish, Stephen J. Schulhofer, and Monrad G. Paulsen, *Criminal Law and Its Processes: Cases and Materials*, 4th ed. (Boston: Little, Brown, 1980), pp. 181–209. R. E. Gahringer, "Punishment and Responsibility," *Journal of Philosophy* 66 (1969): 291, 293, presents an interestingly modified set of the traditional purposes, distinguishing between "high" and "low" conceptions of each. As I say in the text, Peter Brett speaks of these matters rather differently in *An Inquiry Into Criminal Guilt* (Sydney: Law Book Company of Australasia, 1963).

In addition to the traditional four mentioned in the text, purposes of two other kinds are sometimes attributed to the criminal law: (1) those relating to the protection of the individual, such as giving fair warning of what is prohibited and respecting established rights and liberties (e.g., Model Penal Code § 1.02(1)(c) & (d) [Proposed Official Draft, 1962]); (2) those based on the perception that one function of the criminal law is to establish a community of shared values: see, for example, Emile Durkheim, *The Division of Labor in Society*, trans. George Simpson (New York: Macmillan, 1933), pp. 108–9; R. E. Gahringer, "Punishment and Responsibility"; Joel Feinberg, *Doing and Deserving: Essays in the Theory of Responsibility* (Princeton: Princeton University Press, 1970), p. 95.

These kinds of purposes seem to me of a different sort from the traditional four, and I deal with them differently. The first kind is in fact not a purpose of criminal punishment at all, but a principle by which punishment is limited. It is grounded upon values and concerns external to the criminal law proper.

Purposes of the second sort, relating to the creation and maintenance of a community, imply a view of the criminal law as a system of meaning rather than a method of achieving material objectives, and it is, in general, this view of the criminal law that I elaborate and defend in this essay.

The best single work on the traditional purposes of the criminal law that I know is Henry M. Hart, "The Aims of the Criminal Law," 23 *Law and Contemporary Problems* 401–41 (1958). On deterrence see also Johannes Andenaes, "The Morality of Deterrence," 37 *University of Chicago Law Review* 649 (1970); Norval Morris, *The Future of Imprisonment* (Chicago: University of Chicago Press, 1974), chapter 3; Franklin E. Zimring and Gordon J. Hawkins, *Deterrence: The Legal Threat in Crime Control* (Chicago: University of Chicago Press, 1973), chapter 2. More generally, see H. L. A. Hart, *Punishment and Responsibility: Essays in the Philosophy of Law* (New York: Oxford University Press, 1968); Herbert L. Packer, *The Limits of the Criminal Sanction;* Norval Morris, "Punishment and Rehabilitation," in *Equal Justice Under Law: United States Department of Justice Bicentennial Lecture Series* (Washington, D.C.: United States Document Office, 1977).

Finally, I should say that many commentators have of course realized that the usual purposes present a problem of coherence, which they have tried to resolve by placing one purpose over the others, or giving somewhat different roles to each. These efforts fail to persuade me at least, partly because the commentators adhere to the notions that this part of our life is fundamentally bureaucratic and that this kind of public action must be spoken of as if it were motivated, and could be shaped, by a set of fully expressible purposes. But the commentators' awareness of the tension or incoherence among these purposes has not prevented the drafters of legislation from simply saying that the criminal law serves these four purposes (sometimes with others), which can be used as guides to interpretation, all as if that presented no difficulty. See, for example, both the American Law Institute's Model Penal Code and the proposed Federal Criminal Code (cited above).

The examples discussed in the text are sentencing judgments, chosen for their simplicity, but the incoherence that emerges there runs throughout the criminal process. For example, many of the terms by which the power to determine guilt is delegated to the trier of fact are by nature—and on purpose—uncertain in meaning. One thinks of "malice" in murder law, for example, or "breach of the peace" as an offense. These terms must be given content at the trial. When that is done by reference to the aims of criminal punishment, stated as "purposes" of the sort listed in the text, the same contradictions exist at the trial stage as at sentencing. For an analysis of this problem in some detail, see *The Legal Imagination,* pp. 317–63, especially at 358–60. For an attempt to render rational and coherent the choice between different sets of aims, characters, and relations in the sentencing process see D. A. Thomas, *Principles of Sentencing* (London: Heinemann, 1970).

The legislature can try to remove the incoherence from the law by making all judgments itself—defining crimes more precisely and setting fixed sentences. But that merely means that the incoherences go underground, either hiding behind the legislation or buried in silent discretionary acts by judge or juror.

Making Sense of What We Do

NOTES ON THE LANGUAGE OF INSTITUTIONAL PURPOSES

If the language of a purposive mechanism is as simplistic and wrong-headed as I suggest, one can naturally ask how it arose. It seems to me to work this way. What are claimed to be the "purposes" of the criminal law are, I think, not really its purposes at all, but a reduced catalogue of the effects that punishment has been seen to have in practice. These effects come to be regarded as purposes on the following assumption: that our social world is a machine or artifact, in which all action can be perceived and classified in a language of cause and effect, in which every activity can be rationalized by the quantifying mind. This predisposition to assume that the only rational way to talk about social institutions is through the metaphor of the machine converts effects into "purposes," and it leads to the problematic contradictions I have identified. That predisposition (which seems to derive in the modern world from Hobbes's *Leviathan*) of course enjoys enormous academic popularity, especially in what are called social or policy sciences.

Another way to put this point is to say that what I have called the language of systems design elevates one part of the mind over all others, for it assumes that one kind of intellectual activity is the only kind. Its appeal is to the part of the mind that proceeds abstractly and theoretically, that prefers reasoning by definition, distinction, and deduction to what appear to be messier, but which are more comprehensive, ways of thinking; to the part that seeks to expand its claims to understanding and to control by reductive simplifications of experience rather than by speaking and thinking in ways more nearly true to what we know of what we do.

My claim that the activity of the criminal law is comprehensible only when it is regarded as what I call a practice—that is, an organized activity not reducible to the single faculty of ratiocination—is part of a larger point I make throughout this book, that the law is properly regarded as an art, not a science. This is of course not to say that science—or social science—has no place in the world. Both natural and social sciences have much to report about the nature of the world in which we live that may be of interest to legislator, judge, lawyer, and juror. The study of institutions in terms of their causes and effects can no doubt be valuable. But the activity of law is not a scientific activity, nor reducible or convertible into such an activity, any more than activities of history or of argument or of politics or of novel writing are scientific activities. Any account of law which is to make sense of it should reflect that fact, and respect the nature of law as it is.

10 PLATO'S *GORGIAS* AND THE

MODERN LAWYER

A DIALOGUE ON THE ETHICS

OF ARGUMENT

In the *Gorgias* Plato examines rhetoric (represented by Gorgias, Polus, and Callicles) by contrasting it with dialectic (represented by Socrates and implicitly by Plato himself). He asks of each activity what it means from the point of view of the practitioner: what kind of life he can have, what character, what knowledge, what community with others. At every stage the life of the rhetorician is found wanting, and wanting from every imaginable point of view—intellectual, practical, moral, psychological, political, and so on. Elsewhere I have analyzed this dialogue at some length (*When Words Lose Their Meaning*, chapter 4). Here I respond to it by writing a dialogue of my own, in which I recast the Socratic position in modern terms (and apply it specifically to lawyers) and present two possible responses to it.

My starting point is this question: if the devastating things Socrates says in the *Gorgias* about ancient rhetoric and its practitioners are true, are they not equally true of modern law and modern lawyers? For it is the function of the lawyer, like the rhetorician, to persuade about the just and the unjust, about the expedient and the inexpedient, and to do so not among people generally (or in the university), but among those who have power—in the courts, legislatures, and assemblies. Moreover, the lawyer always speaks in the service of someone else whose interests he (or she) represents, and he accordingly says not what he believes to be true or right about an issue he addresses, but whatever will persuade his audience to act in furtherance of those interests. He is, it seems, the modern rhetorician in its purest form, and the law professor is his teacher—a modern Gorgias.

In thinking about how the *Gorgias* speaks to the modern lawyer and how he might respond, we do not have a real Socrates with real lawyers, and we must therefore imagine how their argument would go. The exercise is not wholly impossible, for the outline of the Socratic case is plain enough from what we can read, and one knows something of lawyers oneself. In what follows I will present such an imagined conversation, in which I try to show how two lawyers, of somewhat different types, might respond to the case made against rhetoric in the *Gorgias*. These are two men, Euerges and Euphemes, successful attorneys in a firm with a diverse general practice. They have agreed to talk with Socrates as they walk back and forth through a large city park on a spring afternoon.

Socrates: What I really want to know is who you are and what you do. I know you are called a "lawyer," but what I want to know is this: what do you do in the world that makes you what you are?

Euerges: I would put it this way: I give advice to people who seek it from me about their legal rights and duties, and I represent them in legal proceedings.

Socrates: In whose interests are you acting when you do these things?

Euerges: In the interests of my clients, of course. And in the interest of the law as well, for in my work I help see to it that the law is obeyed and adhered to, and that legal institutions function as they are intended to.

Socrates: Let us take the client first. How does what you do serve his interests?

Euerges: By increasing what can be called his power over the world: his range of choices for action, his liberty, and his wealth. Those are all good things, and my clients show by their appreciation that they know this is true. I use the law to help them get what they want. I am their friend in the law.

Socrates: But is it always in someone's interest to increase what you call his "power"? I suppose you would agree that people sometimes use their "power" in ways that are self-destructive, and in such cases to increase their power is not a help, but an injury?

Euerges: That is a theoretical possibility, I suppose, but, as the world goes, not a real one. My clients are intelligent, practical people who know what they want and are satisfied by my efforts to help them get it. If what you mean is that it might in some way be better for one of my clients to do something else with his time and energy and money, to become a South Seas missionary, for example, or to write the novel he has always talked about, that is, I suppose, possibly so, though I do not often think about such things. I am not even sure what it would mean to say that such a course was "better" for one of my clients, since everyone is entitled to his own views on such personal matters. Anyway, who am I to make such a judgment about someone else, especially when I know so few of the relevant facts?

Socrates: But it remains true that you do not after all serve your client's interests, as you originally said, but instead what appear to him to be his interests, that is, his wants or desires. Isn't that right? And in what you have just said you do not deny this but seek to explain or justify it, by pointing to the supposed competence of your clients (and your own supposed incompetence) at deciding what is good for them, and to the allegedly uncertain character of that judgment, whoever makes it. Strictly speaking, then, it is true that you serve not your client's interests but his wishes or his wants?

Euerges: Strictly speaking, that is true.

Socrates: If so, you are in this respect no different from the keeper of one of those Pleasure Ranches they have out West, who sells his customers whatever they desire, however bad for them it might be: too much food and liquor and drugs, and every kind of sex. In both cases it is not the client's interests that are catered to but his desires, and in the case of the law the desire in question is more dangerous than any other, for it is the desire for power.

Euerges: This is nonsense! Don't you know that an important part of the practice of law is talking with one's client about the wisdom of one course of action over another, in a mutual attempt to determine what his true interests require? We are constantly teaching our clients that they cannot have everything they want and advising them to pursue what is more important to them and to forgo what is less important. We help them to discover their true interests and to shape their wants to suit those interests.

Socrates: If that is so, the present conversation can come to an end, for I have no differences with you, and we should begin on another subject: how do you do what you have just described? For nothing could be more wonderful than to discover a person who knows not only what is best for himself and for others, but also how to teach others what their true interests really are. But I imagine that not every lawyer would make such a claim and that many of those who did would mean by it nothing more than this: that they advised their clients how they could gratify their desires the most—as a really expert keeper of a Pleasure Ranch might do, telling his customers not to drink to incapacitation, or not to combine drug A and drug B, and so on, but having no concern at all for their true interests. Shall I tell you what I would say to such a lawyer? If you permit me, I will make a speech to him, and you can tell me when I am done whether you and I are wrong, or he is.

Here is what I would say: by reason of your training and natural capacities you have what is commonly called a great power, the power of persuading those who have power of a different kind, political and economic power, to do what you wish them to do. Of course your power is not absolute, for there are limits to what even you can achieve. And properly speaking, this is not a true power unless it is exercised in your true interests, but it is a real force, as your record of success and the fees you receive demonstrate, and we can speak as others do and call it a "power" too, though putting it in quotation marks.

Your professional aim is to present your case, whatever its merits, so that those with control over economic and political forces will decide for your client, and you most succeed when you most prevail. You use your mind, as we used to say of the Sophists, to make the weaker argument appear the stronger. Your goal in all of this is to get the most, first for your client, but ultimately for yourself, for what you do with your "power" of persuasion is to sell it, getting in exchange another "power," that of money. Of course neither the power of money nor the power of persuasion is a good thing of itself; that depends upon whether it is used to advance or injure one's interests, and that is no concern of yours, with respect to your client or apparently to yourself.

You say you are your client's friend, but you do not serve his interests; in truth you are not his friend, but his flatterer, which is to be his enemy. For your concern is not with his real interests, but with assisting him to attain whatever it is he may desire. If it should happen that what you do does advance his true interests and thus tends to make him happy rather than unhappy, that still does not make you his friend, because for you that result is accidental, of no interest or consequence. Not having been your object, it can be no ground for your satisfaction. Likewise, you are no friend to the law, for you will always say that justice requires whatever it is that your client wishes, and you use all your skill and art to make it seem that this is so.

In all of this you are least of all friend to yourself, for in return for money that you cannot take the time to learn how to spend, or not to spend, you give yourself the mind and character of one who does these things. You never ask yourself in a serious way what fairness and justice require in a particular case, for to do that would not leave time for what you do. In fact you incapacitate yourself for the pursuit of such a question by giving yourself the mind of the case-maker and brief-writer, the mind of one who looks ceaselessly for the characterization, the turn of phrase, or the line of argument that will make your client's case, however weak, seem the stronger. To persuade those whom you must persuade, you devote yourself with the attention of a lover to the ways in which they can be pleased, to the tricks of voice and manner and tone, to the kinds of argument, that will persuade this jury or that judge, this tax official or that fellow lawyer.

The art of rhetoric is in fact the art of ministration to the pleasures of another, really a species of prostitution. As the sexual responses and energies of a prostitute are debased and debasing by the way they are employed, so also are your intellectual energies and responses, your ways of seeing things and describing them, your ways of making appeals and claims and arguments, the very workings of your mind and the feelings of your heart. When you represent an unjust client, you are in the position of actually wanting an unjust result. And what do you get in return? A prostitute's pay. Like other flatterers you tend to become like the object of your flattery, but since you have so many and various objects of attention, what you really give yourself is the character of none but that of the chameleon, who appears to be whatever suits the moment—like Odysseus in the *Philoctetes*, say. And like him, in your trade you lose yourself.

Well, Euerges, what do you say of my speech? Is it fair or not? I speak not of you, of course, but of those lawyers who serve a client's wants rather than his interests.

Euerges: Of course it is not fair, Socrates, but idiotic. What you do not understand is that the lawyer does not operate alone, but as a part of a community of lawyers and judges, as one component in a larger system. Since the aim of that system is to do justice, it is justice that the lawyer ultimately serves, even such a one as you describe. Of course he wants to make a good living, and of course he wants his client to prevail—that is part of his function in the system—but above these wants is a larger intention, that of serving justice itself. And our adversarial, individualistic, and pluralistic system, although undoubtedly imperfect, has been shown by experience to be the best system for achieving justice yet devised in our imperfect world.

Socrates: I am full of questions about the remarkable claim you have just made—How do you know that this system produces justice? What kind of justice is it? What kind of experience teaches you this? and so on—but I will put these questions aside for the moment to continue with what we were talking about. For even if it were agreed that the "system" does what you claim, that would only justify the sacrifice of character made by the lawyer, not deny it. He would still subject himself to the same deformities of mind and feeling; the only difference would be that he could say that it was all in a good cause, as a soldier might say who died a horrible death for his country. But the self-inflicted deformity would still be there.

Suppose, for example, that you represented a white man in a dispute with a black man, that your client was in the right, and that the judge and jury who were to hear the case were white racists. Your appeals to their bigotry, whether explicit or implicit, whether expressed in words or silence or shrugs or looks or tones of voice, would be in the "cause of justice" in the sense that you mean, but they would still deform both you and your audience, polluting both the process and the community. Argument of this kind can never be truly in the cause of justice, as argument based on falsity can never be in the cause of truth, yet your duty, as you call it, requires you to make arguments that are unjust and false, at least in the sense that they do not represent what you believe justice and truth to require. And you must do this not merely where your client is right, as in the example I have given, but where he is wrong as well.

Euerges: Socrates, you are speaking as if we had made no progress at all since the fifth century, as if the modern lawyer really were like the ancient rhetorician and subject to no constraints of law and custom, indeed, as if there were no substance to the rules he applies and follows and argues about. Actually, doing lawyer's work is a discipline in responsibility and truth. In the first place, there are ethical limits upon the way he can argue: he may not misrepresent either the facts of the case or the law, and he may make only those appeals that are legitimized by our system. Appeals to bigotry and the like, then, are out. And while there is of course some leeway in the interpretation of legal doctrines, they are by no means infinitely pliable—indeed, much of our time is spent applying plain rules with plain effects. This is one way the law is made real in the world. And although the rules that we apply are, like everything else in the world, imperfect, they are rooted in a democratic form of government; having the assent of the people, they are more likely to be just than any other rules. There is a sense, indeed, in which they are by definition just, for they are the product of the most just of all constitutions.

Socrates: But all this, even if I accept it, merely confines and limits the evil; it does not deny it. Your claim essentially is that you are a rhetorician in a good cause, or with good effects, but you remain a rhetorician, with all that that means. Suppose a similar claim were made, for example, by a historian, who said that she did not try to write what she thought was true, but what would most favor a particular person or group or party: every statement of fact, every term of evaluation, was chosen and placed to serve such ends. Suppose further that she were to justify this practice by saying that it was what everyone does, and that experience has shown that what she calls "advocate's history"—and what you and I would call propaganda—produces a more complete and accurate version of the truth than any other kind. Would you have respect for such a historian, and for such history, or contempt? Would you want to be such a historian or want your child to become one? And it would not matter much if there were some ethical limits on the degree to which one could shade things, for the historian would still be a shader of truth, a propagandist, not a historian.

One cannot be a propagandist in the service of truth or an advocate in the service of justice, for the character and the motives are wrong. And character and motive are for these purposes everything, for "truth" and "justice" are not abstract absolutes, to be attained or not in materially measurable ways; these are words that define shared motives out of which a community and a culture can be built and a character made for the individual and his world. They express an attitude, imply a process, and promise a community.

The true historian, who tells the truth as well as she can, exposes herself to refutation: if she is shown to be wrong, it is she who is wrong, and it is she who learns from the refutation. She has a self in the world that can teach and can learn. But the lawyer, or such a rhetorical historian as I describe, can never be refuted, but only beaten. Like Sophocles' Odysseus, he has no self in a world of others.

And is not something like this true even of you, Euerges, when you move from working out with your clients what their true interests require to representing their interests at law? Then you, too, must speak the legal language according to legal conventions: you become an accomplished shader of the truth, and give yourself the facile and shifting mind of the lawyer. Or do you simply say to other lawyers and to judges what you honestly believe that justice requires?

Euphemes: Of course he doesn't do that, Socrates, and neither do I. And I should also say that unlike Euerges I do not spend time with my clients trying to determine what you at least would call their true interests. Of course I do go over and over their problems with them, trying to help them figure out what they want to do, and I will suggest considerations and questions and facts they seem to have left out. But their decision, if it is legal, is final with me. The most I do is to help them organize their affairs in ways that will suit them in the long as well as the short run. I also have to say that I have no faith that our system of justice has been proven by experience to be the best possible one. I'm not sure what Euerges means when he speaks of our "system" or says that justice is its "end," and I don't know whose experience he is talking about, whom it teaches, how it teaches, or what it teaches. As for the rules and principles of law that we apply and argue about, I certainly do not think they are the perfection of justice: some of them seem to be right, others pointless or wasteful, some of them seriously evil. Nor do I think that their origins in our version of a democratic system of government entitle them to automatic veneration. Euerges justifies the activities of his life not in their own terms but by claiming that they are part of a larger system, which has been shown by experience to be the best possible one. But I do not share his faith in the perfection of our legal system, whether it is measured by results achieved or standards applied, and I dare say no one else does either who is not forced to such a position by his choice of profession.

Moreover, I know I do not represent only the noble and the good. Most of my clients are good enough in an ordinary way, but basically unthinking and rather selfish; some are in my view pretty despicable people engaged in pretty despicable enterprises. I help them not only when I think they are in the right, but when I think they are in the wrong, so long as they are not legally wrong or so morally wrong as to be intolerable. In many of the cases I have litigated I am inclined to believe that justice was on the other side, though I have not really asked myself that question in a disciplined way.

In our arguments, whether made to judge and jury at trial or to other lawyers in negotiation, we do not say what we believe justice requires but whatever we think will persuade our audience, subject only to the ethical constraints already mentioned by Euerges. And I have to say that while these constraints to some degree civilize the process, they do not change its fundamental nature. Indeed they permit, and may even be thought to require, a lawyer to discredit witnesses whom he knows to be telling the truth and to suggest false inferences that may plausibly be drawn from true facts, and they give at least some play to motives of bigotry and prejudice of various kinds.

I said before that I do not spend time with my clients trying to determine their true interests, and I acknowledge that sometimes they, and others, are injured by the increase in power they get through my successes. Moreover, I agree that this is important, for it is a question of who they are and who they become. I also think it is important what kind of person I am and what sort of community I help to constitute, and I know that to make myself a lawyer is to give myself a mind of a certain character or cast, and that this is in large measure determined by what happens in argument. But I would describe these things somewhat differently from you and Euerges.

Notwithstanding what you may take to be the implications of what I have just said, I do not think that to practice law is to deform the self. In fact, the character of the trustworthy lawyer seems to me thoroughly admirable, difficult to attain, and, what may surprise you most, to be acquired not in spite of his daily work in the law, but in large measure because of it, by virtue of its discipline and experience. Of course there are really bad people in the law, as in every profession, and perhaps very few people, or even none, fully attain the possibilities I mean to point to with the phrase "trustworthy lawyer." But my point, like yours, has to do with the tendency of the practice of the profession, and I think that its tendency is not to injure but to improve the character, and that it offers possibilities in this respect that most other ways of living lack. I should add that I do not think that this tendency is much affected by the nature of one's clientele, nor even by the substantive rules with which one must deal, but that it is greatly affected by the nature of the ethical community that one establishes both with one's clients and with other lawyers and judges.

I think you and Euerges have simply misunderstood the enterprise in which lawyers are engaged. I would put it this way: in our professional lives we lawyers preserve and improve a language of description, value, and reason—a culture of argument—without which it would be impossible even to ask the questions that you think are most important, questions about the nature of justice in general or about what is required in a particular case. This is because "doing justice," "arguing about justice," and "deciding what justice requires" are never wholly abstract activities, but are always culturally conditioned. They are ways of doing things with preexisting materials and expectations, just as "doing music" and "doing architecture" are; what we lawyers do is to maintain the materials essential to these cultural activities and the conventions and understandings that made them possible.

The first essential resource for the activity of talking about what justice requires is a language in which the social world can be constituted and described, so that a story can be told and an issue stated. At the simplest level we need words to describe the various parties, their situations, and their motives before we can even state a question about what justice requires in a particular case. Similarly, we need procedures and understandings to regulate our talk, such as conventions about representation, the order of speech in the court or assembly, and the like. And we need as well a preexisting language of right and wrong, of expectation and prohibition—rules and maxims and proverbs and stories, and, perhaps, cases—before we can go to work.

Let me try to make this point by using an example familiar to you, Socrates. If I remember my undergraduate reading correctly, the *Iliad* begins with a dispute that arises when Agamemnon is forced to give up his prize girl to her father, the priest of Apollo, after Agamemnon originally refused the ransom request for her. Achilles and Agamemnon divide over whether Agamemnon should bear the loss alone, or whether the community of warriors should in some way make it up to him. Now one could not accurately state the questions presented by this situation, let alone think about what right and justice require here, without words to describe the prize girl, her father the priest, the ransom, and the warriors and their chief. And not just any words will do—think how weakly the English words given above permit one to understand these actors and events; we need the Homeric words themselves, the language that defines the social world and the values that give particular meaning to the dispute. Only in the language of this culture can argument proceed about the issue of justice that has arisen with it.

You yourself, Socrates, show that you know that we need a language of social fact and value, for you invite your auditors not to a languageless looking at the eternal essence of justice, but to a taking apart and putting together of the materials of existing culture, a reconstitution of language in a community of two to which all your loyalties extend. What we lawyers do is both similar and different: in working on our cases we constantly test our language against new facts and circumstances, against its own hidden or overt tensions, against common experience and new formulations, and in this sense we can be said to take it repeatedly apart and put it together again. But our loyalties extend beyond the community of individuals with whom we talk to our legal world, indeed to our culture as a whole.

The object of our work is not to make a new language, good only for two interlocutors, as yours is, but to leave the language we have remade in a condition fit for use by others. It is in fact our method of argument, which you deplore, that enables us to do this, for as we articulate our points of disagreement in a particular case, at the same time we necessarily perform an agreement with the rest of the language in which our disagreement is stated and our arguments framed. In order to assert our differences on some points, that is, we must acquiesce in the language we use to make these differences intelligible and meaningful. The effect of this is to convert the raw human materials of greed and fear and the desire for power, and the like, into questions presented in the language that we maintain. Our work is what makes possible the connections between one case and another, between past and present, that constitute this branch of our civilization.

I say that we not only maintain but improve our language, and in one sense I am sure I am right. For this process ensures, as nothing else could, that congruence between the terms and assumptions of our language and the conditions of social and natural reality which is essential to the survival of a language of justice and the culture it enacts. But we also improve it in another way, I think, for the law as I describe it becomes a repository of shared experiences, a set of experiments and trials and failures, which are by the law made intelligible and sharable. This is a culture of experience and experiment; it is a way of giving experience to ourselves, individually and collectively, the experience of making and remaking language under pressure. For in the law, our language of facts and law is constantly being tested against the real world, against common sentiment, against cases and argument, and being remade in light of what is discovered. This means that the law is a way in which the community defines itself, not once and for all, but over and over, and in the process it educates itself about its own character and the nature of the world. The limits of our minds and imaginations are reached and tested, and a new step is taken. That is what the law is about. The lawyer is not a dialectician, but neither is a poet or an architect, and as is true of them, the meaning and pleasure of the lawyer's life arises from the participation in making and remaking a world of shared significance.

What this view of the law means about the ethics of legal argument is this. First, while I am in a sense "insincere" when I say to a judge, for example, that "justice requires" or the "law requires" such and such result, this insincerity is a highly artificial one, for no one is deceived by it. No one in the courtroom would be surprised to learn that this is a form of argument and not a statement of personal belief. But at the same time I am implicitly saying something else, with respect to which I am by any standard being sincere: that the argument I make is the best one that my capacities and resources permit me to make on this side of the case. This is a statement made by performance rather than in explicit conceptual terms, and it is a statement not about the nature of "justice," but about the nature of the resources our legal culture affords for defending or attacking a particular result. But it is a statement honestly made.

In making this statement the lawyer's audience is the judge, and we serve her directly not by telling her what we actually think she ought to do, but by showing her something about the nature of her own situation in our culture. Together, the arguments of the two lawyers define the boundaries within which the judge operates by showing what even these parties, opposed as they are, must agree to, and they tell her what topics the culture requires her to face and deal with. Our arguments also provide her with a testing ground for her own thoughts. As the judge thinks through the case, at first inclined one way, then the other, she will take up the opposing arguments, oral or written, to learn what she has not yet dealt with in her own thinking and what she has. The briefs and arguments help her think her way into a problem and provide a kind of checklist to tell her when she has thought all the way through it. And there is room for art and invention, too. We tell the judge truthfully not that we think a judgment for our client is the best result—that conclusion is determined by our role—but that the formulations we offer are the best version of our discourse in support of this result that we can find or make.

This kind of rhetoric, despite what you claim, leads to a kind of knowledge and not to mere belief—knowledge about the ways in which the materials of persuasion in our culture can be mobilized. The "trustworthy" lawyer of whom I speak is one who can be trusted to perform this task honestly and intelligently, making the best case he can in light of what can most persuasively and fairly be said on the other side. It is the incompetent or sleazy lawyer who misrepresents or fudges the nature of the material, and his work is of little assistance to anyone. Though on one occasion or another he may prevail through the confusion he creates, over the long run he will fail, in part because those to whom he speaks will see what he is doing. The competent lawyer is by nature trustworthy in the sense I describe, for trustworthiness is essential to his professional standing and success, not only in the long run but in the short run too. It is not too much to say that in his presentation of the best case that can be made in the circumstances, the good lawyer loves to tell the truth.

I have said that the judge is our ultimate audience, and this is true even in negotiating transactions and planning a client's affairs, for the judge is the final authority to whom recourse may ultimately be taken. And although it is true, as you say, that the persuader becomes like the object of his persuasion, it is our practice to address the judge not as the bundle of biases and feelings and predispositions and ideas that she in some sense is, but as if she were an ideal judge. It is what the best judge we can imagine would want to hear and know that we try to provide. (The practice of speaking to the best in the judge we address is in fact enforced by considerations of prudence, for to be caught addressing her any other way is obviously very dangerous indeed.) Thus while at first there may seem to be a huge difference between the justice-loving judge and the advocate who merely wants his client to win, in fact the mind of the advocate is deeply formed by his own conception of what the best judge would be and what she would want to know: it is to an ideal partly of his own making that he gives what you call the attentions of a lover. To do this is not to injure but to improve the self; it is very close to what you mean, Socrates, when you speak of your devotion to philosophy.

This is a way of justifying the lawyer's life by understanding the process of which his activities form a part, as Euerges' was too. But unlike his justification, mine does not depend upon a faith that the substantive rules we work with are the best of all possible rules, or even that they are substantially just. Nor does it claim that our particular procedures for inquiring about and deciding questions of justice are most likely to lead to results that are just. In fact, the justification I advance would support the activity of being a lawyer in almost any legal system, however unjust its rules might be on the merits, for the lawyer's task will always be to make the best case he can out of the materials of his culture in addressing an ideal judge. By its very nature, this is to improve his materials, both by ensuring their congruence with the world of facts outside the law and by moving them toward greater coherence, fairness, and the like.

Socrates: So it may be, Euphemes, but have you not simply substituted one faith for another? Euerges has a faith that the present legal system, as measured by its rules and results, is the best one possible; you have a faith in your capacity to make arguments the tendency of which will always be to improve rather than to damage the culture you have inherited. But upon what does your faith rest? May it not happen, for example, that your particular audience, say your judge, will be persuadable by distinctions and appeals that are, in your view, not better but worse? And in such a case you will make those arguments, for they are what will work, and in doing so you will contribute not to the improvement but to the degeneration of the discourse. Is this not so?

As I understand your claim, it is like that of an artist. You are like the musical composer who makes the best kind of music that can be made, or that he can make, out of the cultural and physical materials available to him. By "materials" I mean the musical instruments on the one hand and the expectations that people bring to musical performance on the other, for it is with both of these that the composer must work. (Indeed, every artist makes his artifact partly out of the materials of nature—stones, bricks, sounds—and partly out of the materials of culture—those expectations that define his audience and enable him to surprise, to please, and to instruct them.) These expectations form a kind of language through which, and only through which, his work can be intelligible. We do not praise or blame the artist for the nature of his materials, of either kind, but only for what he does with them, and the same can be said of the lawyer, and perhaps of the judge as well.

Thus the musical artist—and the same is true of the architect as well, and perhaps of the painter or dramatist—does not collapse into his culture, as Euerges did, when he appealed to the supposed perfection of the system and the respect due to the products of a democratic society, and so forth, but in some measure breaks himself out of his culture, distancing himself from it by claiming to maintain and improve it. The artist, and according to you the lawyer, thus assimilates himself not to the culture as it is, but to his own ideal version of it, and to the processes by which he attempts to make and remake it in that image.

But how can this be so? Where the conventions of the art are not beautiful but ugly, will the work of the artist not be ugly too? And where do the standards by which he establishes his ideal come from? Are they not also formed by the musical or legal culture itself, with all of its defects? Either as a lawyer or musician, then, how can you have any confidence that the changes you make are true improvements, that the ideal to which you assimilate yourself is a proper one? The questions of beauty and justice are in the end the most important ones, and for them rhetoric is plainly useless: only dialectic will suffice.

Euphemes: You state my claim well enough, Socrates, but you evaluate it wrongly, in part because you evaluate dialectic itself wrongly. Of course I do not "know" that my arguments are improvements or that my conception of the ideal judge is best, and of course these are important questions. But you do not know these things either, and what we are really talking about is how such questions ought to be addressed, which is itself another version of the question we have been asking from the beginning: how ought we to lead our lives? The first claim I have been making is not that I do the best possible work with my materials—that is the kind of claim Euerges makes for the "system"—but that this is what I strive for. It is a question of aim and motive, as is proper when the issue is how we should lead our lives.

I also make a second claim about our method, especially as compared with dialectic. For the questions you have asked me—whether the particular argument improves the culture, or the particular conception of the ideal judge is a proper one—dialectic is valueless, because in dialectic you confine your responsibilities to yourself and one other; you remake your language and community on the scale of two. For these questions, dialectic can produce no answer at all, because the questions themselves presuppose a larger world, in which alone they can have meaning. The answers must be good not only for the two of us, but for our whole community, for the others who act in our universe and speak our language. To say, as you do, that it is never good to have any relationship with any person that has any object other than discovering what is ultimately good for each of those two would in fact mean the end of culture; the lawyer is one whose aim it is to maintain and improve the culture that makes possible a larger life, in a larger world.

Socrates: Let us put aside for the moment what you say about dialectic, for you still have not answered my question about what you yourself do. How can you claim to be constantly improving your discourse and culture? Suppose for example that in a particular legal system the ideals to which appeals can be made, the materials for the "best case," are vicious ones? You will then move the discourse in the direction of vicious ideals rather than just ones, will you not? And once you concede that this is so, you will have to tell me how you can possibly know that your own culture is not one of the vicious ones. When you do, you will engage in dialectic, not rhetoric.

Euphemes: To start with, I do have to say that I am not sure that it is a good thing to be a lawyer in any imaginable culture. There is always the possibility that a culture is so horrible that it should be destroyed rather than improved, that one must become an enemy of the political system in order to be a friend to the nation. But I do mean to suggest how that question ought to be thought about, and I think my answer may lead as well to a response to your question about standards and ideals.

In deciding whether we ought to be lawyers in a particular legal culture, we ought to ask not whether there is injustice there, or even serious injustice, for these will be part of any culture. Instead, we should ask about the materials for argument the culture makes available. Does this culture afford the materials with which one can appeal to its better side, establishing and reinforcing standards and values that are incompatible with its evils, and thus counteract them? Think for example of the lawyer in South Africa and the importance of his continually affirming the aspects of that tradition that honor individual autonomy and liberty, that respect each person as an individual, and that are thus wholly incompatible with the country's racist laws. Or think of a lawyer in a Soviet satellite state affirming the principles of legality with which the Party sometimes, but not always, interferes. Or of a lawyer in America appealing to our traditional ideal of equality to correct the hideous inequalities, especially racial inequalities, with which we live. The question for the lawyer is not, does my system achieve justice, but rather, does it afford materials for idealization that, when mobilized by lawyers on both sides of a case, will tend to improve the culture itself? This view corresponds with the common feeling that it is of great importance to have conscientious and high-minded lawyers in regimes that are illegal or corrupt.

Will the answer ever be that the culture must be abandoned? I am not sure it will, for the very act of speaking about justice in a particular case on behalf of one of the parties always affirms the possibility of justice under law, and it necessarily entails, even if it also frustrates, the process of idealization of which I speak. Such speech also makes real an essential equality between the speakers, if only for a moment; and it affirms the practice of reasoned judgment, and that entails certain ethical consequences as well. It may indeed be that it is good to be a lawyer *whenever* one can speak for another and sincerely make the best case that one's materials afford.

This is also, as you can see, a partial answer to your question about my faith in the improvements to be worked by law. Some elements of what we mean by justice are not complex but simple, and the practice of law as I have defined it continually affirms these: the values of equality, of reason, and of the very idea of appealing to right and justice against brute power. I have described the process of idealization that is involved in legal argument, and I think it is part of all legal argument: if an argument lacked that quality, it would no longer be legal, but purely instrumental or expedient. While it is true that some of the particular ideals appealed to may be undesirable or ugly, it is better that the practice itself should exist than that it should not. Indeed, as I said before, only if it does exist can one seriously ask the question that ultimately concerns you, namely, what ideals we ought to pursue.

All this assumes, as you point out, that the lawyer has standards and ideals by which to judge the possibilities for expression and action that a particular culture makes available to him. This returns us to the questions where these standards and ideals come from, how they are to be tested and explained and defended, and so on.

It is implicit in what I have said that at a certain level these things are easy enough, for some injustices are plain and brutal enough to be self-evident to anyone. At this level what we mean by justice is a community that maintains the minimal standards of the rule of law. It is better to have a hearing than no hearing, better to have a tribunal that claims obedience to authorities external to its will than no such tribunal, and so on. As for more complicated issues of justice—the right result in a particular case, for example, or in a particular class of cases, or the proper standards of distributive justice—the question for both of us is not whose answers are right, for neither of us has answers, but how to go about living and thinking in the conditions of uncertainty in which we find ourselves. With respect to these questions, what we mean by justice is a community of a certain sort, a community that proceeds to examine and talk about and decide these questions in a promising way. What really divides us is how to judge the lawyer's way of doing these things.

Here I must return to my earlier claims that the activity of talking about justice requires the existence of a language in which factual and moral problems can be coherently and meaningfully stated and that what we lawyers do is to maintain that language in a condition in which it can be used for those purposes by ourselves and others.

What do I mean by a "condition in which it can be used"? To start with, a language of justice must have within it room for claims both of expediency or self-interest on the one hand, and of justice or virtue on the other, if it is to have a life in the world. You showed that you know this in your famous conversation with Callicles when you showed that his attempts to strip his value words of all but their selfish meanings were doomed to failure, leading to intolerable intellectual and moral confusion. The attempt to use a purely pragmatic language, and to reject the limits imposed by a language of justice, destroys one's capacity to reason sensibly and to function coherently. Indeed, it destroys the very idea of a self upon which the language of selfishness itself depends.

But the converse of this is also true: to strip a language of justice of its congruence with actual facts and sentiments, with the felt needs of those who use it, is to strip it of any force in the world. And this is what you do. You find an intolerable conflict within the central value terms of your own Greek language (*agathos, kalos,* and the like) and seek to strip them of those elements of meaning that reflect the competitive or success-oriented culture in which they had their origins. But when you do that you make a language that is "paradoxical," impossible for others to speak.

The function of the law is to maintain a language that keeps alive this very tension between fact and ideal, expediency and justice, self and other; this tension is in fact essential to the practice of talking about what justice requires. You can see this tension in my own defense of law: when I say that the lawyer makes the "best case" that can be made in the circumstances, does that mean the case that is most persuasive or most just? You would draw a sharp line between them; I would not say that they are the same, but I would say that the answer to that question is always, or almost always, unclear. For to be the "most just" argument it must be a workable one; to be workable, it must be just, at least in the sense that it must maintain the possibility, essential to the existence of self and community, of appealing to ideals that limit the will.

In other words, it is the object of our work to ensure that the language of the law has both the congruence with reality and the element of aspiration that are together essential to any meaningful talk about what justice requires in an actual community. As for the improving character of a particular argument, that is a matter that must be examined in the context of a particular discourse and a particular case; what we do is to establish the conditions and means for that examination. We cannot guarantee the results, but no one can do that. What we can do is justify the practices that make possible thought about justice of a kind that is at once realistic and idealistic.

In the process that I describe, the law converts the raw materials of human nature and conflict into another form of life and language, into argument about justice. This conversion is in fact what marks us as human beings, for it is this above all upon which the life of the polis, of human community itself, depends. Indeed, what is true of the city is true of the self as well: both for the lawyer and for his client, the passions of ambition and conquest and competition are put to work in the service of a larger enterprise, the practice of arguing about what justice requires, without which we would have no city at all, no community, and no philosophy.

The mind the lawyer gives himself is one that loves this process of conversion and translation: the making of a certain kind of conversation and the maintenance of the conditions upon which it can proceed. You should understand the pleasure and meaning of such a life, Socrates, if anyone can.

Socrates: But even if all that you say is true, Euphemes, none of it justifies what you do when you present evidence and argue about the facts, as opposed to engaging in the sort of argument about the law that you have been discussing. Surely making the "best case" on the facts has a different ethical meaning from making the best case that the resources of the law permit you to make on a question of standards or norms. How can you possibly call yourself a friend to the jury when you cross-examine with great skill a witness you know to be telling the truth, or ask them to draw plausible but erroneous inferences from true facts? Whatever may be the case with respect to the judge, then, with respect to the jury you are a pure rhetorician with all that that means: the flattering pleaser and deceiver. Is that not so?

Euphemes: Certainly not in the way you claim, Socrates. It is true that there are important and problematic differences between argument about the law and argument about facts, and I will say something in a moment both about the nature of these difficulties and about what it means to address them correctly. But first I need to correct your assumption that the lawyer will—that he professionally should—do whatever the law permits him to do on behalf of his client. Although some lawyers of course take that attitude, not all do so, and you and I have agreed that our subject is not the ethical quality of the majority of those who actually engage in the practice of law (though that is an interesting question) but the ethical possibilities of the profession.

Let us take the cross-examination of the truthful witness. To some degree what I said about judicial argument also obtains here, for the jury knows that each lawyer is trying to present his case in its strongest light, and the combined efforts of the lawyers do in fact aid the jury in its decision of the case as a whole, for they now know the most that can legitimately be claimed on each side. And in both cases there is a similar duty not to mischaracterize the law or the facts. But you are quite right that there is a critical difference between the two kinds of argument as well, for the judge or other lawyer can effectively check and challenge your characterizations of law, since all have access to the same material, but with respect to the facts some of what you know is simply not available to the other side. This means that the lawyer must indeed take special care in making factual claims, and many lawyers do so. Although it is true that the law would permit the savage cross-examination of a truth-telling witness, that does not mean that every lawyer would do it, or should do it.

Socrates: How can that be? Do not your conventions of argument require you to do for your client whatever the law permits you to do?

Euphemes: No, of course not! That is just what I am trying to tell you. Although most lawyers would be reluctant to admit it even to themselves, different lawyers would respond quite differently to the cross-examination question: some would cross-examine as rigorously as they could, others more softly; some might in fact not cross-examine at all but concede the factual point being made.

Socrates: But how could a lawyer justify to his client any course of action other than the first?

Euphemes: The process of justification would begin with the beginning of their relationship, when the lawyer let the client know that although he had employed her professional skill, he had not obtained the right to dictate how that skill should be exercised. This can be made clear by explicit statement, something like this: "If you want my services you must understand that I observe what I regard as the decencies of life in my relations to other lawyers and parties and witnesses. I will not treat you shabbily; do not expect me to treat others so. I will not be your mouthpiece, but your lawyer." That is, of course, rather pompous, and in many contexts a lawyer would feel that she could establish the essential point implicitly rather than explicitly— by the way she dealt with the client and spoke about the other lawyer, the other party, and the process itself. This kind of statement is not only possible; it is far more common than most people, including most lawyers, are actually aware. Think how often a lawyer refuses to take advantage of a procedural default, for example, or how often, at least in certain branches of the practice—divorce comes particularly to mind—the lawyers on both sides refuse, despite great pressure from their clients, to engage in childish and vindictive litigation.

If challenged, the lawyer could explain her position on two grounds. The first, suggested above, is contractual: this is what I offer you, and you have the right to reject it and go elsewhere. The second is more difficult to talk about, but if anything is even more important; it is ethical in the fullest sense of the term, and also from another point of view strategic. The lawyer might say something like this:

> In the next several months I will repeatedly be speaking on
> your behalf to a wide range of audiences: the other lawyer, the
> judge, the jury, witnesses, other officials, and so on. I want
> these audiences to take seriously what I have to say. I am not a

chameleon or an actor but a single person, and my capacity to
ask them to listen to me in the way I want them to, on the merits of the questions I discuss, is in large part a function of my
sense of myself. If I were habitually sleazy and manipulative,
signs of that would appear and make me less effective as a
speaker for you; if I were habitually ethical but occasionally
sleazy, I am sure that my discomfort would be less than completely hidden. I can hardly exaggerate the importance of what
I am saying: what the Greeks called the "ethos" or character of
the speaker is among the most powerful sources of persuasion.
In any case in which I act, my own sense that I am speaking
properly, asking for what I am entitled to ask for, functioning
out of a sense of fairness, is essential to my ethos and therefore
to my success. And for success in two ways: not only in the material sense of gaining so many dollars by settlement or trial,
but in the much larger sense of helping you to give this difficulty a meaning that is most valuable and appropriate to you.

Let me give you a couple of examples of what such a lawyer would
mean. Often a particular dispute is one of a series of matters with
respect to which the parties must deal with one another. In such
cases proper management of one dispute will lead to quicker and
easier resolution of others, and to the establishment of relations outside the adversarial context that are of real value, economic and otherwise. This is in fact the case whenever there are continuing relations, by reason of commercial connection, common children, or
even residence in the same community.

Even when one puts such considerations aside, there is the question of the meaning of the result in the particular case for this client.
What kind of victory does he really want? Here it is a great mistake
to assume, as many people do, that clients naturally want victory at
any cost, including that of unscrupulous behavior from their lawyers.
Some do, of course, no doubt about it, but others realize that such an
attitude is childish, impractical, and inconsistent with their basic
sense of themselves. Many clients in fact want what they are entitled
to and no more, and welcome the opportunity to deal with a lawyer
who respects the decencies of life, as they themselves do. And they
know in addition that the lawyer who is a shyster to others will often
be a shyster to his client. They know that they can have little confidence in the judgment, knowledge, or skills of such a person.

All this, of course, does not answer the next question, which is
how you decide what the decencies of professional life are and what

practices are beneath you. On such questions categorical rules are of little help, and they must be thought through on the merits each time, or rather, since they arise continually, in surprising ways, and without notice, they must be instinctively responded to by the character that the lawyer has gradually given himself over time by his habits of ethical reflection and action.

My point is not to make the ethical dilemmas of the lawyer's life seem to disappear, but to establish that the lawyer is free to address them as true ethical issues for which he is responsible. Indeed, so far am I from denying the intractable difficulties of the lawyer's ethical life, I would say that they are an important merit of it. Every day the lawyer faces questions of right and wrong that have no ready answer, no authoritative resolution, and this means that his professional life offers opportunities for the building of a character that less problematic lives would lack.

It is true that in our relations with our clients we do fall short of the standards you would have us meet, in that we do not engage our clients in a dialectical investigation of what their best interests really require; in a sense we use them, and their desires, as the material of our art. But it is a corollary to what I have just said about the lawyer's ethical responsibilities that there are important senses in which this relationship, at least in its ideal form, is one of friendship, for it constantly presents the questions, to both of us, how we should behave and who we should be; it involves mutual education and respect and is based upon honesty. As Euerges said, in leaving certain questions of choice to the client the lawyer respects her autonomy; likewise, in reserving some to himself, the lawyer insists upon his own autonomy, and this reservation is a valuable form of teaching. And the lawyer is constantly forcing upon the client new understandings of the nature of the world in which she lives and of her situation within it, either showing her the limits that reality places upon her desires or expanding her sense of what is possible, and he is himself always learning about these things too. On these matters everyone needs continual teaching.[1] And *any* lawyer will tell you that compared with

---

1. The fact that the lawyer finds himself taking now one side, now another, without much regard for his predisposition, is in fact an important source of education for him. It teaches him how much can be said for positions with which he is originally inclined to disagree. For this reason it is a great mistake to think, as some do, that the law professor is somehow freer or better than the lawyer. The danger for the professor is that one will spend one's life writing articles or books that are really little more than a series of briefs all on the side of one's own unexamined biases and attitudes, something a lawyer can almost never do.

at least some of his clients, his role is to insist upon the truth, upon the facts that cannot be wished away. The lawyer is not only a fiction-maker, but a truth-speaker.

And one other thing: the good lawyer is faithful to the obligations he has assumed, to the client and to the law, and there is at once a kind of virtue and a kind of education in that. When he gives advice to his client, makes an argument to the jury, or drafts an instrument, he is engaged in making the world in which others live, and at every moment he is subject to obligations to others and to the law. His advice must be based upon a fair and accurate assessment of a situation; his argument must be punctiliously truthful in every statement of fact; his drafting must meet the needs of those whose life it will affect. A lawyer's life is a constant assumption of responsibility to others, and no one can have contempt for that. I might sum up what I have said by saying that in his relations both with his culture and with his client, the lawyer leads a life that at once requires and makes possible that he have an education of the fullest sort, and, if he takes his responsibilities seriously, he can offer such an education to others. Unlike the life of Callicles, Socrates, that is not a life "worthy of no one," but a life worthy of anyone.

This is one possible set of responses to the challenge that the *Gorgias* makes to the modern lawyer. For obvious reasons—an openness to refutation—I think it important to say that this is the best response that I can make. The reader may, of course, find it unsatisfactory, perhaps especially in its account of the relations between client and lawyer and its version of what it means to give oneself the mind of the brief-writer and case-maker.

What Plato teaches us in the end is that we cannot help speaking a language that is made by others, yet forms our mind; that we are responsible for how we speak and who we are; that self-conscious thought on these questions is among the most important tasks of a mature mind (or people); and that to establish a place of our own making from which cultural and ethical criticism can go on is essential to responsible life. We cannot escape the fact that whenever we speak, we redefine for the moment the resources of our culture and in doing so establish a character for ourselves and a relation with another, the person to whom we speak. Who shall we be? What relation shall we have with others? These are the central questions of human life, and they are present with special force and clarity in the life of the lawyer.

AFTERWORD

LAW AS LAW

My aim in these essays has not been to set forth a conceptual or analytic system, a theoretical model of the law or of rhetoric or of poetry, but to talk my way through a set of questions in a way that exemplifies the view of life and language that lies at the heart of my work. I have proceeded in large part by analogy, by thinking of one thing in terms of another, and as I say at the outset I think it important not to let go of that resource. But at the end of such a book as this it may be useful if I say something, in addition to what I have said in various ways in the body of these essays, about what distinguishes law from the other rhetorical and poetic arts I have discussed.

Some would argue that the main difference is that law is about power, state power, and that the compositions made in the law thus have an importance or consequence of a kind that the poet's or dramatist's or historian's or philosopher's compositions do not. In a sense that is of course true, and the fact that the ultimate legal composition has coercive consequences for others creates pressures in legal discourse—towards objectivity, towards a pretense of total expressibility, total comprehensibility, and so forth—that are less apparent in some other fields. But this point can be exaggerated. It does nothing to undercut my basic view that law is at heart a compositional process, albeit of a distinctive kind; and it greatly overstates the connection between law and power. In some eras—parts of the middle ages come to mind—highly elaborated legal systems were at work whose power to impose results was most doubtful. (Modern international law is another example.) And poetry and history can have great practical power; the burning wit of the skald was feared by Irish and Norse kings as more terrible than the sword; today's poets, the propagandists of Washington and Madison Avenue, have enormous power over the imaginations of our world; and history can have the deepest political consequences. The real power of the army and the police is all too often unresponsive to any law. Law is after all not the only way of constituting and exercising power; and it has the great virtue of limiting what it grants.

What is most deeply distinctive about law, or at least about our law, is I think in fact buried in that last observation, and I would reduce it to two main features: the separation of powers and the obligation to explain (and to explain in a certain way). Both are ways in which the law limits the power it creates. What I mean by the separation of powers is a more general version of the point made in "The Invisible Discourse of the Law," that all lawyers think procedurally: whenever a substantive question is presented, the lawyer asks not only how it should be understood and answered but also by whom, under what authority, and by what procedures. Looked at from the point of view of an official actor, what this means is that he or she must always be asking at least two questions, both of which acknowledge the existence of authorities—of powers—external to the self: (1) Is this question one I am empowered to decide (is it within my jurisdiction)? (2) By what standards am I directed to decide it? What a constitution like ours means is that none of the actors it creates has the plenary power that only the Constitution itself, or "The People" in amending it, can exercise. Powers are separated, distributed, and with the distribution necessarily go standards of decision, more or less clearly framed, by which the powers granted are guided and limited. The legal actor is never merely a center of discretionary power; he or she is always, at least in form, a servant, or trustee.

The legal actor is thus always acknowledging that he or she is part of a community constituted by the law, in which other actors have equal or superior powers. This in turn means (as I suggested in "Rhetoric and Law" [Chapter 2]) that law can never be collapsed to policy science, the premise of which is that a unitary "we" (defined by the language of analysis) faces a "problem" to which various "solutions" are proposed, which can be analyzed and compared. That kind of talk may have value in one legal forum or another, but it can never be the whole story. What is distinctive about law is in fact the insistence that the "we" is not unitary but constituted and that no actor is ever entitled to speak for all of us.

The separation of powers also explains why the activity of interpretation is so central to law. Every legal conversation has at its center the questions: What are the texts that establish the standards by which jurisdiction is defined and regulated? and How should those texts be interpreted? To have a legal system without authoritative texts, as the Athenians very nearly did, is to unite all power in a single actor (in the Athenian case the jury) whose choices are not bound to respect any choices made by others.

In our own judicial system we have for a long time had a second feature, the obligation of the judicial actor to explain what he or she has done. Law is thus not only an interpretive but a compositional process, for the judge as well as for the lawyer, and the composition takes as its subject the disposition of a particular case. This means that its elements must include an assertion of jurisdiction (including an interpretation of the text granting jurisdiction); identification of the legal texts that speak with authority to the substantive question (including an explanation of why certain other texts are not authoritative); and interpretation of the texts so identified, whether they are constitutional provisions, statutes, or judicial opinions—all as applied to the story of a particular case, a narrative of the real world that has been told in different versions. The judge, that is, must make a composition justifying his or her decision and do so by reference not merely to general principles, abstract reasoning, or analysis of circumstance, but to what others, acting in their respective fields of jurisdiction, have said. This explanation, in turn, is meant not only to justify the judgment in terms of an authoritative past but to constitute an authority to be referred to in the future. In this sense the opinion is explicitly embedded in time, mediating between past and present.

The case to which the judge speaks is always a particular narrative, told originally by each of its actors in ordinary English. The task of the court is to make out of these materials a narrative of its own, cast partly in terms of legal conclusion, partly in terms open to more general understanding. The law thus serves as the language into which other languages, and stories told in them, are translated and in that way comprised into a single order. As we saw in the chapter on Gibbon's *History*, each of the stories, in ordinary English and the law alike, is necessarily fictional as well as factual, charged with value as well as objective, and the mind that makes the legal story must be prepared to face these difficulties.

From these facts flow remarkable opportunities for one who composes a judicial text (or addresses another who is to do so), for the judicial opinion has what might be called an archetypal structure, defined by certain basic tensions that the composer must address. These include tensions between the story, told as a narrative, and the legal categories into which it will be made to fit; between the universe of legal discourse and the universe that lies outside it (recognized both by silence and explicitly); between the individual voices of the judge, the lawyer, and the parties, and their institutional voices; between the two centers of life represented by the parties, brought together in the drama of the law; between the sense that one is "deciding facts" and the acknowledgment that all factual accounts are fictive; between the demand of justice in the individual case and the obligation to see one case as a member of a class of cases; between the desire and obligation to explain and the recognition that explanation is impossible. I said in "Reading Law and Reading Literature" that the hearing is the heart of the law, and that is true; but the hearing reaches its fullest significance only where it is coupled with the obligation to explain. Then the judicial opinion becomes a form with wonderful possibilities for meaning. It is a composition in which the speaker must choose a language for telling a story and justifying a result, and must do so against the reasonable claims of the losing side that he or she speak differently. In this sense it offers a perpetual training in the artificiality of culture and the responsibility for what we say and do. It is structurally multivocal, a system of translation that is open, in principle at least, in all directions. It is self-transforming. Since the opinion must make sense as a whole, the ultimate demand is one of integration. The instrument of integration is the voice—one's sense of self, of language, and of another. If one could strike a living balance among all these tensions and be attuned to all the conflicts one addressed, one would be making art of the highest kind, uniting in a single composition the concerns of truth, of beauty, and of justice.

Another word about law and power. It is true that the result of the legal process is a judgment that will be enforced by the state; that this power will be exercised on the basis of a language established and maintained by the legal community; that not everything can be said in this language, which thus becomes a coercive or imposed ideology. But it is also true that this language in principle is open to challenge at every point; that it is made by those who represent the interests of others; and that the very practice of a hearing has elements that enact a politics that can be seen as radically individualistic and indeed subversive of the claims of ideology and power. It is thus foolish to see the law simply as an instrument of oppression (though of course it often is oppressive): many of its practices are, or can become, instruments of liberation. If one turns from the ideal possibilities of legal discourse (which has been my concern throughout this book) to the realities of legal history and legal practice, I think it would be hard to find in our culture another engine of cultural and social criticism that could compare with the law for power, for decency, for correspondence with the facts, for willingness to modify itself, and so on.

In making this apology for law I do not mean to defend our practice of law. Quite the reverse: my aim has been to identify the ideal possibilities of the forms of speech and life we call the law so that they can be called upon as a ground upon which the criticism of what we and others do can rest. My account of the form of the judicial opinion, for example, is not a description of the opinions I read in the reports, but an expression of my sense of the possibilities of the form—never wholly achieved of course, by me or anyone else, but sometimes approximated in the best work, say, of Justice Harlan or of Justice Brandeis. And, even more obviously, my version of the possibilities of the legal hearing, structurally open to different voices, different languages, structurally committed to a recognition of the sense of limits—limits of language, of power, of word—is not a report of what I see in trial courts across the country, but an identification of the largely untapped power of this practice for achieving justice and criticizing our culture, a power that can be realized only as judges and lawyers come to accept more fully their individual responsibility for what they say and do and learn to make their official voices more fully their own.

INDEX

INDEX

Adkins, A. W. H., 26
Aeschylus. See *Oresteia*
Apology, practice defined by Elizabeth Bennet, 92
Areopagus, 176, 180
Argument. *See* Persuasion
Aristotle: conception of friendship, 5; definition of rhetoric, 31, 33; mentioned, 105–6
Art: Gibbon's conception of, as composition, 149–53; language of, in *Philoctetes*, 5; law as, 52–54, 223–28; reading as, 82–83, 107–38 passim; rhetoric as, 44–46. *See also* Composition; Gibbon, Edward, *History of Roman Empire*; Language; Meaning
Audience: criminal law reassures, 201; necessary to narrative, 172–73, 189–90. *See also* Reading
Austen, Jane: Fanny's question about the slave trade, 121; "manners" defined in *Mansfield Park*, 86; mentioned, 89, 94; reading in *Pride and Prejudice*, 92–93
Authenticity, as ethical standard for Neoptolemus, 9–10
Authority: of community of readers, 99–100; of literary and legal canon, 136–37
Autonomy: in law, 236–37; respect for, as central value, 25, 131

Bakhtin, M., heteroglossia, 116
Barfield, Owen, 106, 123
Beauty and justice, related by rhetoric, 228
Black, J. B., 165, 167
Blaming: the criminal law as a practice of, 192–212 passim; not an issue in Philoctetes' final story, 18; and sympathy, 207–9
Bond, H. L., 165, 167
Braudy, Leo, 166, 167
Brest, Paul, 105
Brett, Peter, 210, 212

Brooks, Cleanth, 105, 115
Bureaucracy: authoritarian politics of, 128; cost-benefit analysis and, 30; criminal law analyzed as a, 194–97; institutional purposes as standard of thought in, 214; justification for lawyer's life in terms of, 216–17, 221–23; materialism of, 42–43; as model for legal thinking, 30–31, 35; view of life as composition opposed to, 123–24; why it fails, 41–42. *See also* Art; Criminal law; Ends-means reasoning; Language; Meaning
Burke, Edmund, on "toleration," 84–85; mentioned, 86, 89, 94, 133
Buxton, R. G. A., 26

Canon, authority of, in law and literature, 111, 136–37
Case method: as apprenticeship, 54; described, 49, 51, 110–11
Character: conflict in, not resolvable by compromise or alternation, 198–99, 201–3; formed in composition, 34–35, 126–27; formed in reading, 25–26, 91–99; lawyer's compared to Odysseus', as chameleon or hypocrite, 19–22, 199, 218–19; as proper end of law and life, 23–24, 35, 42, 46–48, 133–35, 208–9; thinking in terms of, as opposed to ends-means, 8–10
Clarendon, Lord, 163*n*
Coleridge, S. T., 114
Community: blaming as way of defining, 207–10; defined in conversation in *Philoctetes*, 8–19; and language, 3–6; and law, 35, 40–43, 133–34; lawyer maintains, 224–37; and narrative, 172–73, 189–90; practices described, 12, 15–16, 20, 21; textual, in *Philoctetes*, 24–26. *See also* Culture; Language; Narrative; Reading; Textual community
Composition: as antitheoretical, 123; equality implicit in relation between

Index

DESIGNED BY RICHARD HENDEL
COMPOSED BY GRAPHIC COMPOSITION, INC., ATHENS, GEORGIA
MANUFACTURED BY CUSHING MALLOY, INC., ANN ARBOR, MICHIGAN
TEXT AND DISPLAY LINES ARE SET IN PALATINO

Library of Congress Cataloging in Publication Data
White, James Boyd, 1938–
Heracles' bow.
(Rhetoric of the human sciences)
Includes index.
1. Law—Philosophy. 2. Law—Language. 3. Rhetoric.
I. Title. II. Series.
K230.W5H47   1985   340'.1   85-40381
ISBN 0-299-10410-0